HOW FOREIGN POLICY DECISIONS ARE MADE IN THE THIRD WORLD

Also of Interest

†*The Dynamics of Latin American Foreign Policies: Challenges for the 1980s*, edited by Jennie K. Lincoln and Elizabeth G. Ferris

†*Latin American Nations in World Politics*, edited by Heraldo Muñoz and Joseph S. Tulchin

†*The Making of Foreign Policy in China: Structure and Process*, A. Doak Barnett

Militarization and the International Arms Race in Latin America, Augusto Varas

†*Cuba's International Relations: The Anatomy of a Nationalistic Foreign Policy*, H. Michael Erisman

†*The Third World Coalition in International Politics*, Second, Updated Edition, Robert A. Mortimer

The Indian Foreign Policy Bureaucracy, Jeffrey Benner

The OAU After Twenty Years, Amadu Sesay, Olusola Ojo, and Orobola Fasehun

†*China and the World: Chinese Foreign Policy in the Post-Mao Era*, edited by Samuel S. Kim

†*Nonstate Actors in International Politics: From Transregional to Substate Organizations*, Phillip Taylor

Economic Diplomacy: Embargo Leverage and World Politics, M. S. Daoudi and M. S. Dajani

†*The Foreign Policies of Arab States*, Bahgat Korany and Ali E. Hillal Dessouki

†*The Caribbean Challenge: U.S. Policy in a Volatile Region*, edited by H. Michael Erisman

†*Latin America and the U.S. National Interest*, Margaret Daly Hayes

†*Japan's Foreign Relations: A Global Search for Economic Security*, edited by Robert S. Ozaki and Walter Arnold

†*Soviet-Third World Relations*, Carol R. Saivetz and Sylvia Woodby

†Available in hardcover and paperback.

ABOUT THE BOOK AND AUTHOR

This textbook analyzes eight crucial foreign policy decisions of the 1970s and 1980s, emphasizing how decision-making is influenced by the social characteristics of Third World states and their position in the global system. Chapter 1 situates the Third World in the global system and traces the evolution and interrelationships of the different Third World groups (from Bandung to the Group of 77) to analyze the pattern of this entity's decision-making at the collective level. Chapter 2 evaluates various decision-making theories and their applicability in Third World contexts. Chapters 3, 4, and 5 provide empirical and comparative analyses of six decisions pertaining to Africa, the Arab-Islamic World, and Latin America. Chapter 6 is devoted to an analysis of the decision-making process of a nonstate but influential Third World actor—OPEC. The concluding chapter pulls the threads together, comparing existing theory with the findings and incorporating analyses from other parts of the Third World, especially India and China.

Written in straightforward language that avoids unwarranted jargon, the book analyzes foreign policy decisions as part of the Third World political process, bridging the subfields of comparative politics, international relations, and political economy. Each chapter ends with a bibliographical commentary that, in combination with the book's bibliography, provides a succinct survey of the literature in Third World studies, development, and international relations.

Dr. Bahgat Korany is professor of political science and director of the Arab Studies Program at the University of Montreal. He is the senior author of *The Foreign Policies of Arab States* (Westview, 1984) and author of *Social Change, Charisma and International Behavior* (1976), which was awarded the Hauchman Prize for 1976.

HOW FOREIGN POLICY DECISIONS ARE MADE IN THE THIRD WORLD

A Comparative Analysis

Bahgat Korany
with contributors

Westview Press / Boulder and London

Chapters 3, 4, and 5 reprinted from the *International Political Science Review*, vol. 5, no. 1 (Beverly Hills, CA: Sage Publications, 1984).

This is a Westview softcover edition, manufactured on our own premises using equipment and methods that allow us to keep even specialized books in stock. It is printed on acid-free paper and bound in softcovers that carry the highest rating of NASTA in consultation with the AAP and the BMI.

All rights reserved. No part of this publication may be reproduced or transmitted in any form or by any means, electronic or mechanical, including photocopy, recording, or any information storage and retrieval system, without permission in writing from the publisher.

Copyright © 1986 by Westview Press, Inc.

Published in 1986 in the United States of America by Westview Press, Inc.; Frederick A. Praeger, Publisher; 5500 Central Avenue, Boulder, Colorado 80301

Library of Congress Cataloging in Publication Data
Korany, Bahgat.
  How foreign policy decisions are made in the Third World.
  Bibliography: p.
  Includes index.
  1. World politics—1965–1975. 2. World politics—1975–1985. 3. Developing countries—Foreign relations administration. I. Title.
D849.K64 1985   327'.091724   85-3259
ISBN 0-8133-7046-9

Printed and bound in the United States of America

10 9 8 7 6 5 4 3 2 1

CONTENTS

List of Illustrations ix
Preface xi

1 Coming of Age Against Global Odds: The Third World and Its Collective Decision-Making, *Bahgat Korany* 1

2 Foreign Policy Decision-Making Theory and the Third World: Payoffs and Pitfalls, *Bahgat Korany* 39

3 The Political Economy of Decision-Making in African Foreign Policy: Recognition of Biafra and the Popular Movement for the Liberation of Angola, *Cyril Kofie Daddieh and Timothy M. Shaw* 61

4 The Glory That Was? The Pan-Arab, Pan-Islamic Alliance Decisions, October 1973, *Bahgat Korany* 87

5 The Primacy of Politics: Comparing the Foreign Policies of Cuba and Mexico, *Jorge I. Domínguez and Juan Lindau* 113

6 Decision-Making in a Nonstate Actor—OPEC, *Bahgat Korany and Selma Akbik* 138

7 The Findings, the Two Asian Giants, and Decision-Making Theory, *Bahgat Korany* 166

Bibliography 184
About the Contributors 197
Index 199

ILLUSTRATIONS

TABLES

1.1	Membership in Nonaligned Summit Conferences, 1961–1983	16
4.1	Percentage Share of Saudi Arabia in Crude Oil Production of the Middle East, the OPEC Countries, and the World	105
4.2	Saudi Arabia: Oil Revenue	106
5.1	Examples of Latin American Foreign Policy Decisions, 1970–1982	116
5.2	Cuba's Trade with Angola and Ethiopia	124
5.3	Mexican Trade with the Central American Common Market	129
6.1	OPEC Member Countries' Oil Revenues (1961–1980)	141
6.2	OPEC Official Development Disbursements (1973–1981)	143
6.3	Oil Output of Major Oil Companies in the Gulf (1971)	145
6.4	OPEC Members and Their Characteristics	154

FIGURES

1.1	The Organizational Structure of the Nonaligned Movement (December 1981)	24
1.2	Time Pattern of High-Level Meetings of Nonaligned Countries Between Summits	26
1.3	The Multicentral Structure of the Group of 77, December 1981	33
2.1	Rosenau's Pre-Theory	43
2.2	Brecher's Input-Output Model	46
2.3	The Decision-Making Diagram	50

4.1 The Network of Ownership of Major Oil Companies
     in the Gulf Prior to 1974............................108
6.1 Proved Oil Reserves of Middle East Nations..............144
6.2 OPEC's Organizational Structure.......................150

MAPS

Biafra..61
Angola..62
Africa..63
Middle Eastern and Arab countries in
   Africa and Asia..86
Central America and the Caribbean.........................114
The OPEC Countries..139
India and China, the Asian giants.........................167

PREFACE

Specialists and nonspecialists agree that both the Third World and decision analysis are crucial political topics. The last all–Third World conference (the Seventh Nonaligned Summit, New Delhi, March 7–12, 1983) had a membership of 101 countries as well as 18 observers and 28 guest delegations from another 19 countries, international organizations (including 15 branches of the UN), and various national liberation groups. Decisions are the microcosm of politics: They deal with such basic questions as how political outcomes emerge and how choices are made. Analysis of decision-making is indeed among the approaches most widely used in both political analysis and the conduct of daily affairs, since policy-makers do make decisions, either explicitly or implicitly.

Yet not a single book exists on foreign policy decisions in the Third World. Data are either inaccessible or, because archival facilities are lacking in many Third World countries, unavailable. But we do not have the relevant concepts and analytical tools to determine, for example, why China invaded India in 1962 or why the Iran-Iraq War started in 1980. Thus it was thought useful to publish a revised and enlarged edition of the results of a project that has existed within the International Political Science Association since 1979. Chapters 3, 4, and 5—or less than half this book—were published as a special issue of the Association's journal, the *International Political Science Review*, Vol. 5, no. 1, January 1984. The book thus aims to unearth data on how *principal* decisions in the Third World were made, but also to evaluate critically the conceptual apparatus used in present decision-making theory.

In short, conceptual problems appear in dealing with any Third World country. For example, Tunisia (whose political importance has greatly increased since it became the new headquarters of the twenty-one-member Arab League in 1979) is representative of many countries in the Third World. A North African state of around 7 million people, Tunisia gained its political independence in 1956 after more than seventy years of French colonization. Since then it has been headed by Habib Bourguiba, a president-monarch now eighty-one years old. Bourguiba, then, is a basic facet of Tunisia's political life.

For instance, in downtown Tunis the main street is called—naturally—Bourguiba Street. When taking the metro downtown, I asked a local fellow-passenger which stop was nearest Bourguiba Street. He did not seem to understand, and it took some discussion before I grasped the fact that in almost every small town, there was probably a Bourguiba Street. Indeed, Bourguiba is omnipresent: as an imposing statue on horseback in the center of the capital, or on the currency, in the press, on the radio, and in official political culture. Every day before the main eight o'clock news one can see "Guidelines from the President," a program in which Bourguiba talks to his people about all that has been accomplished in Tunisia since he headed the independence movement in 1934 and advises his people on the path Tunisia should take when he is no longer there. Bourguibism is not only everywhere but appears alive and well, unaffected even by the health problems of the ailing president. In this book I call such a conceptual lens the "great man" theory of history. This approach reduces all political and social phenomena in Third World countries to the man at the top. It is a personalistic and simplistic view, one that confuses appearance with reality.

Yet, if we scratch just beneath the surface, this same Tunisia can tell us another story: that of the social groups and factions around the president, which truly control Tunisia. There is first and foremost Wassila Bourguiba, the president's wife. She is a permanent companion, a constant gatekeeper, and an imposing political influence. There is also Habib Bourguiba, Jr.—the president's son by his previous, French wife—who for a long time was Tunisia's foreign minister and is now the president's special adviser. But Bourguiba, Jr., is frequently forbidden by Wassila Bourguiba from even entering the Presidential Palace. Then there is the present prime minister, Mohammed Mzali, who is also minister of the interior and who has been explicitly confirmed by Bourguiba as his successor. And, finally, there is the relatively young and energetic Mohammed El-Sayyah, an ex-communist and a man of the Neo-Destur party and its militias, who has been in charge of youth organizations and is now minister of equipment.

Each of these four "patrons" has around her or him certain clients, clans, and allies. But what complicates the picture is that these different patrons enter into various shifting alliances with each other. The picture can be further complicated if we include less visible but nonetheless influential "shadow elites" such as the military or religious movements. The situation becomes even more complex if we try to trace the social bases of the different elites or analyze the impact on decision-making of the counter-elites. In addition to the great man theory of history, or the psychological level of analysis, then, there is a second level: that of society and its dynamics.

Of course, Third World societies do not function in a vacuum. The countries of the Third World were integrated into the world system a long time ago. The "colonial intrusion" has disorganized these societies, interrupted their normal evolution, and is still shaping what is taking place within them. Moreover, the vagaries of the contemporary world economy are conditioning the rates of development of these countries, in addition to their systems of government; even the day-to-day survival of the people is affected by the larger economic picture. These countries are often described as "dependent"; indeed, there exists a whole school of analysis, the Dependencia-Imperialism School, that originated in the Third World itself (first in Latin America). This school even affirms that its perspective is the *only* one from which to analyse the Third World. It isn't, of course, but this third level of analysis—the impact of the global system on weak states and penetrated societies—cannot simply be brushed aside either.

So much has been written on economic dependency that we do not need to emphasize this aspect here. Instead, to illustrate the possible impact of the global system on decision-making, we can draw attention to another dimension of this same dependency: external but dominant cultural norms. Of course, cultural norms constitute the frame of reference within which options are evaluated and specific decisions adopted. In this connection, to continue with the Tunisian case, 70 percent of Tunisia's political elite have studied in France; many more than that speak French fluently and tend to look down on those unfamiliar with French language and values; and high-school students still receive a major part of their education directly in French. In 1975, Tunisia had 2,110 French "cooperants," the highest per capita ratio for the whole of north Africa (1/2718), and as late as 1978 France still received 86 percent of all Tunisian students abroad (i.e., Tunisia's future elite). Other indicators of cultural dependency, such as films, point in the same direction. In 1970, for instance, Tunisia produced two "long metrage" films, a documentary, and six short films. But it imported 346 "long metrage" films, of which 71 percent came from four Western countries (the United States, France, Italy, and Great Britain) and only seven from India, the world's biggest film producer.

Briefly, instead of perpetuating the present conceptual orthodoxy, which "explains" Third World decisions exclusively by reference to the leader's caprices, whims, and other idiosyncracies, this study aims to bring in the other two levels of analysis: the national-societal and the global. To counterbalance the one-sidedness of present literature, the present study also emphasizes the importance of "objective" or "real-life" factors (as distinct from the psychologistic-subjective), the plurality of actors participating in decision-making, and the impact of external influences. This objective has determined the way the decisions were both selected and analyzed. The aim was not to accumulate every piece of data on each of the major decisions included and their following subdecisions. Students and scholars may soon realize, in fact, that the data presented here are available for the first time between the two covers of one volume. As for the specialists on a country or even a geographical region, it is hoped that new data presented on other decisions and regions may provide the comparative perspective and hence make the volume useful for them too. Moreover, the decisions chosen are not isolated cases in the actor's foreign policy but are closely related to its general objectives and behavioral patterns and hence should improve our understanding of regional and international politics.

Accordingly, the book is organized in the following way. In Chapter 1 the Third World is situated within the global system; the emergence of "Third Worldism" against global odds is discussed; and the general context shaping decision-making at the collective level is considered. Chapter 2 presents an overview of influential decision-making theories in which they are critically evaluated from the point of view of their relevance to our subject matter. Chapters 3, 4, and 5 are devoted to an analysis of state decisions in specific regions: Africa, the Arab-Islamic world, and Latin America. Inasmuch as international politics has been unduly dominated by a state-centric frame of reference, Chapter 6 focuses on the importance of Third World nonstate actors and reveals how their decision-making mechanisms function. In this context, two basic OPEC decisions—those concerning oil prices and oil output—are analyzed. Finally, in Chapter 7 we find an inventory of the findings of the different chapters, a comparison between these findings and those of existing theory, and suggested avenues of future research involving the cases of India and China. With respect to the last concern, the basic question is this: If existing decision theory is too narrow and deficient, is it advisable to make of it a tabula rasa and start from scratch? Alternatively, is there a possibility of conceptual sorting out to choose the best parts of existing theory and throw out the rest? The answers to both questions are suggested in the last chapter, in which I divide decision analysis into the general mechanism of decision-*making* and the much more limited one of decision-*taking*.

Overall, the research contained in this volume concentrates on the data collection and analysis of eight major foreign policy decisions made in the 1970s and 1980s. Given the poverty of existing theory, and the question as to whether general findings are still possible, no conceptual framework was imposed on the different chapters from the outset. However, all the decisions had to adopt a comparative perspective emphasized by the analysis of two major decisions in each empirically oriented chapter. In the general and conceptually oriented chapters (1, 2, and 7) I emphasize the wider aspects of this field of analysis and indicate both where we are and where we are heading in the realm of foreign policy. The organization of the book is designed to attract the reader's attention to the mutual feedback between data collected on principal decisions and the state of the field.

More specifically, I believe that we should exploit every bit of help we can get from the conceptual literature, but we should also aim—through empirical analysis—to understand how underdevelopment influences Third World decision-making. Particularly with respect to those societies in the throes of social change, we must explore the impact of societal groups, of informal networks, and of patron-client relationships.

In a field lacking empirical analysis and suffering from conceptual onesidedness, the author is faced in a small study like this one with a kind of damned-if-you-do, damned-if-you-don't dilemma. But I hope that through the singling out of limitations and imperfections, I will help make it easier for others to pick up where we leave off and go further in the analysis of Third World foreign policy decisions.

I am grateful to Professor John Meisel, the general editor of IPSR, who during the 1979 IPSA Moscow Meeting invited me to head the project. I am indebted, as well, to Joan Sarazzin for her editorial assistance. The cooperation of my fellow authors transformed the project from an idea into a reality. Gamil Matter of the Arab League made my stay in Tunisia both pleasant and useful, and our constant dialogue helped to sharpen many of my ideas. Dean Birkenkamp of Westview Press has shown patience and perseverance, both of which were crucial to the publication of the book. It was a result of Christine Arden's editing of the manuscript that the book's fine distinctions in conceptualization and analysis are now available to the reader. Christiane Aubain of the Université de Montréal slaved over the manuscript and the different tables. And last but not least, Margaret Korany did not simply sit and watch, but read, argued, and criticized—thus helping me to clarify and improve much of what I wanted to say.

Bahgat Korany

1

COMING OF AGE AGAINST GLOBAL ODDS

The Third World and Its Collective Decision-Making

Bahgat Korany

INTRODUCTION

Students and scholars interested in the Third World face a series of problems at the very outset. First, they must face the multiplicity of terms used to describe the same group of countries. Second, they must decide on the ratio of factors of assimilation to those of differentiation among Third World countries: On the one hand, how many factors are in common within these countries and, on the other, how many set them apart and separate, say, India from Lesotho, or Bangladesh from Kuwait? Finally, some might even ask whether the Third World actually exists in the first place. Related questions may follow: How and when did "Third Worldism" (i.e., the idea of a Third World collective identity and the corresponding belief in its common interests) emerge in the postwar period? What is the structure of the group (or groups) representing it? How does this group function (i.e., what are the characteristics of its decision-making process)?

In dealing with these issues, we shall first examine the plethora of labels used in the field and attempt to sort out the defining characteristics of the Third World as an object of study. Then we will trace the evolution of the different groups (the Afro-Asians, the Nonaligned group, and the Group of 77) and investigate the relationship of possible hierarchy, cooperation, or competition among them. Last, we shall turn to a discussion of the various attempts made to institutionalize the Third World and examine how these attempts influence the Third World's collective decision-making process.

THE THIRD WORLD AS AN OBJECT OF STUDY

LABELS

In Third World analyses, elastic labels abound: *nonaligned states, underdeveloped countries,* the *world periphery.* "In the interests of readability," Hill (1977: 11) tells us in an introductory chapter that "the terms 'developing countries,' 'new states,' 'Third World,' 'unmodernised states' and occasionally, 'LDCs' [Less Developed Countries] are used interchangeably." Such practice leads many to wonder when these labels were coined and whether they guide—or mislead—analysis of the Third World.

Even the first use of such a standard term as *nonalignment* is in doubt. Krishna Menon, India's distinguished political leader, affirmed that he had used the term for the first time in the UN and that Nehru had not liked it. But Nehru himself had already used the term during a debate on foreign affairs on March 28, 1951 (Nehru's Speeches, n.d.: 191-203).

The phrase *underdeveloped countries* was probably first used officially in the 1951 UN document "Measures for Economic Development of Underdeveloped Countries (E/1980 ST/ECA of 10/3 May 1951) (Wolf-Phillips, 1979: 105-117). It was soon to be regarded as a derogatory term by the governments of these countries. *Developing* or *less developed* was preferred, leading Gunnar Myrdal to qualify this change in labels in his *Asian Drama* as "diplomacy by terminology."

The term *Third World* came to the English language from the French *Tiers Monde.* In fact, the French phrase was used in italics in English writings until books such as those of Peter Worsley (1964) and J.B.D. Miller (1966) popularized the term. But English users tended to respect its French connotation as expounded by the French demographist A. Sauvy when he employed it at the height of the cold war in the mid-1950s to refer (by analogy with the French *Tiers Etat*) to noncommunist countries that purported to remain outside the Western system of alliances. In this sense of political nonalignment, *tiers-monde* was used by African leaders (such as Kwame Nkrumah) when they suggested the formation of a "nonnuclear Third World" between the two world blocs.

Tracing the use of labels does not help to establish a consensual use of their meaning. Writing in the early 1960s on this subject, P. Lyon (1963) quoted diverse authorities and concluded that "neutralism has been used so often by so many people, in such different circumstances and with such different intentions, that its meaning seems to change, chameleon-like, depending on the context in which it appears."

Twelve years later the Legal Committee of the Group of Experts on the Establishment of the Solidarity Fund for Economic and Social Development in Nonaligned Countries (Kuwait, January 14-15, 1975) could not resolve the problem of definition of nonalignment and had to adopt an ad hoc solution: "An understanding was reached" the Legal Experts affirmed, "that a country which is invited to attend a Conference of the Heads of States or Governments of the nonaligned countries pursuant to a decision of the latter should be regarded as a nonaligned country for purposes of this convention" (Jankowitz and Sauvant, 1978, vol. III: 1727). The labels as well as their definitions are increasingly related to one of the biggest controversies in contemporary social science literature: development and underdevelopment. The controversy proliferates not only into articles and books but also into theories and paradigms (Chilcote, 1984; Gendzier, 1985; Oxaal, 1975; Roxborough, 1979). The debate over labels, definitions, and approaches will undoubtedly continue.

In a chapter on Latin America, Edy Kaufman (1977: 131-164) attracted attention to the overhomogenizing aspect of the term *Third World* and stressed the differences between Afro-Asia and Latin America. This emphasis on differences is in keeping with what E. Williams (1969: 342-353) had done eight years earlier when he analyzed religion, the role of the church, and interest groups as well as other conventional political development indicators (e.g., per capita income, literacy, and energy consumption) to emphasize the distance separating Latin America from Afro-Asia and to draw the conclusion that Latin America is a connecting link between Europe and Afro-Asia. In trying to get the "Labels Straight" among "Third, Fourth, and Other Worlds," Rothstein (1977: 42-70), too, drew attention to the differences between Latin America and Afro-Asia:

> On the broadest level, there are so many underdeveloped countries, and there are so many differences between them, that any single label is bound to be misleading. Whatever indicator we choose to highlight, the range of variation is enormous: level of development, per capita income, political forms, culture, historical experience, or ideology. In fact, the variations among underdeveloped countries are probably much wider than those among developed countries, if only because of the absence of the advanced technology and heavy industrialization that tend to create similar institutional patterns and problems (p. 48).

Even Third World sociologists committed to the Third World both as an object of study and as a reference group are forced to agree, as expressed by this most recent example (Hermassi, 1980: 170):

> The term "Third World" almost defies conceptual analysis. It is elusive for several reasons. . . . The issues covered by the term "Third World" have rarely seemed clear enough to be taken as objects of discriminant thought and judgement. Thus, instead of providing mature generalizations, those

involved in Third World affairs have presented grand schemes and intensely held personal opinions, which, in the absence of a fixed object, cannot be sustained for long.

Indeed, after all this emphasis on intra-Third World differences by serious specialists, is it not legitimate to ask if the Third World really exists? "No one raised the question in the 1950's and through much of the 1960's," Rothstein tells us (1977: 47).

DEFINING CHARACTERISTICS OF THE THIRD WORLD

During the 1950s and much of the 1960s, in fact, the literature was dominated by a "power assumption" that divided all countries into "big powers" and "small states." These latter were analysed—much like any related phenomenon at the heyday of the cold war would have been—as a function of the dominant East-West conflict, as objects or pawns in the superpowers' competition. Such a "Prussian historical school" mentality, with its emphasis on the strength of the state, resulted in a negative assessment of the small state (Amstrup, 1976: 163-182). Thus, for instance, Morgenthau classified the foreign policies of newly independent states into three categories: "escapism pure and simple," "moral indifference," and "surreptitious alignment with the Soviet bloc" (Morgenthau, 1961: 76-77). Briefly, "small states" could not be conceptualized as having purposeful and self-contained foreign policies.

The emphasis on the small/great power dichotomy followed an established tradition in the analysis of eighteenth- and nineteenth-century European politics. Some students of the European scene manifested interest in the small state as representing both a political phenomenon and an attractive alternative to the big absolutist state, but they fell victim to the problem surrounding the concept of size (Amstrup, 1976: 163). We can identify at least six approaches, manifesting various degrees of arbitrariness, in defining the size factor. They range from the view shared by Annette Baker Fox (1968-1969: 751-764) and David Vital (1967) that a strict definition is, after all, unnecessary or irrelevant, to R. Vayrynen's five-dimension classificatory scheme of small-state status (1971: 91-120).

Not only political scientists but also economists (Khalaf, 1971; Lloyd, 1968; Robinson, 1960), who have been more successful in refining and operationalizing the size concept, could not reach conclusive findings. After analyzing economic data from eighty countries, Khalaf (1971: 232) summarized his conclusions:

> Size does not have any clear impact on economic stability nor on economic growth and development. "Smallness" is not a source of extra instability,

nor is smallness necessarily an obstacle to economic growth and development. The impact of size on dependence on trade and concentration in trade is relatively less ambiguous. In some instances significant inverse relationships were observed between size and concentration in trade. These relationships, however, were not as significant as is often claimed or suggested by plausible a priori reasoning. But regardless of the strength of these relationships, both dependence on trade and concentration in trade turned out to be neither sources of extra instability nor important obstacles to economic growth and economic development.

Social scientists realized at last that size as a variable suffered from a case of overdetermination, from a monovariable approach to explanation. Indeed, if size is analyzed in isolation, out of context, the result is an aberrational categorization of the kind that puts Sweden and Switzerland in the same basket as Kampuchea and Zimbabwe, since these countries are roughly equivalent in respective population (one of Vital's criteria of size). Many social scientists are also beginning to realize the qualitative differences between "small" but old European countries and equally "small" but new states in Afro-Asia and, consequently, have started to stress these differences in their analyses. To start with, clear differences exist in the problem supposedly facing all "small" states, that of security. But there is much more to consider than these differences in security, especially at the structural-societal level, as Rothstein (1977: 43) has suggested:

> The European small countries . . . shared political tradition and political language with the European Great Power. Their leaders came from the same social class, they were committed to the same ideas about the necessary primacy of foreign policy, and they did not question the value of preserving the existing international system. The Afro-Asian small countries could hardly be more different: Western forms of government have been loosely imposed on much different indigenous political traditions, the leaders of the new states do not come from a single social class (and they are frequently much younger than their counterpart in the industrial world), domestic politics is more important than foreign policy, and there is little commitment to the preservation of an international system identified with imperialism and exploitation.

Accordingly, analysts switched the focus of their inquiry in the 1970s from "smallness" to "weakness" (East, 1973: 556–576). The title of M. Singer's 1972 book, *The Weak in the World of the Strong,* is significant in this respect. The switch is even more revealing in Rothstein's case: His 1968 book on the subject, *Alliances and Small Powers,* emphasized smallness, but he replaced this term with *weakness* in one of his titles ten years later. Both Singer and Rothstein equated "weak" with underdeveloped countries, and Rothstein (1977: 47) explained that he was concerned in his book "solely with underdeveloped countries." The "weakness" label, then, should be limited to underdeveloped countries, not only as an economic datum but also as a structural (objective) and perceptual (subjective) characteristic. Rothstein, in agreement, emphasized the general (objective) common characteristics that make of the underdeveloped countries a proper object of study—namely, "the dominance of subsistence production and self-employment, low per capita incomes and unequal distribution of incomes, imperfect markets, low productivity, dependence on export earnings and foreign capital flows, and small public sectors and minimal modern industrial sectors" (1977: 50). But the subjective elements are equally important. They are two: (1) "a strongly felt sense of deprivation and resentment against the developed countries and a growing conviction that the rules of the international system are deliberately against them—so much so that fair treatment is impossible without a fundamental restructuring of the principles of world order" (Rothstein, 1977: 31); and (2) the common psychological attitudes that this situation engenders. J. Scott's analysis of Malaysian civil servants and Pye's study of the Burmese elite substantiate this view. Tanzania President Julius Nyerere's metaphor is much more to the point: "Small nations are like indecently dressed women. They tempt the evil-minded." Similarly, in their interviews with Weinstein (1976), Indonesian political elites came back again and again to the pretty-girl image to emphasize danger to their country.

GLOBAL PRESSURES AND THE EMERGENCE OF THE THIRD WORLD COLLECTIVITY

Notwithstanding national variations (although they are very important), this context of vulnerability—that is, previous colonial domination and present weakness, poverty, and insecurity—tends to cement the Third World countries together and to make of them an eligible object of study and analysis. Indeed, it is this global-systemic context that accounts for their various regroupings into the categories of Afro-Asians, Nonaligned, and Group of 77.

The Afro-Asian group reached its zenith in April 1955 when twenty-nine states from Africa and Asia convened their first (and only) summit in Bandung, Indonesia, and made this Javanese town world-famous overnight. The first summit of the Nonaligned group took place not in Africa or Asia, but in Europe when twenty-five like-minded states (albeit mostly African and Asian) met in September 1961 in Belgrade. In March 1983, the Nonaligned group assembled its seventh summit in New Delhi with a membership of one hundred one countries—an increase of over 400 percent. As for the Group of 77 (G-77), the year of its creation seemed to be less clear-cut (1963? 1964? 1967?) but it was more specific in its object: the economic sphere. It came into being with the convening of UNCTAD I (the United Nations Conference on Trade and Development, Geneva, March–June 1964). However, a group of sorts was already present in the UN in 1963 and seemed to be behind the convening of UNCTAD, but this group included the non–Third World New Zealand. As New Zealand had little in common with these developing countries, it dropped out in 1964 when the Group of 77 coalesced much more concretely during UNCTAD I. The G-77 took an independent form when it convened in Algiers in October 1967 to codify a common Third World position in international economic negotiations, which were to take place shortly afterward within UNCTAD II in 1968 in New Delhi. At the Algiers Conference, G-77 published its charter, which contains the basics of the Third World position in North-South negotiations up to the present time. By 1984, the membership of the Group of 77 had grown to 126 countries, but the name has been retained.

During the thirty-year span between Bandung (1955) and the present, Third World meetings have mushroomed (Mortimer, 1980; Jankowitz and Sauvant, 1978; Sauvant, 1981), membership has increased (with greater numbers of Latin Americans and, especially, of Africans), fields of concern ranging from "pure" politics to political economy have multiplied, particularly given the role and impact of multinational companies, and the leaderships of Third World countries have changed. For instance, the 1950s and early 1960s were dominated by such leaders as Nehru of India, Nasser of Egypt, Tito of Yugoslavia, and, to a lesser degree, Sukarno of Indonesia as well as Nkrumah of Ghana. The second half of the 1960s and especially the 1970s saw the confirmed leadership of such personalities as Boumedienne of Algeria, and Castro of Cuba. Both the Nonaligned group and the G-77 tended to be influenced by the revolutionary national experiences of such new leaders, and thus emphasized in their public positions as a group not mere international accommodation but international restructuring. During this time, the Third World was increasingly frustrated by existing "outdated" world mechanisms and thus became radicalized.

Although such a pattern of Third Worldism seems clear in retrospect, the great overlapping in the membership of the different groups should not lead us to confuse them or to treat them as interchangeable. True, all these groups gave expression to one and the same Third World reality. But their emphases have differed, their ups and downs have reflected different periods in the evolution of the Third World as a collective entity, and the groups have even competed among themselves.

THE AFRO-ASIAN MOVEMENT

Chronologically speaking—but with reference only to the most inclusive post–World War II manifestations (see Queille, 1965, for more historical and regional ones)—the first grouping of the Afro-Asian movement materialized at Bandung in April 1955, giving rise to the "Bandung Spirit," which reflected an emphasis on Third World togetherness and its affirmation at the international level. Contrary to widespread misconceptions among many students and analysts, this conference was one not of nonaligned countries but of Afro-Asians. In other words, the criteria of invitations were based on geography rather than on political orientation toward the two blocs (as they were six years later in preparation for the First Nonaligned Summit). Accordingly, both nonaligned and aligned members were present at Bandung. Among the participants, then, were prominent Afro-Asian advocates of the Western alliances (e.g., representatives of Iran, Iraq, the Philippines, and Turkey) and those of the Eastern alliances, too (specifically, advocates from China, the most populous country in the whole world and still known as "Communist China").

Given the application of geographical criteria to membership, one can indeed say that the participants were "in" but not necessarily "of" the Third World (Mortimer, 1980: 8)—particularly if the term *Third World* is taken to denote nonalignment and a third distinct political regrouping outside the two existing blocs. However, Bandung still occupies a place of unequalled prestige in Third World annals (Ghali, personal communication, January 1985); it is indeed a Third World precursor.

Yet there are still other reasons for this prestige. First, the Bandung Conference indicated that nonalignment is (as we shall soon see) the "natural," genuine, and almost inevitable position of the Third World in the global system. Even those participants aligned with the West insisted at Bandung that their position was forced upon them by the "aggressiveness" of Communist powers; in other words, this position of alignment was not an inherent factor in their policies and could indeed change. (This change from alignment to nonalignment is precisely what has happened, inasmuch as Afro-Asian pillars of Western alliance systems like Iraq, Iran, and Pakistan have not only defected but are presently members of the Nonaligned Group's Coordinating Bureau.) As for Communist China, its brand of communism was different from that of the Soviets, as indicated by, among other things, the deterioration of its relations with Moscow. Even China's most vehement critics insisted on the distinction and went to such pains to emphasize the differentiation that Chou En-lai had to note it officially. Briefly, this implicit identification of Third Worldism with nonalignment makes of Bandung a precursor not only of the movement as a whole but of the future pattern of the policies of its members.

But there is yet another reason for the special prestige that Bandung enjoys in Third World historiography, a reason related both to those who convened and attended the conference and to its location in Bandung. In short, this was the first and largest international gathering convened and attended *only* by representatives from Third World countries—by the excolonized, black, yellow, or olive-skinned people. No whites attended. As Indonesia's Sukarno, the convenor of the conference, put it: This is "the first intercontinental conference of coloured peoples in the history of mankind." Thirty years ago, that was a feat in itself, not only from the political perspective but from the administrative-technical standpoint, too: Accommodations had to be provided for 340 delegates and 655 pressmen, secretarial and interpretation services had to be organized, and so on.

Invitations to the Bandung Conference came from representatives of the five Asian powers (Burma, Ceylon [present-day Sri Lanka], India, Indonesia, and Pakistan), who had met in Colombo, Sri Lanka, at the end of April 1954. Their Joint Communiqué of May 2, 1954, indicated that "the prime ministers had discussed the desirability of holding a conference of African-Asian nations and favoured a proposal that the prime minister of Indonesia should explore the possibility of such a conference" (for the text of this communiqué, see Jansen, 1966: 414).

The almost hostile U.S. reaction to the idea behind this conference reminded the convenors that others still wanted to dictate when and with whom they should meet. The then Secretary of State J. F. Dulles talked about the invitation as an "ambiguous document" for a "so-called" Afro-Asian conference. Washington even tried to discourage its allies and friends from participating, thus killing the idea itself. The United States was worried, of course, about political contamination of its allies on the part of the nonaligned countries, but, above all, it did not want China to escape from the imposed *cordon sanitaire* and attend an international gathering (Jansen, 1966: 184). Thus the U.S. allies in Asia dragged their feet about attending, but upon discovering that the conference was going to meet in any case, they hurried to participate so that, as the *New York Herald Tribune* put it (20 March 1955), "America's friends will outnumber her enemies and they will defend the United States when necessary" (Jansen, 1966: 185).

The attempts to sabotage the Bandung Conference were not only political and indirect, but also physical and quite direct—especially those made against China's representation. The Chinese government had chartered an Air India plane to fly from Hong Kong to Jakarta. But Beijing took precautions to inform the British colonial authorities in Hong Kong of the plane's timing and insisted on the necessity of protecting it against possible attempts at sabotage, thereby arousing suspicions about the presence of Chou En-lai on board. When the plane was approaching the coast of Indonesian Borneo, an explosion took place on board and the plane had to crash in shallow water. All on board died except two of the crew members, who provided details about the explosion. A bomb was indeed found in the wreckage. The committee of inquiry found that no precautions had been taken at Hong Kong, and the Easter weekend was mentioned as one factor responsible for this fatal negligence. But some weeks later, the committee gave the police the name of the suspected saboteur, a well-known Kuomintang agent who was still in Hong Kong, yet allowed to get away to Taiwan (Jansen, 1966: 189-190).

Thus the brutal gang-warfare attempts of external powers to prevent the convening of the conference and even to eliminate physically some of the participants symbolized the risks against which the Third World had to stand. In this sense, the convening of the Bandung Conference would test whether a Third World political will existed or not, and whether, by persisting in the face of odds, it could become an action.

Less symbolic politically, but equally difficult to overcome, were the administrative-technical obstacles. One of the conference participants (Jansen, 1966: 188) put it in this down-to-earth way:

> The international Secretariat which arranged the conference had two principal difficulties to overcome—its being in Bandung, and the cheerful insouciance of their Indonesian colleagues. Bandung . . . is not a large town, and to squeeze a large and high-powered international conference into its limited accommodation was a genuine problem, solved only by obliging most of the delegates and all pressmen to share rooms. Telegraph and telephone communications into and out of it had to be expanded many times over. All the important sections of the Secretariat were headed by officials lent by other countries, and . . . the mechanics—typing, interpreting and so on, were also handled by foreign staff. . . . [Problems of organization] greatly worried Mr. Nehru, and one of his directives the author cannot forbear to quote at the risk of infringing the Official Secrets Act. Mr. Nehru wrote: "Above all one fact should be remembered . . . this fact is an adequate provision of bathrooms and lavatories. People can do without drawing-rooms but they cannot do without bathrooms and lavatories. I am writing about what might be considered trivial matters. But these trivial matters upset people, and frayed tempers are not good when we consider important problems."

In this sense, the mere convening of the conference, apart from any of its results, represented the birth of the Third World, a birth that had not been a foregone conclusion. It demanded political stamina and technical know-how against substantial global odds, and victory was far from guaranteed. The Bandung Conference is thus important above all as a historical precedent and for its "psychological impact." As President Senghor of Senegal later put it, it resulted in the death of the Third World's inferiority complex. And the Indonesian chairman concluded the conference proceedings by saying, "We are now about to enter the gate that leads to the Rebirth, Revival and Rennaissance of the coloured Nations" (Jansen, 1966: 217). Even Nehru, a "westernized" leader not known for his political rhetoric, agreed. Talking to the Indian parliament a few days after the conference, he emphasized that "Bandung proclaimed the political emergence in world affairs of over half the world's population. . . . It would be a misreading of history to regard Bandung as though it was an isolated occurrence and not part of a great movement of human history" (Jansen, 1966: 224). Indeed, the Third World was acquiring self-confidence and becoming aware of its worth; according to the Syrian delegate, A. El-Shukeiry (himself a Palestinian), "We are the two greatest continents on earth. We have the greatest pool of manpower, the greatest pool of all, materials. We have the greatest pool of fuel. We have every strategic military base and area. If we are determined, all of us, with our collective will, no strategic war will take place—if we do not participate in any sense" (Jansen, 1966: 210).

Given the great symbolic importance of the Bandung Conference for the global system, but especially for the Third World, the latter countries were keen to repeat the experience. Accordingly, the final act of the political committee, before going into the closing plenary session, was to approve a proposal from China to convene Bandung II. Indonesia suggested that the second conference should occur "within the next year," and apparently Bandung II was to meet in Cairo in March 1956. But the proposal to hold another Bandung Conference took ten years to be accepted, and when it was about to materialize in Algiers in 1965, President Ahmed Ben Bella was ousted in a bloodless coup by Colonel Honari Boumedienne. Although Algeria made a great subsequent effort to convene this second Afro-Asian summit, the attempt never succeeded.

Why did Bandung stop at one conference? One answer is that its program was taken over by other Third World groupings, such as the Group of 77 and the Nonaligned group.

NONALIGNED MOVEMENT:
THE INCARNATION OF THIRD WORLDISM

In retrospect, it was an alternative grouping—one designed around the concept of nonalignment—that pulled the carpet out from under Bandung, thus relegating the conference to the status of a historic precedent (albeit a prestigious one) rather than that of a living and dynamic international institution. Nevertheless, the first stage in equating nonalignment with "genuine" Third Worldism occurred at Bandung itself.

Anticolonialism and the urge for "togetherness" aside, two "theories" of international politics were in opposition at Bandung: that concerning the Nonaligned group and that concerning the states aligned with the West (Korany, 1976: 50–51). The first point of view was advocated by Burma's U Nu, Egypt's Nasser, and especially India's Nehru. All three stated that the existence of two rival military blocs not only increased tension in the system but in fact threatened its maintenance. Consequently, if every state joined one or the other of the two conflicting blocs, rigid bipolarity would increase and war might become inevitable. Hence one had to create in Afro-Asia an "area of peace" whose "mobilization of the moral violence of people" (as Sukarno called it) against "situations of strength" and military alliances would introduce an element of global flexibility, act as a bridge builder and a communication channel, and mediate to reduce the level of conflict. The practical means of action for the nonaligned countries were consolidation of the universal actor (i.e., the UN) and a strengthening of the principles of peaceful coexistence as norms governing the functioning of the international system.

The second theory, concerning the actors allied to the West, was mainly expounded by the conference participants from Turkey, Iraq, Iran, and the Philippines, who agreed with those from the nonaligned states in their diagnosis of the international system. They also expressed, as the latter had done, their desire to contribute to the reduction of conflict and to global regulation, but they differed with the nonaligned actors as to the means of achieving this goal. For instance, although the nonaligned actors proposed to remain aloof from both the two blocs, the actors allied to the West believed that it was more "realistic" to take all preventative measures in the form of military pacts to frustrate the "aggressiveness" of the Communist bloc. Their starting point was the belief that newly independent states should not trust the Communists, who were aiming at "world supremacy," and that the concept of peaceful coexistence was nothing but a device used by the Communists to drug their victims until they became ripe for "Communist revolution." That, they maintained, is why small states had no choice but to join defensive military pacts with the anti-Communist bloc.

Two factors contributed to the emergence of the concept of nonalignment to replace Afro-Asianism as the sole incarnation of Third Worldism. The first concerns the evolution of interaction between some Third World countries and the colonial powers; the second factor is related to the political will and active lobbying of certain states—notably nonaligned Yugoslavia, which was not invited to the Afro-Asian gathering at Bandung.

The impact of the first factor is best revealed by the controversy in the mid-1950s surrounding the Middle East's inclusion in Western alliances and its strategy of "containing" the Soviet Union. Although the controversy revolved specifically around the so-called Baghdad Pact, it epitomized the basics of the debate about the political orientation of newly independent countries within the global system and revealed opposition in interests, perceptions, and modes of thinking between the system's big powers and its small, marginalized states. The controversy thus has a significance far beyond its specific regional context, for which its immediate results foreshadowed the events to come later in the rest of the Third World.

The Baghdad Pact project started formally with the Turko-Pakistani Treaty on April 4, 1953, followed by British attempts to incorporate Iraq and Iran into the new "anti-Communist" organization destined to stretch from the Bosphorus to the Indus. Britian was enthusiastic in its welcome of this arrangement because it offered Britain a new treaty in place of the existing Anglo-Iraqi one, which was due to expire by 1957. Thus, on February 24, 1955, Turkey and Iraq signed their mutual assistance pact, and Britian joined on April 5, 1955, followed by Pakistan and Iran in September and November, respectively.

Nasser reacted vehemently to Iraq's "defection," and this issue was to dominate policies in the Arab region for almost the entire year. Nasser's arguments were diffused through the widely heard Cairo Radio, which gave them added weight. He also contacted Arab nationalists throughout the region, explaining that Iraq had violated the solidarity of the Arab League in committing itself to "outside" obligations and had threatened to withdraw from the League itself (a move that would have brought about its demise). Nasser's line of attack was simple. He emphasized Pan-Arabism as against "imperialism and zionism" and said that the Baghdad Pact was not aimed at the "real" enemy of the Arabs (i.e., Israel) but was instead an alliance with those who had created and still supported this "imperialist base" against the Arabs (i.e., the Western states).

Not only was the pact unrelated to the Arabs' defense against their "real" enemies, but it was also an "imperialist formula" permitting "imperialist forces" to come back into the Arab world through the back door. The appeal of this argument to excolonial people was strengthened when "material evidence" was cited to "prove" its truth; according to the agreement governing British accession to the Turko-Iraqi pact,

> the airfields in Iraq occupied by Great Britain in accordance with the 1932 treaty were to pass under Iraqi sovereignty; but the existing facilities of

overflying, landing and servicing British aircraft in Iraq were to be maintained and British military personnel would remain in Iraq, under British command, for this purpose, and would enjoy appropriate amenities. Furthermore, the installations on the airfields retained for British use were to remain British property (Survey of International Affairs, 1955–1956: 28).

It followed, according to a British analyst who summarized the new agreement, that "the effects of the new agreement were therefore juridical rather than practical; in other words, although sovereignty and legal ownership passed to Iraq, effective use by Great Britain remained largely undisturbed" (ibid.).

Thus, as far as the relationship between the Arabs and the Western powers was concerned, and as Nasser insisted, Iraq's step meant a return to the old treaty relationships that had brought the newly independent state back into the "imperialist sphere of influence." Instead, an alternative strategy could achieve the Arab nationalist aim of independence by materializing solidarity on the basis of the 1950 Arab League Collective Security Pact. In practice, as the Egyptian delegate Salah Salem expressed it, efforts have to be focused on arranging and organizing the "Arab house," consolidating Arab military and economic capabilities, and coordinating Arab efforts and plans. At this stage, no commitments should be concluded with foreign states, for which reason Arab states should not participate in the Turko-Pakistani alliance or any other defense arrangements outside the Arab region.

Moreover, according to the Turkish newspapers, this "unification of an Arab policy" would put an end to the Arabs' dispersion of their capabilities and their "wasting of energy" through disunity. In addition, a "unified Arab stand" would make of the Arab states a "weighty" interlocutor, and give them an elevated status in the international system (*Al-Ahram,* July–August 1954).

Finally, Nasser emphasized why such an "Arab strategy" would appeal psychologically to the masses: "The Arabs have been colonised for a long time and they are always afraid of falling back again under Western domination." For this reason, "defence of the area . . . has to spring from the area itself"; otherwise, the Arabs would not feel that "they are defending their own families, their own children, their own property . . . [but] British or American interests" (Nasser, vol. II, n.d.: 454–464). Accordingly, if the Western powers were really interested in having independent states that would provide the Middle East with a defense against "Communist danger," they should supply the Arabs with weapons, but without pressure and without requiring political commitments. In particular, they should not insist on retaining the power of command in the field of defense; the

Arabs themselves were capable of assuming the power of command even in the absence of any alignment.

The Baghdad Pact controversy is significant in at least two respects: (1) Nasser maintained that he was talking not only for Egypt but also in the name of a unified Arab strategy and of excolonized people and "underdogs" generally. Characteristic of his speeches at that time was his identification with general nationalist aspirations and the transcendence of the interests of individual states and governments. (2) The controversy between the supporters of pro-Western alignment and those of nonalignment was depicted as synonymous with the battle of "imperialism, zionism, and their stooges" against the forces of independence and Arab nationalism. If anyone questioned this equation, the Israeli attack of February 28, 1955, on the Egyptian-controlled territory of Gaza (killing thirty-eight people and wounding thirty-one) was to "prove" that Egypt was paying the price for its opposition to "imperialist" alliances. The attack confirmed that Nasser, an "Arab champion," was the "target of the Arabs' enemies," thereby enormously strengthening his position in the Arab region. With the defeat of the 1956 "Tripartite aggression" at Suez, his popularity expanded throughout the Third World.

Nasser—and behind him most of the Arabs—thus came to see nonalignment as a form of true independence. Nehru thought the same, and both men aired such views within the Afro-Asian gathering at Bandung. But nonalignment's third friend, Yugoslavia's Tito, could not be accommodated within such a gathering—and this brings us to the second factor favoring nonalignment over Afro-Asianism.

It was precisely Yugoslavia that pushed for a nonaligned gathering and attempted the institutionalization of the Nonaligned Movement (NAM). A year or so after Bandung, Tito invited his two colleagues for a summit in July 1956 at the Yugoslav island of Brioni. For the Yugoslavs, this tripartite summit among the high priests of the nonalignment cause was to lay the foundations of nonalignment as a Third World movement. Despite Nehru's hesitation, the institutionalization of NAM was indeed to take place with the First Nonaligned Summit at Belgrade in September 1961.

As others in addition to myself (e.g., Acimovic, 1969; Burton, 1965; Jansen, 1966; Korany, 1976; Lyon, 1963; Rubinstein, 1970; Sayegh, 1964; Willetts, 1978) have analyzed this conference in detail, what needs to be emphasized here is its contrast with Bandung. In particular, the First Nonaligned Summit at Belgrade signaled the continuation, consolidation, and increasing institutionalization of NAM, as indicated by three factors: (1) membership increase, (2) "economization" and sophistication of the

TABLE 1.1 Membership in Nonaligned Summit Conferences, 1961-1983

Summit Conference	Full Member	Observer	Guest	Total
Belgrade 1961	25	37	0	62
Cairo 1964	47	12✦	0	59
Lusaka 1970	53	12	13	65
Algiers 1973	75	29	3	86
Colombo 1976	86	21	7	114
Havana 1979	93	20	19	132
Delhi 1983	101	18	27	146

movement, and (3) its formal institutionalization. The last two phenomena relate to the competition between NAM and G-77.

With respect to the accelerated membership increase, Table 1.1 shows the evolution of the different categories of participants from the First Nonaligned Summit to the Seventh. At another level, a look at this table indicates that the nonaligned countries have shown a certain regularity in convening their summit conferences (usually every three years), with the exception of the Second and Third Conferences, which were separated by six years. The mid-1960s thus witnessed the Nonalignment Movement's lull, a lull that coincided with certain developments both in the international environment and within the Nonaligned group itself.

1. The Nonaligned Movement seemed to be facing a *crisis of orientation*. As a result of increasing communication and de-escalation between the superpowers following the 1962 Cuban missile crisis, nonalignment seemed to lose one of its basic functions—that of bridge building. On the eve of the Second Nonaligned Summit Conference (Cairo, 1964), some even raised the question as to whether nonalignment was still needed.

2. This crisis of orientation was aggravated by the presence of another crisis: the *crisis of leadership* following Nehru's death in May 1964, coupled with India's preoccupation with its conflict with China after their 1962 war. Some believed that this momentary eclipse of "moderate India" within the Nonalignment Movement might help the movement's reorientation by facilitating the task of the "radicals." But the radicals had their own problems: Algeria's Ben Bella was toppled in 1965; a year later Kwame Nkrumah faced the same fate, as did Ahmed Sukarno, finally;

then, after yet another year, the Arabs went down to a humiliating defeat and Nasserism was weakened.

3. A change in the *dominant mode of analysis* occurred in the study of Third World countries, from an emphasis on "modernization" to one on "dependency" (Korany, 1984b; Valenzuela and Valenzuela, 1978). The decolonization and rise of Third World states have been paralleled by the upsurge in courses and theories to analyze them (Bill and Hardgrave, 1973); some analysts have aspired to provide *the* paradigm to study these new polities (e.g., Hagen, 1962; McClelland, 1961; the Social Science Research Committee volumes inspired by the Almond and Coleman classic, 1960; and, of course, Rostow, 1960). All these works share some general but basic assumptions about the issues involved in the developmental process of the Third World and how to overcome them. Rostow's *The Stages of Economic Growth* (with a subtitle, *A Non-Communist Manifesto*, that shows the study's ambition) encompasses these issues:

- As the developmental process is unilinear, it does not involve incompatibilities between developed and developing countries. On the contrary, developed countries are the model to follow and will give "aid and advice" about how to reach the same end (i.e., development) as that reached in the West. In short, becoming modern meant becoming like the West.
- Modern is good and traditional is bad, and the two dichotomies are separate in society.
- Also separate are the processes of development and underdevelopment at the international level. This international dichotomy, or dualism, between development and underdevelopment is a reflection of the modern/traditional one within the societies of the Third World. Accordingly, Third World leadership must do away with the psychological and cultural obstacles to development—obstacles intrinsic to the traditional sector. In this way, Third World societies can accelerate their modernization (i.e., westernization) and increase their rate of integration into the global system.

Against this analysis is a counterparadigm that has adopted a global level of analysis and a historical-structural approach (Amin, 1969; Cardoso and Faletto, 1979; Chilcote and Edelstein, 1974; Frank, 1966; Ibrahim, 1982; Wallerstein, 1974) in addition to certain opposing assumptions:

- The starting point is not the study of underdevelopment in the national society but, rather, an analysis of the mode and results of interaction between developed and underdeveloped countries (see Frank's "The Development of Underdevelopment" [1966] or Rodney's "How Europe Underdeveloped Africa" [1974]). Accordingly, the Third World's economy as well as its social stratification patterns can be considered functions of this relationship (in this connection, refer to Amin's or Galtung's center/periphery relations).
- The interconnectedness among nations is paralleled within the Third World society itself by an interconnectedness among sectors, notably the traditional

and modern sectors of the Third World economy. Beyond the aforementioned dualism, the foreign-oriented modern sector has economically exploited the traditional sector and appropriated its surplus value for the benefit of the West (see Jallee's "The Pillage of the Third World").
- Hence the process of development is a conflict-laden one, not only with respect to the given national society but also as it relates to the outside system, whose structures and processes are adverse to developmental efforts because of the inherent historical patterns of unequal exchange (Emmanuel, 1972) or unequal development (Amin, 1973). Necessary, therefore, is a global restructuring—a new international order governing economy, of course (Mortimer, 1980; Reubens, 1981), but also other fields such as mass media (*Annuaire du Tiers-Monde*, 1976). The objective is economic growth not as an end in itself but, rather, as a means to satisfy the basic human needs of adequate food, safe water, health care, shelter, clothing, and education. This change in emphasis signaled the increasing dominance of a counterparadigm as frame of reference—that of political economy.

The fact that this counterparadigm so effectively reflects the daily life of the majority of the Third World population has made it a powerful analytical instrument that reoriented and revitalized the movement. Moreover, the adoption of this counterparadigm by Third World countries has changed it from an abstract concept to an explicit policy objective. In the process, both Third World academics and policy-makers have come closer together, and the nonaligned subsystem has become increasingly preoccupied with developmental issues. Hence we find that the Nonalignment Movement, now in keeping with the new economic context of Third World countries and much more functional in the face of their immediate problems and demands, has been revitalized.

Turning next to the second phase of NAM's evolution—its economization and sophistication—we find that it is not that economic issues were disregarded in the documents and deliberations of the nonaligned countries; even on the agenda at Bandung, economic questions figured significantly. Rather, it is the central place increasingly occupied by these issues in the conferences' agenda and deliberations, as well as their increasing primacy within international organizations, that matters here. Thus, without giving the false impression of neglecting politics, the Fifth Nonaligned Summit at Colombo (August 1976) emphasized an integrated approach:

> The increased importance given to economic affairs at nonaligned meetings does not imply acceptance of the view that the political aspects of international affairs should be left to the rich and powerful states, while the poor and weak should mainly concern themselves with economic affairs. That view has to be regarded as part of an imperialist strategy aimed at preserving

an international order favourable to the rich and powerful (item 157 of the Political Declaration, Colombo Nonaligned Summit, 1976).

This continuing preoccupation with politics is all the more justified in the new "economic era" of nonalignment, given that "a complete change of political attitude and the demonstration of a new political will is an indispensable prerequisite for the realization of the new international economic order" (ibid., item 156). Such preoccupation with political matters is therefore valuable as a means to attain the objective of economic development. Indeed, "the conference noted with satisfaction that nonaligned meetings are giving increased importance to economic affairs. This is a reflection of the fact that the great majority of the nonaligned states are poor or underdeveloped. Economic affairs must, therefore, be their primary concern if political independence is to have real meaning" (ibid., item 155).

Hence we find an increasing saliency of economic questions in the conferences' final declarations. For instance, the 1961 Belgrade Final Declaration amounted to 4.5 pages in the form of a general statement devoted primarily to political questions, with occasional references to economic aspects. This was followed by a declaration on war and peace, and by messages to Khrushchev and Kennedy. But the 1979 Havana Final Declaration contained two parts: a twenty-seven-page political section and a twenty-page economic section, as well as an Action Program for Economic Cooperation. This latter part dealt with sixteen areas of cooperation, ranging from policies concerning fisheries and agriculture to such topics as the role of women as well as the issues of public enterprises, monetary-financial cooperation, and scientific and technological cooperation. Moreover, the Action Program took care to specify the coordinating countries responsible for organizing (and usually chairing) the various meetings as well as the central headquarters for each area.

Coupled with the saliency of economic issues and the adoption of a relevant paradigm is the *growing degree of sophistication* and increasing role of technicians in the structure of NAM. For instance, the following seven technical groups held no fewer than thirty meetings in the four-year period from 1973 to 1977—that is, more than seven meetings per year. These meetings break down as follows: (1) Experts on Private Foreign Investment: two meetings; (2) Intergovernmental Group on Raw Materials: six meetings; (3) Information and Press Group: four meetings; (4) Science, Technology, and Research: three meetings; (5) Public Enterprises and Multinational Companies: six meetings; (6) Solidarity Fund for Economic and Social Development of Nonaligned Countries (Committee of Experts):

two meetings; and (7) Action Program for Economic Cooperation (Meeting of Coordinator Countries): seven meetings.

The revitalization of NAM in the 1970s was associated with some problems concerning the global institutional representation of the Third World. For instance, given its emphasis on economic issues, NAM was increasingly encroaching upon, and indeed undermining, the raison d'être of another well-established Third World group: the G-77. There thus existed a potential for competition, and some "old hands" were reminded of the previous competition between Bandung (symbolizing the Afro-Asian gathering) and Belgrade (symbolizing NAM). Accordingly, before considering NAM's institutionalization, we must discuss the third group claiming to speak for Third Worldism—the Group of 77.

THE GROUP OF 77: THE THIRD WORLD'S TRADE UNION

In contrast to the multifaceted objective of NAM, the G-77 had from the very start a specific focus: economic issues—so much so, in fact, that some analysts (Sauvant 1982: xiii) affirmed that "North/South negotiations about the international economic system in general and its impact on the development process of the Third World in particular are thus unthinkable without the Group of 77." Yet, until very recently, the G-77 lacked all the elements of a basic institutional infrastructure (i.e., a permanent secretariat, a headquarters, and even a constitution). The group thus remained multicentral in character. Its original chapter is in Geneva, where UNCTAD's headquarters are centered, but other chapters have developed in Vienna and Rome. The arrangements of the G-77 have thus been very informal, with a high degree of organizational flexibility.

As mentioned before, different dates have been given as to the emergence of the G-77. In fact, its emergence developed in three stages. The first stage occurred in 1963 on the occasion of the convening of a UN preparatory committee responsible for the first session of UNCTAD. At the closing of the second session of this committee, Third World representatives (but including some from New Zealand) submitted a Joint Statement summarizing the views, needs, and aspirations of the Third World with regard to the impending UNCTAD session. This statement was submitted to the UN General Assembly later in the year as a Joint Declaration on behalf of seventy-five developing countries that were UN members.

The second stage in the creation of the G-77 materialized in the spring of 1964 when UNCTAD I (March 23–June 16) was convened in Geneva. Interests had clearly crystallized along geopolitical lines—hence the strengthening of the original Group of 75, which became 77. In fact, New Zealand dropped out and later joined OECD, but Kenya (which by then had become independent and joined the UN) was added to the original seventy-four signatories along with South Korea and South Vietnam, which were members not of the UN but of UNCTAD (Raghavan, 1985: 54). In the "Joint Declaration of the Seventy-seven" adopted on June 15, 1964, the signatories referred to UNCTAD as "an event of historic importance" and found unity to be its "outstanding feature." It was "this unity that has given clarity and coherence to the discussions of this Conference" (Sauvant, 1981). They thus pledged to maintain and consolidate it through "joint programs of action" and "specific arrangements for contacts and consultations" (Sauvant, 1981: 2). The choice of Raoul Prebisch, from Argentina, as UNCTAD's first secretary-general (1964-1969) certainly gave a boost to the ideas of the G-77.

The third phase in the establishment of the G-77 occurred in October 1967 in conjunction with its first Ministerial Meeting in Algiers. Its membership had already grown to eighty-six countries (Grimaud, 1984: 216), and over seventy developing countries sent delegates to Algiers with the immediate task of synthesizing "3 documents that had been drafted in each of three continent-wide meetings, a task that reflected perfectly the regional nature of the Group of 77 at the operation level" (Mortimer, 1980: 26). The Algerian leaders, who wanted very much to play host to a second Bandung Conference, which never convened, used this meeting as a substitute to air their views on the international system. At the beginning of the meeting, Boumedienne's inaugural speech set the tone by affirming that "the principal confrontation in to-day's world is between imperialism and the Third World" (i.e., the North and the South). On October 24, 1967, after two weeks of deliberations, the G-77 published its charter (UN Document TD/38), which reiterated many of the topics of the original Algerian document and set forth for the first time the comprehensive views of the Third World on development and international economic relations. These views still govern the negotiating position of the Third World with respect to trade in raw materials, manufactured goods, and services; finance and development aid; and the structure of international economic relations generally.

Following this third phase, the Group of 77 consolidated itself through several meetings, either at the level of UNCTAD as a whole or at the more limited ministerial and/or expert level. Up to this point, UNCTAD had held six sessions—namely, UNCTAD I (Geneva in 1964), UNCTAD II (New Delhi in 1968), UNCTAD III (Santiago, Chile, in 1972), UNCTAD IV (Nairobi, Kenya, in 1976), UNCTAD V (Manila, Philippines, in 1979), and UNCTAD VI (Belgrade, Yugoslavia, in 1983). With the exception of UNCTAD V, the sessions were scheduled on a quadrennial basis.

Between UNCTAD sessions, the G-77 holds meetings at the ministerial and/or expert level. For example, between November 1963 (when the Group of 77 submitted their Joint Statement to the eighteenth session of the UN General Assembly) and the meeting of the group during the thirty-fifth session of the UN General Assembly (October 1, 1980), I counted no fewer than 171 meetings, including 4 meetings of the group's ministers of foreign affairs (for an excellent chronology, see Sauvant, 1981: 217-224). Given the burgeoning number of meetings, the questions of overlappings in membership, basic issues, and jurisdiction between the Group of 77 and NAM were bound to arise, especially when G-77 tried to institutionalize its structure.

This brings us to the topic of Third World institutionalization, a subject of prime and direct importance to the issue of decision-making as such.

INSTITUTIONALIZATION, INTRA-THIRD WORLD COMPETITIVENESS, AND CONSENSUS BUILDING

INSTITUTIONALIZATION

The first attempts at institutionalization of NAM became clear at the Third Summit in Lusaka in 1970, when President Kenneth Kaunda was appointed chairman of the Nonaligned group. However, this issue had plagued NAM even before its establishment and the convening of the First Summit at Belgrade.

From the very beginning, there were two views. One school of thought held that if NAM was to play an effective political role among conflicting blocs, a minimum of coordination in views and concerted action was necessary among NAM members. This argument in favor of greater coordination seemed justified when in 1960 the nonaligned countries witnessed certain typical decolonization problems following the political independence of the ex-Belgian Congo (Zaire)—an "independence" that brought with it foreign invasion, the nascent state's disintegration, the assassination of Prime Minister Patrice Lumumba, and the controversy over the UN role in the crisis. NAM became badly divided, and there was a total absence of any collective action (Korany, 1976: 186-187).

However, with respect to the second school of thought, other NAM members (championed by Nehru in India) opposed even a minimum level of institutionalization, for fear of giving the impression that the nonaligned countries were constituting a third bloc. Nehru hesitated to attend both the 1956 Tripartite Brioni Meeting and the First Summit at Belgrade. He finally went along because he realized that, with or without him, the trend toward conference gathering would continue; thus he attended and tried to keep the decision-making machinery as informal as possible. Even when "moderates" such as Tunisia's Bourguiba suggested meetings among NAM ministers of foreign affairs, finance, development, education, and information so as to "give each other mutual assistance," widen "the circle of uncommitted countries," and achieve a "moral striking force" (Bourguiba's speech at Belgrade), these attempts were resisted. However, NAM finally acquired some institutional teeth, as indicated in Figure 1.1. In this connection, three institutional mechanisms have been elaborated and emphasized: the scheduling of periodic meetings at the summit and/or ministerial or technical level; the requirement of a three-year chairmanship or presidency of NAM to keep the Nonaligned Movement going and its members in contact between summit meetings; and, finally, the establishment of a Coordinating Bureau. Each of these mechanisms merits a brief description.

Periodicity of Meetings

The Second Summit of 1964 met very soon after Nehru's death and was occupied by discussions about changes in the global environment and the possible change in orientation of NAM. Thus it was at the Third Summit in Lusaka in 1970—six years after Nehru's death and following a change in leadership—that NAM took the first steps in establishing an institutional structure. At this time, the conference approved a "resolution strengthening the role of the Nonaligned Countries" and spoke of the meeting of the "3rd Summit of NAM" at its *third regular* session at Lusaka (Conference of Nonaligned Countries, 1970, emphasis added). This final communiqué also spoke of insistent demands from various delegates to increase "the effectiveness of Nonaligned Countries through *appropriate machinery*" (my emphasis) and to entrust the *chairman* to maintain contacts among members to ensure implementation of decisions and directives and enhance continuity until the next meeting (Korany, 1976: 196–206).

It might have been unwarranted to take literally such press reports as "Third World nations set up headquarters" or "Zambia Chief heads permanent secretariat" (*Christian Science Monitor*, editorial, 15 September 1970), but the trend to come was inevitable. The deliberations and resolutions of the Conference of Foreign Ministers of NAM held in Georgetown (August 8–12, 1972) explicitly reiterated the trend toward institutionalization by interpreting decisions of previous conferences as steps going in the same direction. Moreover, the conference adopted an "Action Program for Economic Cooperation Among Nonaligned Countries," identified "institutional arrangements for such cooperation and coordi-

Figure 1.1 The Organizational Structure of the Non-Aligned Movement (December 1981)

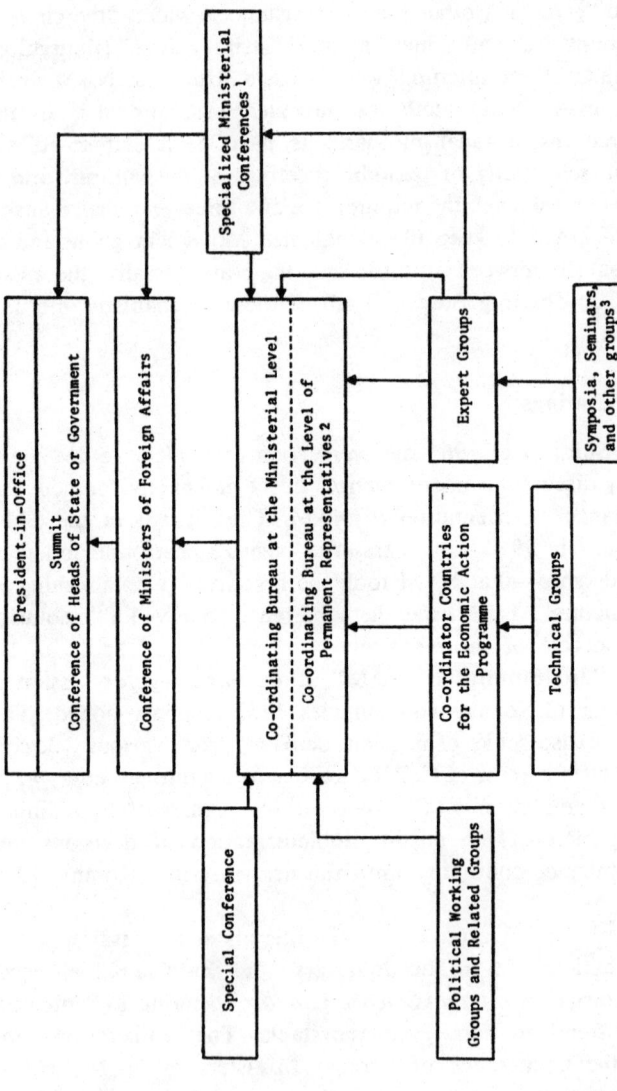

[1] The First Special Conference, Cairo 1962, took place before the establishment of the Bureau.
[2] The Co-ordinating Bureau at the Level of Permanent Representatives also functions as preparatory committee for summits, foreign minister conferences, and meetings for the Bureau at the ministerial level.
[3] If no competent expert group exists, these meetings may report to any other body of the non-aligned movement.

SOURCE: Sauvant, 1982.

nation," and decreed that "the Ministers of Nonaligned Countries should meet every two years" to follow up the economic arrangements. In addition, the ministerial conference approved a "Resolution on Coordination," which, after extending the mandate of the Preparatory Committee that assisted the government of Zambia, coordinated all further activities in the preparation of the next (Fourth) Summit. The conference coordinator then made the following proposal to the next summit conference:

> A. September Meeting of Non-Aligned Countries: A meeting of Non-Aligned Countries at a Ministerial level shall be held in the last week of September, as deemed necessary and desirable from 1974, at the United Nations Headquarters a few days after the opening of the General Assembly, to coordinate participants' approaches to the matters of common concern.
>
> B. Standing Committee of Non-Aligned Countries: To consider the desirability of creating a Standing Committee composed of seven Non-Aligned Countries which shall be elected every year by the September Ministerial Meeting on the basis of geographical distribution and of rotation. Its main task will be to review all preparatory work of the yearly September Ministerial Meeting and any other matter they consider necessary to bring to the notice of the yearly Foreign Ministers' Meeting.

It is usually the country assuming chairmanship that keeps track of all these meetings (see Figure 1.2) and summons new ones. This brings us to the second aspect of the institutional mechanism: the chairman (or chairwoman).

Chairmanship or Presidency

Although both *chairmanship* and *presidency* refer to the same institutional mechanism, only one such term applies in a given situation; the term chosen generally indicates whether the chairperson in question is going to be active or not. Castro, for instance, usually used the term *president,* and, indeed, his pattern of behavior was different from that of Sri Lanka's Mrs. S.W.R.D. Bandaranaike (who was the first chairwoman) and of India's Indira Gandhi (who was the second). The chairperson, in combination with his or her foreign ministry and his or her country's permanent UN delegation, most closely resembles a NAM Secretariat; indeed, some countries, such as India, have established within their foreign ministeries a Department of Nonalignment Affairs.

At the beginning of NAM and long before the establishment of the chairmanship, this role was assumed *informally* by the triumvirate of Nehru in India, Nasser in Egypt, and Tito in Yugoslavia. Nehru's resistance notwithstanding, these three high priests of NAM, by meeting at Brioni in 1956, initiated the institutional trend, albeit informally. Both before

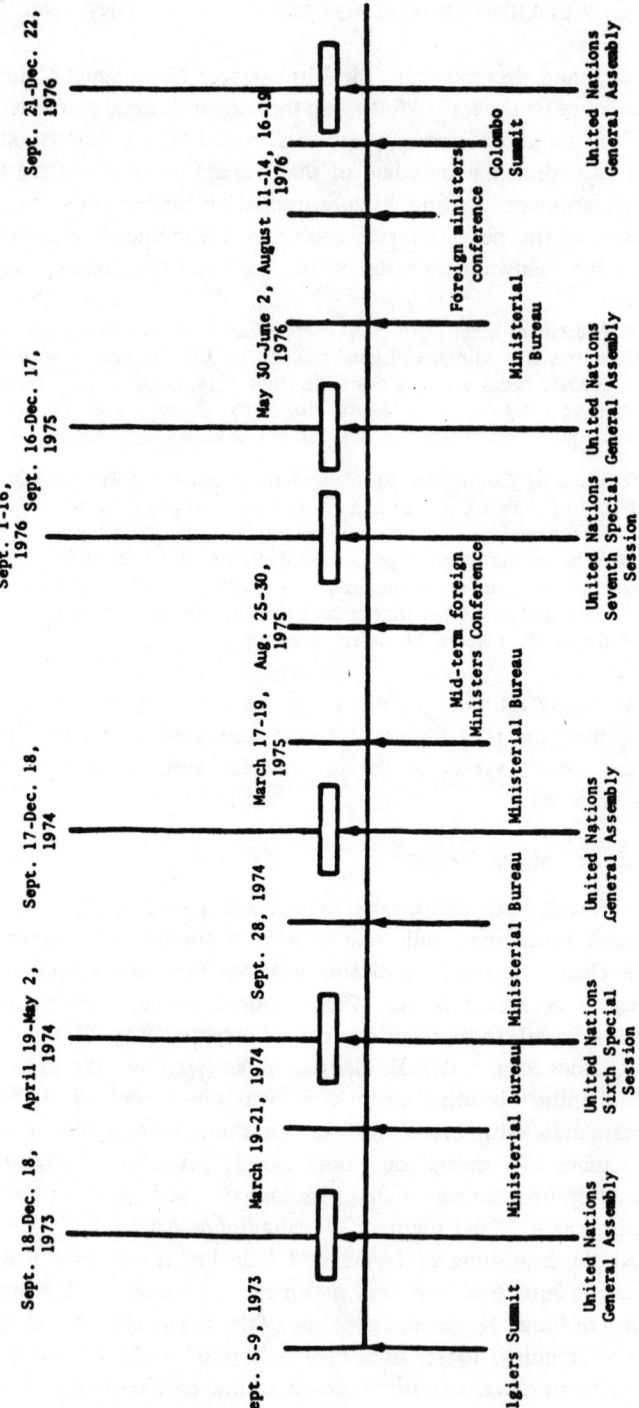

Figure 1.2 Time Pattern of High-Level Meetings of Non-Aligned Countries Between Summits, Exemplified for the Period Between the Algiers and Colombo Summits

SOURCE: Sauvant, 1982.

Shaw in this volume), and in 1978 it sent about 17,000 troops to bolster the Marxist regime in Ethiopia. Moreover, some NAM members inferred from Castro's speech during the Congress of the Cuban Communist party (December 17, 1980), in which he explicitly endorsed the entry of Soviet troops into Afghanistan and the application of the Brezhnev Doctrine to Poland, that Cuba was putting its role in the cold war before its chairmanship of NAM. Consequently, Castro's chairmanship was perceived by many within NAM as excessively favoring one school of thought rather than acting as a median rallying point to promote consensus.

Such a perception—if not dissipated promptly and convincingly by the chair—tends to be dysfunctional for the Nonaligned Movement as a whole, because resistance among the rank and file could develop against the elected leadership. Thus, for instance, Cuba was not able to wield nonaligned approval (as a function of the UN "automatic majority") to put the issue of Puerto Rico on the agenda of the UN General Assembly. More important, these "radical" aspects of Cuba's chairmanship fueled demands by some members to reconsider the role and mode of functioning of NAM's Coordinating Bureau.

The Coordinating Bureau

The Coordinating Bureau, formally instituted at the Fourth Summit in Algiers in 1973, was not so much a new invention as a continuation of an already existing arrangement—true especially of the Preparatory Committee, which was initially instituted to help Zambia host the Third Summit. The Bureau evolved very quickly to include more members and wider jurisdiction. Its mandate was to supervise the increasing economic deliberations and activities of NAM, coordinate policy at the UN, and prepare the next (i.e., Fifth) summit in Colombo.

According to the decision of this latter summit "regarding the composition and mandate of the Co-ordinating Bureau," the Bureau works at two levels. The first of these is the ministerial level, in keeping with instructions from the Colombo Summit to continue meeting once a year (in a nonaligned capital) at the level of the ministers of foreign affairs. This was already the practice, as the record shows: March 1976 in Algiers; April 1977 in New Delhi; and May 1978 in Havana. The second level is that of the permanent representatives at the UN, who meet regularly (in principle, once a month) in New York to coordinate moves on the submission and drafting of different resolutions, including negotiations with other groups and the mobilization of NAM members. In addition, the Bureau was authorized to meet in emergency session pending the occurrence of "special crisis situations . . . directly concerning the Non-

and after Brioni, they kept in close contact and met relatively frequently either *à deux* or *à trois* to keep the movement going and on the "right track." Thus, between 1955 and 1964 (the year of Nehru's death), Nehru went to Belgrade three times, and Nasser went five times. But the number of *actual* meetings was, of course, much higher. For instance, during the period 1955–1968, Nasser and Tito met more than twenty times, and Nasser's biographer affirms that the number of their meetings went beyond thirty (see Korany, 1976: 177, and the references cited therein).

The leaders of these three countries, however, held three tripartite conferences: Brioni (1956), Cairo (1961), and New Delhi (1966, when Indira Gandhi replaced her deceased father). In this last meeting, the three leaders presided over the reorientation of NAM toward a greater emphasis on economic aspects. Indeed, 40 percent of their Final Communiqué was devoted to economic issues. "Perhaps the most outstanding result of the meeting," Indira Gandhi declared, was the collective approach "to the economic challenges to nonalignment and peaceful coexistence." Consequently, the three leaders decided to explore the possibilities of giving a *formal* core to NAM in this sphere. Two months after the Tripartite Summit, the ministers of economy of the three states met in New Delhi (Korany, 1976: 181).

This informal tripartite leadership reflected the pattern of decision-making in the 1950s and 1960s. The 1970s, of course, were to tell another story. With the increase in and diversity of membership, NAM lost the simplicity of its "small-club" structure, which could be oriented and managed by the political directives of the triumvirate. Formal chairmanship was, by necessity, a part of the revitalization of NAM in the 1970s, after the lull of the late 1960s.

Neither the chairmanship of Zambia's Kaunda (1970–1973) nor that of Sri Lanka (1976–1979) had much impact on NAM. Kaunda as first chairman had little in terms of precedents and rules to guide him. Moreover, he was the head of a relatively small country that had difficulties hosting the Third Summit for even a few days; others had promised financial and technical help to enable Lusaka to accommodate the delegates. The administrative-diplomatic infrastructure at Kaunda's disposal could not enable him to play an active and effective chairmanship role, even if he had desired to do so.

In the case of Sri Lanka, when Bandaranaike's Freedom party lost the 1977 elections, she was succeeded by J. R. Jayewardene and the United National party. There was no noticeable difference between either the two parties or the two leaders regarding nonalignment. The transition prompted most of the nonaligned countries to adopt an attitude of wait-and-see, thus putting Jayewardene very much on the spot and possibly limiting his maneuverability. In short, Sri Lanka's chairmanship was an entirely uneventful one (Jackson, 1983: 55-74).

Nevertheless, Sri Lanka was the first Asian country to host the Nonaligned Summit and to occupy the chair. India is now the second, although its chairmanship is too recent to be evaluated. But with the assassination of Indira Gandhi, India, much like Sri Lanka, has experienced a leadership change while occupying the chair of NAM.

The other two cases of chairmanship, that of Algeria (1973-1976) and Cuba (1979-1983), transferred NAM leadership to its radical wing. The two countries, however, occupied the chair at different junctures in the evolution of NAM and manifested different patterns of leadership. Unlike Cuba (and also Iraq), Algeria did not make a sustained claim to host the Fourth Summit. At the Lusaka Meeting, no formal decision was made concerning either the location of the following summit or the NAM presidency. But by informal agreement between Bandaranaike and Presidents Tito and Kaunda, Sri Lanka was to be the host in 1973. This choice of Sri Lanka would also have taken care of the informal rotation system concerning the regional group or continent hosting the summit. However, at the 1972 Georgetown ministerial conference, the African Group rallied round Algeria, and their majority ensured a formal endorsement of this country.

Algeria took over NAM chairmanship when the collectivity experienced a leadership vacuum and was still groping—after the lull of the 1960s—for a consensual orientation that would revitalize the Nonalignment Movement and integrate its membership. Algeria's active role in the G-77 and the regional African and Arab spheres of activity allowed it to assume the NAM leadership smoothly. Indeed, the Fourth Summit constituted a watershed that renewed the movement and left Algeria's imprint on its evolution. Thus, in the summer of 1973, Algeria established an organizational committee to guarantee the largest participation. In July, a few ambassadors were sent around the world to encourage attendance at the highest level. A month later, Algeria's ministers were sent on similar missions throughout the Nonaligned group. As a result, seventy-five countries attended and as many as sixty delegations were led by their heads of state (Korany and Dessouki, 1984: 106).

During the conference itself, Boumedienne set the tone in his inaugural speech, emphasizing the primacy of North/South relations. Unlike Kaunda, Boumedienne (both as summit host and as chairman for the ensuing three years), backed by his dynamic foreign minister, Abdel-Aziz Bouteflika, and a large political staff, lobbied actively and successfully for a specific action program. For instance, the Algerians, for the first time in the history of NAM, "used tight control of Conference procedures to manage the Summit's outcome and to sidetrack extraneous issue The result was a more coherent and anti-Western generalizations and sometimes conflicting positions o (Jackson, 1983: 64). After the summit, Algeria—in the World—followed up its conclusions at the world level l primacy of North/South issues. Thus Algeria, with c summoned a Special UN Session in 1974 and had it iss on the Establishment of the New International Econor As chairman of NAM, and quoting the deliberations of t Boumedienne delivered the opening speech of which used in the declaration itself (see Korany and Desso a systematic comparison between the two documents)

Algeria's radicalism, however, did not lead to any sch or to the alienation of the "moderate" wing. For althou as being anti-Western, Algeria also emphasized Third W the primacy of economic issues, the necessity for world the avoidance of the "two imperialisms" of West and I while profiting from the leadership vacuum to exerci mandate of chairmanship, it gave NAM a specific ec rallied the Nonalignment Movement's membership.

Cuba's chairmanship was different. Even previous cations and "disinformation campaigns" that occurred Sixth Summit at Havana, Cuba had always been in th war. From the very beginning, the participation of Cu NAM have been closely linked to its relations with Moscow, in addition to being affected by the state of the two superpowers. Indeed, Cuba's "admission as Latin American member in 1961 was a direct result invasion earlier in the year. The image of a small invasion by a Superpower ensured NAM acceptance" (

But the end of the invasion did not lessen Cuba's s the United States and its consequent growing depen Thus, while Cuba enjoyed sympathy and prestige, a of NAM members considered it "too radical" and not same way" as they were. These opinions affected Cu reactions "from the floor," and even the functioning o Bureau.

Although Cuba was usually seconded by countries li Korea, or Ethiopia, its specific ideological goals set i fringe far even from Algeria's goals. For instance, in Soviet support sent about 20,000 troops to Angola Neto's radical movement (see Domínguez and Lindau, aligned Countries" and "if need be to recommend any action which should seem appropriate" (Mortimer, 1980: 89).

When the Bureau was formally established at the Fourth Summit in Algeria, seventeen members were present. This number increased to twenty-five at the Fifth Summit in Colombo, increased again to thirty-six at the Sixth Summit in Havana in 1979, and finally reached its present total of seventy-four seats at the Seventh Summit in New Delhi. This continuing increase in the Bureau's composition was dictated not only by the increase in NAM membership but also by the desire to keep a careful regional balance and thus ensure the Bureau's political representativeness. Of the seventy-four seats approved at the New Delhi Summit, then, thirty-six are designated for Africa, twenty-three for Asia, twelve for Latin America, and three for Europe (Jackson, 1983: 51).

It is this insistence on the Bureau's political representativeness that defeated notions by some countries (such as Iraq, Libya, and Tanzania) to transform the Bureau into a permanent, centralized secretariat. Those opposed to such a move feared that the Bureau would become a nucleus of activist or "first-class" NAM members, or, as Sri Lanka's Foreign Minister put it, a "cabinet—an inner circle—a cabal of decision-makers" (Jackson, 1983: 52). Such an elitist aspect would lessen the Bureau's political accountability and its control. For many members, this continues to be a serious issue, especially in those instances when the chairperson conceives of his or her role as one taken up with proselytizing (as in the case of Cuba's representative) rather than with mediation and consensus building among the different orientations. As a result, there were pressures to "democratize" decision-making in NAM and to open the Bureau meetings to all members. Consequently, the Bureau's sessions have come to resemble plenary meetings—a clear case of conflict between the democratization of NAM decision-making and its maximum usefulness.

Debates concerning the role and mode of functioning of the Bureau notwithstanding, this organ continues to wield an important influence within NAM. It supervises the work of the "coordinator countries" responsible for twenty-one economic subjects, as well as that of nine political working groups on issues such as Cyprus, Korea, and Palestine. In addition, it has assumed primary responsibility over the ever-present and controversial issue of membership (concerning such questions as which government's delegation should occupy Kampuchea's seat, whether Egypt should be suspended following the conclusion of the 1978 Camp David Accords, and so on). Moreover, its growing number of extraordinary ministerial meetings allows it to anticipate and orient NAM strategy on crucial issues. Finally, "relegation of disputed issues to the Bureau for recommendations has consolidated its central policy-making role" by making it the arbiter of last resort (Jackson, 1983: 53-54). In this respect, it has not only prevented divisions within NAM from being aggravated but has also helped the group to maintain unity in its ranks and to talk with one voice to other groups, with representatives from both developed countries and developing ones (e.g., the G-77). It should be remembered that the Havana Summit specifically charged the Bureau to meet as an entity within the G-77 to ensure NAM's catalytic role at this level (Jackson, 1983: 53). This brings us to the last point in our analysis of decision-making structure and characteristics at the Third World level: the potential for competition between NAM and G-77, which are the two groups representing Third Worldism at present.

INTRAGROUP COMPETITIVENESS

With the eyes of the world increasingly turned toward economic issues, the role of the Group of 77 became more prominent in Third World annals, thus leading the G-77 to attempt to institutionalize itself and emerge as a serious competitor, if not yet an alternative, to NAM (see Figure 1.3).

The drive for institutionalization came primarily from the Asian Group, which—in contrast to Africa and Latin America—did not have a regional organization. The most enthusiastic were countries such as Iran and Pakistan (before they joined NAM), the Philippines, and certain Latin American countries such as Mexico (Mortimer, 1980: 80). Despite opposition, the campaign to institutionalize G-77 picked up speed with the passage of time and the support of such leaders as Nyerere of Tanzania (as evidenced by his opening speech to the group's 1979 Arusha Conference) and Manuel Perez Guerero of Venezuela, who is the current secretary-general of the UN, but was UNCTAD's secretary-general in 1979.

Briefly stated, the high-level meeting of the G-77 in Caracas in 1981 emphasized the importance of the South-South Cooperation principle (i.e., the principle of cooperation among Third World countries) and brought the foreign ministers in to give political thrust to its drive. It ended by approving the Caracas Program of Action (CPA), which called for the following institutional elements:

> an Intergovernmental Follow-up and Coordination Committee of senior officials, for review, policy-making and general monitoring, to meet once a year; sectoral review meetings at the level of senior officials once in two years; and annual ministerial meetings of the Group in New York at the time of the U.N. General Assembly, concentrating every second year on a thorough review and appraisal of ECDC (Economic Cooperation Among Developing Countries) Programmes in order "to provide the necessary

Figure 1.3 The Multi-Central Structure of the Group of 77, December 1981

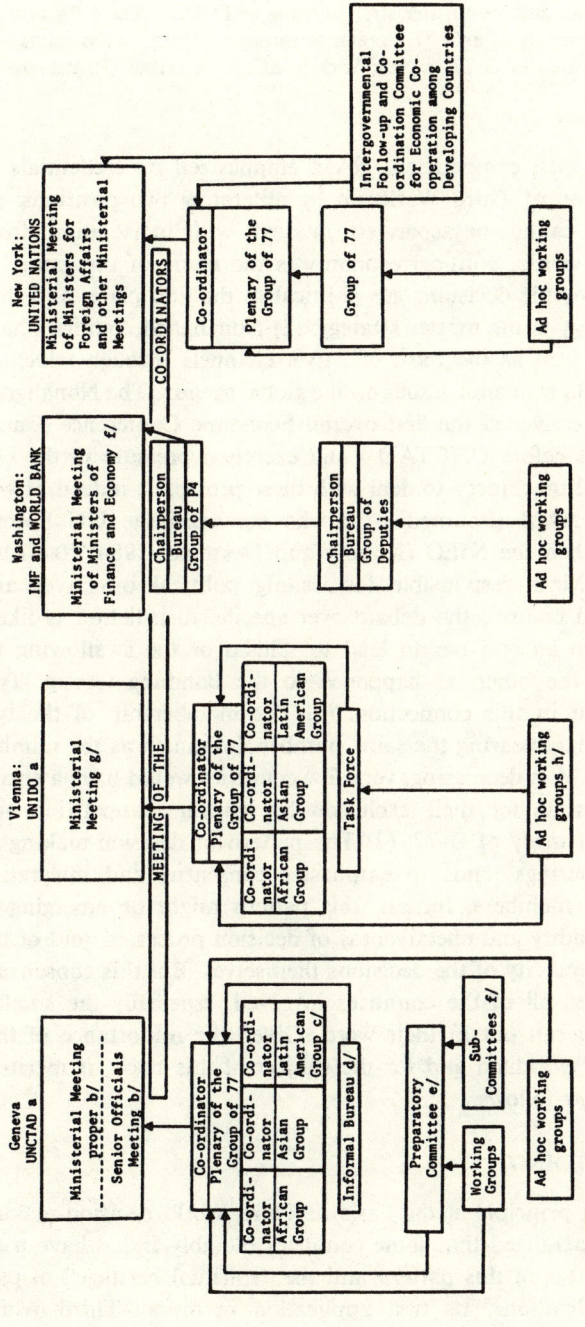

a/ And other international organizations of the United Nations system headquartered in that city.
b/ Only in preparation of UNCTAD sessions.
c/ Romania is an associate member.
d/ Consisting of the co-ordinator of the Group of 77 and the co-ordinators of the regional groups.
e/ Only in preparation of Ministerial Meetings.
f/ Established by the Preparatory Committee.
g/ Only in preparation of UNIDO General Conferences.
h/ A working group in reference to the Committee on Assurance of Supply of the International Atomic Energy Agency has a somewhat more permanent character.
i/ So far, only one such meeting, on 29 September 1979, took place.

SOURCE: Sauvant, 1982.

guidance and take other decisions required with respect to policy issues and operational matters and for further strengthening of ECDC." The CPA also provided the rudiments of a G 77 secretariat through a "core of assistants" to help the Chairman of G 77 in New York in ECDC activities (Raghavan, 1985: 60).

In the face of such competition, NAM emphasized its credentials as the very incarnation of Third Worldism by reiterating two positions: (1) Economic aspects cannot be separated, or dealt with in isolation, from politics. In other words, political economy is the name of the game. In fact, so-called economic decisions are political in the first place, and thus the political strategy is the master strategy. (2) Nonaligned countries have been the first, as well as the most effective, channels through which to impose Third World economic issues on the global agenda. The Nonaligned countries as such convened the first overall Economic Conference (Cairo, 1962) twelve years before UNCTAD I and exercised pressure in the UN to establish special machinery to deal with these problems; indeed, it was the chairman of NAM (Boumedienne) who convened the UN Special Session and launched the NIEO (Korany and Dessouki, 1984: 104-108).

Now that NAM is responsible for issuing political directives and exercising political control, the debate over specific jurisdiction is likely neither to come to an end nor to lead to schism or the swallowing up of one group by the other, as happened to the Bandung Group. Two points are relevant in this connection: (1) The membership of the two groups is increasingly nearing the same number. Inasmuch as the number of outsiders in NAM is decreasing, very few countries would have a strong reason to compensate for their exclusion by igniting competition and working for the primacy of G-77. (2) The pattern of decision-making in Third World gatherings tends to emphasize consensus and integrative tendencies among members. Indeed, this pattern might be emerging at the expense of rapidity and effectiveness of decision processes, and of the optimality and specificity of the decisions themselves. But this consensual pattern has allowed all of the countries involved, especially the smaller states, to feel they can put in their word. Given the importance of this pattern for Third Worldism and for the subject of this book, it merits a longer comment, as follows.

CONSENSUS BUILDING

The consensual principle at the basis of Third World decision-making seems to be so generalized that some countries (notably India) have tried to create a link between this pattern and the "spiritual heritage" of past Third World civilizations. Its first application in an all-Third World gathering took place at Bandung in 1955. It was Nehru, upon his arrival at Bandung airport, who stated that the conference should not decide anything by vote—a principle that, indeed, had already been adopted by the Colombo powers who had convened Bandung and, ultimately, the precedent followed by the Commonwealth Prime Ministers' Conference (Jansen, 1966: 193). Nehru was an important pillar of both, and the practice continued. As a representative at the 1979 Havana Summit put it:

> The practice of adopting decisions of the Nonaligned Countries by consensus [must] be continued. Consensus has a certain indefinable quality hard to express in words although we all know instinctively what it means. It presupposes understanding of and respect for different points of view including disagreement and implies mutual accommodation on the basis of which agreement can emerge by a sincere process of adjustment among member nations in the true spirit of Nonalignment. Consensus is both a process and a final compromise formula, shaped by prior consultations, discussions, and negotiations into a generally agreed position. In other words, consensus is a general convergence and harmonization of views reflecting the broadest consent of the conference, or meeting, enhancing or at least preserving the unity and strength of the Movement (Willetts, 1981: 210).

Not only is this procedure time consuming, however, but it may also prevent decisions from being recorded (unless they are accepted unanimously). In other words, a single dissenter may impose a veto on a decision being reached (Jansen, 1966: 194). Hypothetically, this handicap could paralyze Third World action at a time when its institutions were proliferating and its membership increasing.

Consequently, although the consensus was maintained and a minority/majority vote did not become necessary, an additional practice was adopted to avoid paralysis in decision-making: Each country could express its own reservations about the decision adopted. As the Havana procedure stipulates, "reservations should be avoided as far as possible because they tend to weaken the consensus," but such reservations are kept because they "cannot block or veto a consensus" and because they allow "the maintenance of the democratic character of the Movement and sovereignty of every one of its members." Reservations were few at the early meetings, but at the Colombo Summit in 1976, thirty-six states recorded reservations; at the Sixth Summit in Havana the number increased to forty, and at the Seventh Summit in New Delhi it increased to forty-three (Jackson, 1983: 41).

In the case of both NAM and the G-77, the process of consensus formation is one of negotiation based on the presence and acceptance of regional groups within the whole (e.g., the African Group, with fifty-one members, constitutes more than half of NAM). Their importance is so evident that Sri Lanka's foreign minister proposed in New Delhi in 1983 that "the NAM Chairman be backstopped by 4 regional chairmen who hold regular and separate meetings" (Jackson, 1983: 45). In the case of G-77, the consensus takes place at three levels (Sauvant, 1981: 16–18). Negotiations usually start at the level of the regional group and work upward. Within each regional group, different countries have to exchange support for their different positions and, by this means, facilitate the reaching of compromise. The same principle applies at the second level (i.e., in negotiations among the regional groups)—hence the trading of support and package deals. This trading process, of course, takes time and can lead to factionalization, but since each regional group needs the support of the others, compromise (or agreement on a maximum position) is, again, usually valued. Finally, the third level is the plenary of G-77, where compromises have to be found that are acceptable to all—"even if these should require renewed consultations with the regional groups" (Sauvant, 1981: 17). Then follows a fourth level: negotiations between G-77 and the developed countries, whether market-economy or centrally planned. As these groups have also elaborated their fragile consensus, their prenegotiation positions are wide apart and could even be inflexible. Consequently, in order to promote further compromise while maintaining the unity of the group, the hard-liners are usually sent to negotiate with other groups.

The decision-making process is of course cumbersome, tiring, and very time-consuming. Moreover, even if "solutions" do finally emerge, they are only partial ones or vague compromises. The various issues on the agenda are thus bound to appear again and again. Yet the procedure has substantial advantages. It avoids the isolation of individual members and the calling into question of their continued participation, as well as the divisions that might otherwise endanger the group's survival.

CONCLUSIONS

Integrative tendencies among Third World member nations form the basis of both the Third World's emergence and its collective decision-making. Concerning the latter issue, three characteristics should be emphasized:

1. The Third World's self-assertion and the manifestation of its collective identity have come of age, as a function, above all, of the common position of its countries within the global hierarchy. No longer formally integrated

into colonial empires, these countries are vulnerable, suffer from an acute sense of threat, face serious economic problems, and feel that the "system" is somehow rigged against them.

2. Notwithstanding the presence of common characteristics and interests within the Third World, the analyst should avoid any overhomogenization (i.e., glossing over of differences) among its different countries and clusters. Although Third Worldism is equated with NAM, the groping toward expression of a collective identity at the global level has had a multigroup involvement from the very beginning. These groups can be general (Bandung) or specific (G-77), ideological (radical versus moderates) or geographical (African, Latin American).

3. To keep these groups together, the Third World—while becoming increasingly institutionalized—has emphasized consensus building in its collective decision-making processes.

BIBLIOGRAPHICAL NOTE

Although the problem of defining the Third World seemed to pertain only to the 1950s or early 1960s, even the late 1970s saw its resurgence (Wolf-Phillips, 1979). Most early books were straightforward introductions, giving basic information, but there were also a few that centered on analysis and debated the choice of appropriate conceptual lenses with which to define and study the Third World (Worsley, 1964).

Among those oriented toward conceptualization, two schools in particular confronted each other. The 1950s and early 1960s were dominated by the "modernization" paradigm or approach (Almond and Coleman, 1960; Hagen, 1962; McClelland, 1961; Rostow, 1960), but the late 1960s and the early 1970s witnessed the emergence and consolidation of a counterparadigm built around the concepts of imperialism and dependency (Amin, 1969 and 1973; Cardoso and Faletto, 1979; Emmanuel, 1972; Frank, 1966; Jalee, 1968; Rodney, 1974; Wallerstein, 1974). Despite variations in emphasis, authors in this latter category are united in their opposition to the modernization orthodoxy, and share basic assumptions about how external factors (e.g., imperialism, exploitation, foreign investments) have caused underdevelopment. Chilcote (1984) and Gendzier (1985) offer admirable syntheses of both the conceptual debate and the dependency or "radical" school of thought.

International relations involving the Third World are not yet at the stage of debates between schools of thought. The objective of early books on the subject was to document the appearance of the Third World as an international entity. Quielle (1965) concentrated on the Afro-Asian movement and dealt with its historical origins, whereas Jansen (1966) was concerned with the much more contemporary aspects, especially Bandung and the early nonaligned conferences up to the Second Summit in Cairo in October 1964. Whereas Jansen concentrated on the Asian dimension, Mazrui (1967), still one of the most insightful and beautifully written studies of African togetherness, emphasizes the manner in which nonalignment is stipulated in the charter of the 1963 Organization of African Unity (OAU).

Concerning nonalignment in general, Lyon's pioneering study (1963) is still valid, Burton's text (1965) is one of the very few on theories of international relations that deals extensively with the place of nonalignment and demonstrates the poverty of the power school à la Morgenthau or Aron. Korany (1976) proposes a much more adaptable framework, which he applies to the analysis of nonalignment both as a collective movement and as a country's foreign policy behavior and in which he establishes links between nonalignment and the societal processes of Third World countries. Willetts (1978), who is much more concerned with empirical analysis and its methodological aspects, concentrates on nonalignment as an international movement and unearths crucial data on such indicators as UN voting and the role of the Coordinating Bureau. Jackson's work (1983) is a return to the traditional power school by an American diplomat who, though less rigorous, brings the story on nonalignment up to the 1983 New Delhi Summit. As for the basic documents on nonalignment, the Yugoslav bimonthly *Review of International Affairs* (available in English and French) is a basic regular source. Willetts (1981) has conveniently collected the documents of the 1979 Havana Conference and provides a long solid introduction. Jankowitsch and Sauvant (1978) are collecting all the papers of the various conferences and meetings of both the Nonaligned group and the Group of 77, and their eighth volume has just come out.

Concerning the Group of 77 itself and the debate on the New International Economic Order, the various writings of Sauvant are basic; in fact, his study (1981) on the Group of 77 is still the only book-length one available on the structure and functioning of the G-77. Mortimer's work (1980), which is much more general in character, deals with other groups as well and is still the best introduction for the beginning student. Finally, Grimaud's published Ph.D. dissertation from the University of Paris (1984) is the only all-book study of the foreign policy of Algeria, an influential actor in all instances of Third Worldism in the 1970s.

2

FOREIGN POLICY DECISION-MAKING THEORY AND THE THIRD WORLD

Payoffs and Pitfalls

Bahgat Korany

INTRODUCTION

Decisions are only one part of a country's foreign policy. They can be the most visible, dramatic, and newsworthy events in this context, but they are by no means the totality of foreign policy. Decisions are discrete, easily identifiable, and delimited phenomena: declaring war, signing a peace treaty, withdrawing from an alliance, or recognizing a state. For purposes of analysis, their beginning, making, and terminating can be isolated from other events and assigned a date. A country's foreign policy, on the contrary, is a continuous, wider phenomenon, embracing general objectives, stated strategy, and a series of routine actions: trade exchanges, cultural encounters, exchange of diplomatic notes. Whether representations of, or departures from, a country's foreign policy, decisions are best analyzed as part of this amorphous whole.

For this reason, I begin Chapter 2 by reviewing the barren state of Third World foreign policy studies and demonstrating the limited help that established foreign policy theory can offer in this regard. I then move to an in-depth analysis of the two main schools of foreign policy decision-making—the psychological and the bureaucratic—tracing their conceptual evolution, and comparing their advantages and limitations. Since the psychological model seems to be the only conceptual lens offered in the literature to analyze Third World foreign policy decisions, this dominant orthodoxy will be submitted to an extensive critique. At the basis of my analysis is a plea to dislodge the unhealthy monopoly of psychologism that reduces all social processes to the perceptions and idiosyncrasies of the "great man."

FOREIGN POLICY THEORY AND THE THIRD WORLD: A CASE OF MUTUAL UNDERDEVELOPMENT

The conceptual confusion between specific decisions and general foreign policy indicates the problems in the field of foreign policy analysis. Reviewing the field in the mid-1970s, Bernard Cohen and Scott Harris could not help emphasizing its meager achievements: "When scholars characterize the study of foreign policy as in a primitive theoretical stage, and when they feel compelled to insist that our first steps be the definition and classification of foreign policy . . . , those over fifty may be swept by despair, while those under thirty may sense unlimited opportunity" (Cohen and Harris, 1975: 381-437).

Systematic analyses of Third World foreign policies, let alone the anatomy of decisions, are in an even worse state. Commenting on available analyses of Asian foreign policies, Michael Leifer has stated that "in the main, the States of South East Asia either individually or collectively have not attracted the attention of authors concerned specifically with testing theoretical propositions about foreign policy" (Leifer, 1977: 39). The state of Middle Eastern foreign policy studies is no different. As Adeed Dawisha put it: "The vast majority of scholarly works dealing with the region have been primarily concerned with the domestic politics of the Middle Eastern States, and many of these have been essentially biographical essays of the various leaders of these countries" (Dawisha, 1977: 70). Edy Kaufman was even more detailed in his list of complaints about the study of Latin American foreign policies:

> Studies in international relations in Latin America have mostly been undertaken by Western scholars, and these have tended to focus on U.S. influence in Latin America, and to a lesser extent on the Latin American policies of other outside powers. Contributions made by Latin Americans have for many years approached the subject from a legalistic or historical angle, though recently an emphasis on economic factors has become apparent. Very few scholars have integrated internal and external variables in the study of foreign policy in Latin America. The reason for the overwhelming emphasis on external determinants of policy is undoubtedly related to the fact that for most countries the domestic setting does not seem to play an important role in foreign policy decisions. Correspondingly, studies of domestic politics and government scarcely touch on foreign policy decision making (Kaufman, 1977: 158-159).

Even at the general Third World level, some authors think there is nothing worthwhile in the literature to build upon. In dealing with the nonaligned movement, Peter Willetts asserted that "the extent of the neglect of the subject is shown in that it is believed to be the first time in this book that the simple distinction has been made between membership and nonmembership of the Movement in the Third World" (Willetts, 1978: xvii).

Basic handicaps in the analysis of Third World foreign policies, especially of the decision-making process, are the lack of data and the cult of secrecy practiced by many state authorities. In many Third World countries, the press is both technically less developed and more "guided" than that in the West. Moreover, the inadequacy of documentary and archival facilities makes the analysis of decisions very hazardous. Even information reported by the international and "elite" press is sometimes of poor quality or low credibility; it may even be just plain incorrect. For instance, the *International Herald Tribune* reported the number of countries attending the Fourth Nonaligned Summit (Algiers, 1973) as some sixty instead of seventy-five; it also stated that Saudi Arabia was not represented, although, in fact, the country's delegation was headed by King Faisal himself. Difficulties increase when we search for systematic data from which to build indicators of international behavior or scales of diplomatic interaction. Such standard data sources as *Facts on File, Keesing's Archives,* and the various yearbooks can frustrate the efforts of the most dedicated researcher in this field because their data on these countries are too general, incomplete, or incorrect.

Such data problems are not unique to the Third World. At the same time, however, they have not prevented the publication of well-documented research on the USSR, for instance, or of some solid works on the Third World itself by scholars in comparative politics and political economy. This discrepancy directs attention to the state of foreign policy theory (Korany, 1974 and 1983). Tim Shaw, in reviewing the field of African foreign policy study, could not help emphasizing "the inappropriateness, bordering at times on the irrelevance of the sub-field . . . characteristic of the widespread misconceptions about . . . the 'periphery' in the contemporary global system . . . and symptomatic of the deficiencies and mistakenness of much (most) of the field as defined by the prevailing paradigm" (Shaw, 1983: 2).

The problems, then, are related not only to accessibility of data; they go much deeper to the epistemological level, as the analyses of scholars in other subfields reveal (Chilcote, 1984; Gendzier, 1985). Since the appropriateness of our conceptual models seems to be at issue, it is imperative that we start with that problem.

As far back as 1975, the standard review of foreign policy analysis expressed confidence that the emergence of the much-awaited general theory on the subject was just around the corner (Cohen and Harris, 1975). Charles Kegley and Richard Skinner (1976: 303–318) went even further: "A field of scientific (comparative) foreign policy analysis has not only emerged but is also proceeding in the 'mopping up' activities of '*normal* science.'" James Rosenau concurred (1976: 369–377), arguing that "mopping up" activities were complete and that the science of foreign policy was already with us:

> All the evidence points to the conclusion that the comparative study of foreign policy has emerged as a *normal* science. For nearly a decade many investigators have been busily building and improving data banks, testing and revising propositions, using and departing from each other's work. It has been an astonishingly rapid evolution . . . because of the steady and growing flow of research products . . . and of the convergence around particular variables and methodologies. Our differences now are about small points (Rosenau, 1976: 370).

Have we advanced so far that "great debates . . . have faded into an obscure past" (Rosenau, 1976: 369–370) and only the most trivial points remain to be settled? To ascertain the veracity of Rosenau's claims and to avoid overemphasizing differences in foreign policy theory building, we offer an overview of his conceptualization in comparison with that of another North American authority, Michael Brecher. Both Brecher and Rosenau have worked for the same objective, roughly at the same time; both now have disciples and direct transnational projects on foreign policy. In addition, the endeavors of both authors are a product of the "behavioral persuasion" in politics and have drawn on the concepts, methods, and hypotheses of contemporary social science literature.

ROSENAU VERSUS BRECHER

Rosenau stated that "there can be no real flourishing of theory until the materials of the field are processed, *i.e.*, rendered comparable, through the use of the pre-theories of foreign policy" (Rosenau, 1980); he also assumed the task of elaborating a pre-theory that would provide "a basis for comparison in the examination of external behaviour of various countries in various situations." This pre-theory (see Figure 2.1) is based on five sets of independent or explanatory variables: (1) the idiosyncratic or individual factor: all those aspects of the decision-maker, "his values, talents and prior experiences, that distinguish his foreign policy choices or behaviour from those of other decision makers"; (2) role: "the external

FIGURE 2.1 An abbreviated presentation of Rosenau's pre-theory of foreign policy, in which five sets of variables underlying the external behaviour of societies are ranked according to their relative potencies in eight types of societies

Geography and physical resources	Large country				Small country			
State of the economy	Developed		Developing		Developed		Developing	
State of the polity	Open	Closed	Open	Closed	Open	Closed	Open	Closed
Rankings of the variables	Role Societal Governmental Systemic Idiosyncratic	Role Idiosyncratic Governmental Systemic Societal	Idiosyncratic Role Societal Systemic Governmental	Idiosyncratic Role Governmental Systemic Societal	Role Systemic Societal Governmental Idiosyncratic	Role Systemic Idiosyncratic Governmental Societal	Idiosyncratic Systemic Role Societal Governmental	Idiosyncratic Systemic Role Governmental Societal
Illustrative examples	United States	U.S.S.R.	India	China	Netherlands	Czechoslovakia	Kenya	Ghana

Source: Korany, 1974.

behaviour of officials that is generated by the roles they occupy and that would be likely to occur irrespective of the idiosyncrasies of the role occupants"; (3) the governmental factor: "those aspects of a government's structure that limit or enhance the foreign policy choices made by decision-makers"; (4) the societal factor: those "non-governmental aspects of a society which influence its external behaviour"; and (5) the systemic factor: the "external environment or any actions occurring abroad that condition or otherwise influence the choices made by its officials."

But Rosenau went beyond such listings to establish the "relative potencies" of each independent variable (i.e., foreign policy determinant) according to some specific classificatory criteria: size (large or small country); state of the economy (developed or underdeveloped); political accountability (open or closed political system); penetration or nonpenetration; and issue area (status, territorial, human and nonhuman resources) (Rosenau, 1966: 27-93).

Three years after the publication of Rosenau's article, Brecher (1969, 1972, 1974, 1979) and his colleagues at McGill University published a multivariable model of an input-conversion/output-feedback foreign policy system consisting of fourteen independent variables clustered in five groups (following the example of Harold and Margaret Sprout) embracing the psychological and operational environments (see Figure 2.2). Although Brecher does not neglect the operational environment (i.e., the world as it "really" exists), his emphasis is clearly on the psychological environment (i.e., each person's perceptions or images of the "real" world), which includes two closely related sets of data: an attitudinal prism (i.e., the psychological predispositions of the decision-makers); and images of the elite (i.e., the cognitive representation of reality). On the other hand, the independent variable—the foreign policy output—is classified according to four issue areas: military-security, political-diplomatic, economic-developmental, and cultural-status (a research design that Brecher followed up by applying it in a 1,800-page, three-volume study of Israel's foreign policy and decisions).

Although a unified list of explanatory variables can be sorted out through a comparison between the frameworks of Rosenau and Brecher, the same cannot be said about the most important independent variable. Brecher et al. have assigned priority in their research design to the individual-psychological variable, and Brecher has confirmed this priority status in his empirical analysis of Israel's foreign policy system. "Elite images," he has affirmed, "[are] the decisive input of a foreign policy system" (Brecher, 1972: 11). If we compare Brecher's assignment of priority to the psychological-perceptual determinant with the potency established in Rosenau's "pre-theory," we find that Israel—Brecher's empirical domain—falls within the category of "small, developed and open political system[s]." The most potent independent variable in this case is the global-systemic one, whereas the individual-psychological variable occupies the fifth and last rank.

Given that Brecher and Rosenau have a cultural area in common and are pillars of the same "scientific," or behavioral, school, might not this sheer opposition between the two theory-builders raise questions about the credibility of "foreign policy theory" and its capacity to offer clear guidelines and operational hypotheses to those who are interested in its application?

One of the reasons for the lack of cumulativeness between the two schools and their leaders is their implicit and divergent definitions of what needs to be explained: foreign policy itself. In referring to foreign policy as an output or dependent variable does one mean the state's objectives and general strategy on the international scene, its diplomatic actions or commercial and military transactions, its major war or peace decisions, or all of these aspects together? Rosenau's theory is the most deficient insofar as his lengthy discussion of the independent variables (sources or determinants of foreign policy) contrasts with his neglect of definition or discussion of the dependent variable: the foreign policy output. It eventually became evident that by foreign policy output he meant general behavioral transactions, and the result of his omission in the definition of the object of analysis has been not only the difference in ranking the independent variables, but also the adoption of different analytical techniques. Rosenau and his adherents have used events data as a technique of analysis (Azar and Sloan, 1975; Burgess and Lawton, 1972; Munton, 1978) to describe a country's general behavioral pattern at the international level, whereas Brecher and his school have concentrated on the subject of specific decisions (Brecher, 1978 and 1979). In doing so, the latter group has focused more and more specifically on crisis situations, all the while subjecting such concepts as attitudinal prism, stress, and coping to content analysis. Yet even the study of decisions is fraught with differences in approach and lack of cumulativeness among foreign policy analysts.

THE DECISION-MAKING APPROACH TO FOREIGN POLICY

As the decision-making approach has been very successful, we must agree with Rosenau that "the habits it challenged have been largely abandoned and the new ones it proposed have become so fully incorporated into the working assumptions of practitioners that they no longer need

FIGURE 2.2   Brecher's Input-Output Model

INPUTS

    OPERATIONAL ENVIRONMENT

EXTERNAL	—Global System	(G)
	Subordinate System	(S)
	Other Subordinate Systems	(SO)
	Dominant Bilateral Relations	(DB)
	Bilateral Relations	(B)
INTERNAL	—Military Capability	(M)
	Economic Capability	(E)
	Political Structure	(PS)
	Interest Groups	(IG)
	Competing Élites	(CE)
COMMUNICATIONS	—The transmission of data about the operational environment by mass media, internal bureaucratic reports, face-to-face contact, etc.	

    PSYCHOLOGICAL ENVIRONMENT

ATTITUDINAL PRISM	—Ideology, Historical Legacy, Personality Predispositions
ÉLITE IMAGES	—of the operational environment including competing élites' advocacy and pressure potential

PROCESS

FORMULATION	—of strategic and tactical decisions in 4 ISSUE AREAS:	
	Military–Security	(M–S)
	Political–Diplomatic	(P–D)
	Economic–Developmental	(E–D)
	Cultural–Status	(C–S)
IMPLEMENTATION	—of decisions by various structures: Head of State, Head of Government, Foreign Office, etc.	

OUTPUTS   —The substance of acts or decisions

Source: Brecher 1974.

Figure 2.2 continued

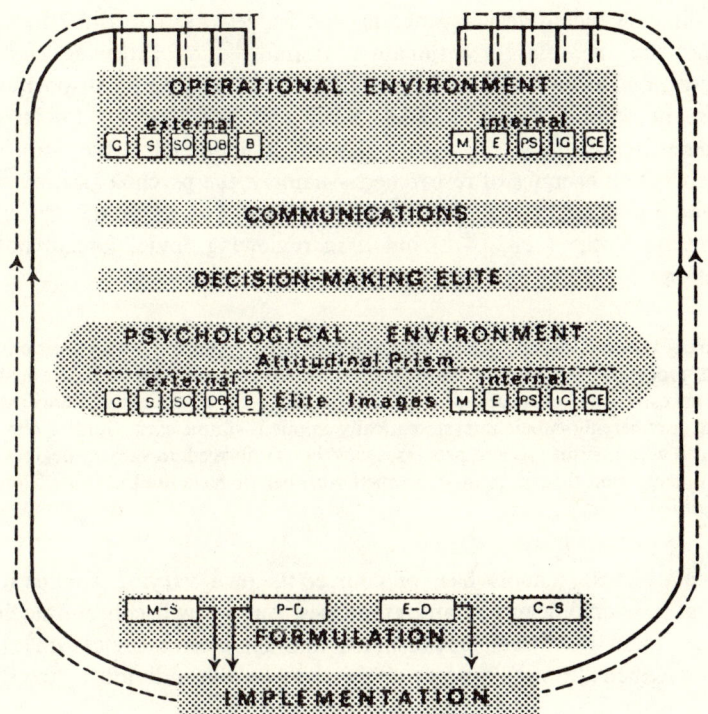

to be explicated or the original formulation from which they came cited" (Rosenau, 1967: 211). This does not mean that we have an established empirical theory of foreign policy decision-making, whether general or even partial. Indeed, different frameworks do exist. Some analysts emphasize the presence of four such frameworks (Quandt, 1976: 4-36), whereas others may mention lower or higher numbers depending on the author's criteria of classification and epistemological premises. Although none of these frameworks attempts to concentrate on the role of global-systemic factors in influencing decision-making, the frameworks still differ in their emphasis on the roles of rationality, of information gathering and its processes, and of organizational mechanisms or personality dispositions. Two main schools (for a possible third one, see Korany, 1984a: 12) dominate the debate in the field and seem to monopolize the empirical and conceptual energies of researchers—namely, the psychological-perceptual and bureaucratic-organizational schools of foreign policy decision-making. As Cutler (1982: 418) put it in reviewing Soviet foreign policy formation:

> During the past decade much attention has been given . . . to institutions and processes on the one hand and to beliefs on the other. Theoretical advances in the social sciences have provided each of these two concerns with a coherent—albeit unsystematically applied—framework. Studies concerned with institutions and processes have been informed, to varying degrees, by organization theory; those concerned with beliefs have used insights from cognitive theory.

Each of these schools has, of course, its own varying applications, formulations, qualifications, and emphases, but we will concentrate here on their main premises, propositions, and distinctive basics—in other words, on their "forest" aspects rather than on the individual "trees."

THE PSYCHOLOGICAL-PERCEPTUAL SCHOOL

This framework, which is part and parcel of the "behavioral revolution" in political science (Dahl, 1961), goes back to the early 1950s. Snyder and his colleagues expressed their ideas privately first in 1954, when they offered an outline of categories for the collection and processing of data on foreign policy decision-making; before the publication of this research in book form in 1962, excerpts from it were widely reprinted, and the study was soon cited in different works ranging from treatment of disturbed communication to publication on judicial behavior.

The study's popularity was due not only to the decision-making model it elaborated but also to its explicit concern with a number of issues in methodology and the philosophy of science that were current in American political science in the 1950s. Certain of these issues represent important difficulties common to research in international relations:

> the absence of a frame of reference for relating the several aspects of the field; the random nature of the search for important variables; the tendency to construct entire systems of explanation around single factors (for example, power); the lack of a clear definition of purpose and the consequent tendency for policy, empirical, value, and scientific questions to be thoughtlessly thrown together in the same investigations; the failure to make explicit the assumptions and concepts employed in research; the habit of confusing analytic and concrete structures; the preoccupation with questions that are not stated in researchable form (McClosky, 1956: 281-295).

An illustration of the popularity and enormous impact of the decision-making model is that the term *decision-making* has been used in standard textbooks on international relations and related subjects; even historical material was studied in terms of this approach (Zinnes et al., 1961). The assumption of Richard Snyder and his colleagues is that "the nation-state is going to be the significant unit of action for many years to come" (Snyder et al., 1962) and, thus, that strategies of action and commitment of resources will continue to be decided at the national level. Consequently, action in international relations can be best understood by focusing on the decisions of these basic actors, and the strategic focus for research becomes the point at which these inputs are transformed into outputs, through the decision-making process. Hence, rather than concentrating primarily on the ends or forms of foreign policy, the authors are concerned with the process of foreign policy itself. In fact, they define decision-making as "a process which results in the selection, from a socially defined, limited number of problematical, alternative projects, of one project intended to bring about the particular future state of affairs envisaged by decision-makers" (Snyder et al., 1962: 90). This selection or choice process is determined both by those variables which can explain how and why the actors in the international system behave as they do, and by those which embrace a wide range of concepts and disciplines (e.g., the economy, psychology, sociology, and, of course, political science). The diversity and multiplicity of these variables can easily be seen in Figure 2.3.

The exposition here is oversimplified for the sake of clarity and communication, inasmuch as each of the "major determinants" is in itself a complex cluster of variables with its own potential ramifications and expanding rate of proliferation. Among these major determinants one might deal with

> a host of questions concerning such matters as the general setting in which a decision is made; the actors' perceptions of their roles and the actual authority they are free to exercise; the information, attitudes, and beliefs they bring to the decision-making event; the actors' views of the alternative choices and consequences; the actual and perceived goals of the organization and its actors; the personality, skills, and needs of the decision-makers; and dozens of other matters of a similar order (McClosky, 1956: 281-295).

FIGURE 2.3 The Decision-Making Diagram

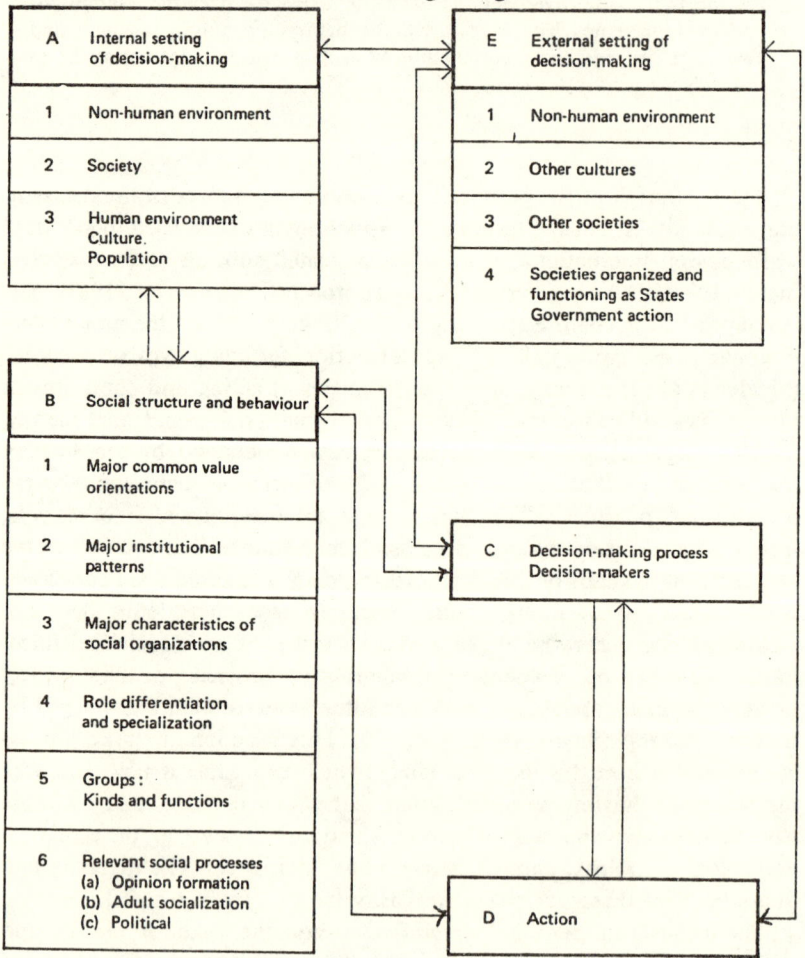

Source: Adapted from Korany, 1974.

The continued impact of the decision-making model almost twenty years after its exposition is due not only to its pioneering aspect but also to some of the advantages it has offered in the way of useful concepts and constructs: (1) The study by Snyder et al. (1962) proposed uniform and comparable categories for the collection of data, thus making comparative foreign policy research feasible. (2) The same authors explored in depth the psychological environment (i.e., the images and beliefs) of the foreign policy elite. (3) They also provided a rigorous conceptual analysis of the decision-making process. (4) Given the importance the authors attached to methodological-conceptual issues, they avoided such problems as the reification of the state. As they themselves affirmed, "We need to . . . rid ourselves of the troublesome abstraction 'State.' It's one of our basic methodological choices to define the State as its official decision-makers—those whose authoritative acts are, to all intents and purposes, the acts of the State." Such a stand has permitted the authors to combine many assets. *Operationally,* they have given form and substance to such a widespread (albeit controversial) concept as that of "national interest," and they have indicated the way to discern and investigate it: "The key to the explanation of why the State behaves the way it does lies in the way its decision-makers as actors define the situation. The definition of the situation is built around the projected action as well as the reasons for the action" (Snyder et al., 1962: 60-74). *Methodologically,* by identifying the state with its top political officials, they have reaped the benefits accruing from the combination of two levels of analysis: the individual and the collective entity. And *conceptually,* their dual level of analysis has facilitated the borrowing of some basic organizing concepts from two pioneering social sciences: sociology and psychology. As a source of enrichment for a young, empirical political science, these borrowed sources have paved the way for integrating foreign policy analysis into the social sciences and for giving it interdisciplinary applications. (Unfortunately, however, this interdisciplinary trend has been limited to increased borrowing from psychology, at the expense, for instance, of political economy or even sociology.)

Thus, whether it is based on Boulding's "image" (1959), Brecher's "attitudinal prism" (1969, 1972, 1974, 1980), Ole Holsti's "belief system" (1962), or the "definition of the situation" coined by Snyder et al. (1962), this school is anchored in the Sprouts' distinction between the "operational" and "psychological" environments (1957, 1965). The cornerstone of the school is the proposition that decision-makers respond not to the real world but to their perceptions and images of this world, which may or may not be accurate representations of that world reality: "Decision-makers act in accordance with their perception of reality, not in response to reality itself" (Brecher, 1972: 11-12). Moreover, the "relevance of particular [environmental] factors . . . will depend on the attitudes, perceptions, judgements and purposes of state X's decision-makers, that is, on how they react to various stimuli" (Snyder et al., 1962: 65-67). Indeed, it is in this way "and in this way only . . . that environmental factors can be said to influence or to condition or otherwise to affect human values and preferences, moods and attitudes, choices and decisions" (Sprout and Sprout, 1965: 11).

This consistency and continuity among principal theorists across time and countries results in the quasi-exclusion of the operational environment, the real world, which is replaced by the decision-maker's perception of the world. According to Snyder and Paige (1958: 17), "we make a basic choice to take as our prime analytical objective the recreation of the 'social world' of the decision-makers as they view it. Our task is to devise a conceptual scheme which will help us to reconstruct the situation as defined by the decision-makers." Hence the operational environment as represented by, say, the state structure, is divorced from its interactive properties and structural complexities and reduced to the office of its decision-maker(s). "State action is the action taken by those acting in the name of the state" (Snyder et al., 1962: 65).

Despite its psychological one-sidedness and reductionism, the psychological-perceptual school has been dominant in Third World foreign policy analysis for at least two reasons: First, it coincided with an important characteristic of the political systems of the Third World countries—their personalized political processes (Asso, 1976; Dibaco, 1977; Moulin, 1978); and, second, competing models from the other school were, in the main, explicitly limited to industrialized countries (Allison and Halperin, 1972; Allison, personal communication, 1979).

THE BUREAUCRATIC-ORGANIZATIONAL SCHOOL

The bureaucratic-organizational school has reacted to the psychological-perceptual school in two ways: It has enlarged the arena of decision-making to include top bureaucrats, and it has refused to see decision-making as a deliberate choice to be made by any individual, even the president or the top decision-maker. State action is not a deliberate choice—rational or otherwise—but an outcome. As Graham Allison has noted, decision-making is not a matter of why a given nation did X, but rather "Why did X happen?" (Allison, 1969 and 1971).

Allison is indeed the name most associated with the bureaucratic-organizational school, although he is not its only advocate. In its contemporary formulation, the school was initially championed by Richard

Neustadt (1970), who used this model to examine alliance relations between the United States and Britain; by Roger Hilsman (1958, 1971), whose short descriptive text was revealingly entitled the *Politics of Policy-Making in Defense and Foreign Affairs* (1971); and by I. M. Destler (1974), who characterized the policy-making process as essentially organizational and bureaucratic in nature. Still, the literature is dominated by the works of two authorities: Allison, whose *Essence of Decision* (1971) followed the publication of his widely quoted article in the *American Political Science Review*, and Morton A. Halperin, whose *Bureaucratic Politics and Foreign Policy* (1974) has made him one of the foremost exponents of the bureaucratic politics approach in the time since his departure from the foreign affairs bureaucracy in 1969. Allison and Halperin joined forces in 1972 to provide a succinct statement of their model.

In looking at the work of these prestigious advocates and at the wide diffusion of their writings, one might readily surmise that the bureaucratic politics model is not merely one of the approaches to policy-making, but, rather, has emerged as *the* influential paradigm in the field. Allison's influence is due not only to the fact that he subjected an important event (the shattering 1962 Cuban missile crisis) to minute scrutiny, but also to his ability to synthesize the writings of a whole school into straightforward language. For instance, at the beginning of his book, Allison stated that "professional analysts of foreign affairs (as well as ordinary men) think about problems of foreign and military policy in terms of largely implicit conceptual models that have significant consequences for the content of their thought" (1971: 3-4). Indeed, these conceptual models determine the analyst's explanation, for they fix "the mesh of the nets" that the analyst drags through the material and direct him to "cast the nets in select ponds and at certain depths in order to catch the fish he is after" (Ball, 1974: 73).

Allison explicated three of these conceptual lenses (1969) and examined the missile crisis three times over from the perspective of each lens. Model I, the rational actor model, pervades the literature of diplomatic history and of conventional power politics (à la Morgenthau or Aron) strategic formulations such as those of Schelling (1962), Kissinger (1957), and even the *New York Times*. This standard frame of reference defines the state as a unitary value-maximizing actor. As the analogy is between a government and a reasonable person, the explanation of governmental actions is given in terms of the means a rational person would adopt to achieve his or her ends. In this way, the Soviet placing of missiles in Cuba is perceived as the reasonable choice given Soviet strategic objectives.

Allison goes on to reveal the unrealistic assumptions at the basis of such a conceptual lens (e.g., the assumptions of accessibility of perfect information, availability of unlimited time, and presence of clear preference schedules for the decision-maker). More important, he exposes the shortcomings of the aforementioned analogy: Governments are *not* individuals, he claims, but, rather, are clusters of organizations that act on imperfect information under pressure of time, and that decide not on the best choice but on the reasonably satisfactory one in the light of their established routines or standard operating procedures. One might say that Allison is in a strong position to argue for an alternative to the Rational Actor model.

In both his 1969 article and the book that followed two years later, Allison did indeed offer two alternative models: the organizational process model (Model II), and the bureaucratic politics model (Model III). Both aim to provide a base for improved explanation and prediction of the decision-making process. As Allison (1969: 690) put it:

> Although the standard frame of reference has proved useful for many purposes, there is powerful evidence that it must be supplemented, if not supplanted, by frames of reference which focus upon the large organizations and political actors involved in the policy process. Model I's implication that important events have important causes, *i.e.,* that monoliths perform large actions for big reasons, must be balanced by an appreciation of the facts (a) that monoliths are black boxes covering various gears and levers in a highly differentiated decision-making structure, and (b) that large acts are the consequences of innumerable and often conflicting smaller actions by individuals at various levels of bureaucratic organizations in the service of a variety of only partially compatible conceptions of national goals, organizational goals, and political objectives. Recent developments in the field of organization theory provide the foundation for the second model. According to this organizational process model, what Model I categorizes as "acts" and "choices" are instead outputs of large organizations functioning according to certain regular patterns of behavior. Faced with the problem of Soviet missiles in Cuba, a Model II analyst identifies the relevant organizations and displays the patterns of organizational behavior from which this action emerged. The third model focuses on the internal politics of a government. Happenings in foreign affairs are understood, according to the bureaucratic politics models, neither as choices nor as outputs. Instead, what happens is categorized as outcomes of various overlapping bargaining games among players arranged hierarchically in the national government. In confronting the problem posed by Soviet missiles in Cuba, a Model III analyst displays the perceptions, motivations, positions, power, and maneuvers of principal players from which the outcome emerged.

For many analysts, the differences between Model II and Model III were not clear-cut; hence Allison clarified the distinction in his book (1971: 145): "What moves the chess pieces is not simply the reasons that support the course of action (*i.e.,* as rational actor or Model I presupposes) or the routines of organizations that enact an alternative (as the organizational Model II indicates) but the power and skill of proponents and opponents of the action in question (Model III)."

Yet because it is the *politics* of policy-making that really matters, and because politics is the product that Allison is attempting to sell, the bureaucratic politics model (Model III) was emphasized at the expense of the organizational model (Model II). Thus, when Allison and Halperin joined forces in their 1972 collaboration, Model II was swallowed up by Model III in the authors' efforts to emphasize the basic principle of this whole school: that the plurality of players and their interests determine the final outcome. In other words, "players choose in terms of no consistent set of strategic objectives, but rather according to various conceptions of national security, organizational, domestic and personal interests. Players make governmental decisions not by a single rational choice, but by pulling and hauling" (Allison and Halperin, 1972: 43).

The influence of the bureaucratic politics model is such that its framework has been subjected to extensive reviews and critiques by opponents and proponents alike (e.g., Art, 1973; Ball, 1974; and Freedman, 1976). Some of the criticism has been extremely detailed and has gone into the numerous layers of data as well as the evolution of the Cuban missile crisis itself. In analyzing decision-making in the Third World, we can emphasize three points:

1. The bureaucratic politics model took a serious crisis decision—one in which psychological factors were supposed to reign supreme—and showed the presence of other factors. But then it fell into the trap of overkill. That is, if the psychologistic paradigm has gone to one extreme by singling out the weight of the president's personality dispositions and idiosyncrasies, the bureaucratic politics model has gone to the other extreme by underestimating, if not negating, the president's influence. At best, according to this model, he is just another player, not even *primus inter pares*.

2. The same model has opened the black box and emphasized a dynamic factor inherent in the decision-making process: the politics of policy-making. It is thus a step in the right direction—that is, away from psychologistic reductionism and toward an emphasis on the role of groups. However, its conception of politics is very limited. All politics is confined to the top of the state. No attempt has been made to specify, or even to indicate, the state-society links (i.e., the links between bureaucrats and the different domestic or external forces). Bureaucrats are thus considered an autonomous group, virtually isolated from the structure and processes of their society. We are not allowed to know whether pressure groups,

economic interests, or the press bear on the decision-making process, or whether these influences even exist.

3. Although Allison and Halperin explained that their model was conceptualized with only the industrialized countries in mind (Allison and Halperin, 1972; Allison, personal communication, 1979), some researchers suspect that the model is even much more culture-bound. In other words, this model of discrete decisions leading to disjointed incrementalism is inspired only by, and applicable mainly to, the U.S. decision-making process.

THE GREAT MAN THEORY OF HISTORY: AN UNHEALTHY MONOPOLY

What the inapplicability of the bureaucratic model means for Third World countries is that we are left with the psychological-perceptual model, without even the benefit of a debate among advocates of the two existing models. In analyzing Third World decision-making, we have no alternative model with which to supplement, let alone supplant, the excesses of psychological reductionism—a situation that amounts to a victory by acclamation (or by default) for the psychological-perceptual school. No wonder, then, that the psychological-perceptual school has been accepted as the established and standard frame of reference in Third World foreign policy analysis both by model builders and by other, more "conventional" analysts (Choucri, 1969; Heikal, 1978a; Thompson, 1967; Vatikiotis, 1962; Zartman, 1966). Accordingly, in an effort to attenuate the conceptual one-sidedness of foreign policy analysis, to avoid the cul-de-sac represented by the monopoly of psychologism in this field, to encourage debate, and to prompt the search for applicable and relevant approaches to Third World decision-making, we must examine the shortcomings of psychological reductionism. For, despite its apparent empirical relevance to the Third World context, this approach suffers from the following gaps:

1. Its overemphasis on the psychological environment has led—at least at the empirical level if not explicitly at the conceptual level—to the exclusion of the operational environment. This research strategy imbalance, in turn, has resulted in a psychological reductionism verging on monovariable analysis—a major handicap in any serious endeavor at theory building.

2. By basing its advance on detailed answers to complex psychological questions related to the decision-maker's perceptions, stress, and coping, psychological reductionism has complicated rather than eased the problem of data accessibility in Third World foreign policy analysis. For instance,

one of the main researchers involved in the applications of Brecher's worldwide international crisis behavior model to Zambia warns us that "much of the primary evidence needed for any exhaustive analysis is unattainable, unrecorded or beyond the recall of the principal participants" (Anglin, 1980). Another researcher, working on the same project but concerned with another Third World country, invested several months in research only to find himself unable to collect the needed data. He confided to me that he needed to live several days and nights with the head of state, his family, his secretary, and perhaps other members of the immediate entourage. (Indeed, my own research confirms such difficulties.) In analyzing Egypt's 1973 October War decision, this researcher managed to interview both President Sadat's press counselor and the official spokesman immediately before, during, and after the October War—namely, Ambassadors Ashraf Ghorbal and Tahseen Bashir, respectively. Neither of them could answer specific questions concerning the stresses on the president. Would Sadat himself have been able to answer these questions? In the various interviews that Sadat has given concerning his behavior on the first day of the war, or even the day on which the Israelis crossed to the other side of the canal, he consistently excluded the possibility of behavior under stress. It seems probable that, in the Third World, interviews with the main decision-maker, even if attainable, will not always yield the desired results. But does this mean that the required data can be obtained only through individual feats of resourcefulness, perseverance, long-term investment, and lucky, high-geared connections such as those exhibited by Snyder and Paige (1958) in their analysis of the Korean decision or by Brecher in his work on Israel? These feats have not yet been matched by other researchers; hence the model's reapplicability remains inert. Content analysis (the other technique, in addition to interviews, favored by this school) is even less helpful. Egypt and Syria, at the time of the October War, were engaged in a carefully planned deception campaign. What was said and published during this campaign was geared not only to camouflage the preparation of the imminent attack until the last minute but also, in fact, to indicate exactly the opposite—namely, the absence of such preparations.

3. Even if these data problems are tackled, and even if we manage to accumulate enough information to analyze the attitudes of decision-makers, the crucial problems involved in the attitude-behavior correlation must still be faced. That is, we know that a change in leadership is not always followed by a change in behavior. We also know that in many cases of politics, as well as in daily life situations, there is a difference between "said" and "done," between expressed attitude and actual behavior—an inconsistency that psychological research has been struggling with for some

time. But rather than facing this problem, which is at the basis of the conceptualization and findings of the psychological model, the psychological model has chosen to ignore it. Indeed, it has assumed an attitude-behavior correlation rather than demonstrated it.

4. Related to this last problem is the absence of any answer—although the question has not really been asked—as to why individual decision-makers sometimes act out of character. To continue the Egyptian example, if any behavioral change took place in President Sadat's style of dealing with the Arab-Israeli conflict up until the October War, it occurred in the direction of narrowing, rather than widening, the differences between his behavior and his predecessor's (militant) behavior. It was, after all, the "moderate" Sadat who had to launch the war—hence the implication that psychological variables are only a residual determinant, superseded by "operational environment" factors that, in the final analysis, condition the decision.

5. Equally perplexing is the explanatory potential claimed by the psychological model. If psychological factors explain the need for action (in this case, the need to launch the October War), why didn't the war take place earlier? For instance, in 1971 the psychological crisis was so acute that Sadat had to declare 1971 "the year of decision," only to be ridiculed later on and to lose yet more credibility for not carrying out his threat. And why did the country feel compelled to go to war at the time it did? More important, what were the factors that made Egypt switch from the long-respected Arab strategy of total war to plan and launch a limited offensive? What were the real goals as distinct from the declared ones? Last but not least, why did the war take the form it did? Which groups or individuals participated in its elaboration, and how did they succeed or fail in advancing different points of view? These are some of the basic questions to be asked in any analysis of the decision-making process. But the psychological model not only leaves them unanswered, it fails even to raise them.

Perhaps the psychological model is guilty of functionalist logic (Jones, 1967; Smith, 1973), which engages in a form of tautology instead of full-fledged explanation. Functionalist logic answers a question such as "Why did X die?" by stating that "X died because his heart stopped beating." Technically, the answer is correct, but it fails to indicate, for instance, either the properties of the disease or the mechanisms that led finally to death.

CONCLUSIONS

To counter the serious deficiencies plaguing the established model, analysts of Third World foreign policy decision-making must turn to other schools of social analysis for inspiration. They must also be frankly innovative and attempt to adapt available frameworks to maximize potential payoffs. Thus, if the analyst is not to be dazzled by the psychological filter, the approach emphasized in this book can be used. It calls attention to the significance of the operational environment (i.e., the "real life" or objective factors as distinct from the subjective ones), especially those factors characteristic of developing countries. It seems that the best way out of the present conceptual cul-de-sac is to turn to the field of decision-making activity itself and see what the data say. Through a dialectical process of interaction between existing theory and rigorous empirical research, we can advance both. With the passage of time, it is hoped, data-based generalizations will be numerous and cumulative enough to achieve a more credible theory of foreign policy decisions in the Third World.

BIBLIOGRAPHICAL NOTE

The literature on Third World international relations and foreign policy is still quantitatively limited and modest in quality. Scholars of Africa, however, have tried to face up to some of these problems: DeLancey has provided a much-needed annotated bibliography, and Shaw (1983) has produced a lengthy evaluation of the field. Korany (1974, 1983c) has twice evaluated the state of the art on Third World foreign policies, emphasizing the ethnocentrism of the general international relations literature.

Concerning conceptualization in international relations, Holsti's textbook (1967), now in its fourth edition, is still one of the best introductions to the field. It was Singer (1961), in a pioneering and well-quoted article, who pushed scholars to distinguish explicitly between the macro level of the international system and the much more limited level of actor behavior, thus helping to establish foreign policy study as a distinct field of analysis. Both Brecher (1969, 1972, 1974, 1979) and Rosenau (1973, 1975, 1976, 1980, 1984) have determined the recent evolution of this field and shaped the basic issues, not only through their own prolific writings but also through those of their adherents. Cohen and Harris (1975) have provided an effective survey of the state of the field up to the mid-1970s; Burgess and Lawton (1972) and Munton (1978) have offered good reviews and analyses of the problems inherent in measuring (i.e., providing events data) international behavior; and Azar and Sloan (1975) have developed a fourteen-point scale to apply to the interaction of thirty-one nations between 1947 and 1973. The work by Snyder et al. (1962) is, of course, the standard reference for decision-making analysis.

The two major decision-making schools compared in this chapter are, however, dominated by the works of Brecher et al., Allison, and Halperin. Despite their differences, the leaders of these two schools have not limited themselves to pure conceptualization but have actually applied their approaches to the field; indeed, they have already influenced a whole young generation of foreign policy analysts. For instance, both Karen Dawisha (1979, 1984) in her work on the USSR and Eastern Europe and Adeed Dawisha (1976, 1980) in his work on Egypt and Syria have attempted applications of Brecher's framework.

Regarding Third World foreign policy analysis in general, the attempt to combine conceptual frameworks with empirical data is still nascent. Singer's work (1972) is a good example of the use of some basic concepts and indicators; Zartman's work (1966) represents a pioneering departure from the standard journalistic treatments of the mid-1960s in attempting at this early date an analysis of African foreign policy decision-making centering on the president; Weinstein's works (1972, 1976) provide an effective application to Indonesia; and Korany (1976) and Korany et al. (1984b) provide applications of role analysis to the foreign policies of Egypt, India, and Tunisia. Clapham's collection (1977) concentrates specifically on policy-making in four regions of the Third World (Africa, Southeast Asia, Latin America, and the Middle East). Although it does not provide a systematic analysis of a specific foreign policy decision, the book is a good general introduction to the field (given the credentials of the authors and the insights of the editor) and it helps to map issues for future research.

3

THE POLITICAL ECONOMY OF DECISION-MAKING IN AFRICAN FOREIGN POLICY

Recognition of Biafra and the Popular Movement for the Liberation of Angola

Cyril Kofie Daddieh
Timothy M. Shaw

A completely new start had to be made, for the basis of the state had been dissolved in the complete breakdown of law and order, and the intertribal violence which existed (Tanzania, 1968:3).

Yet, once Lagos—reacting as much to domestic pressures as to Pretoria's intervention—reversed itself on 25 November and came out in support of Neto, it was only a matter of time before the majority of African governments, and therefore the OAU as an organization, followed suit [on 11 February 1976] (Anglin and Shaw, 1979: 313-314).

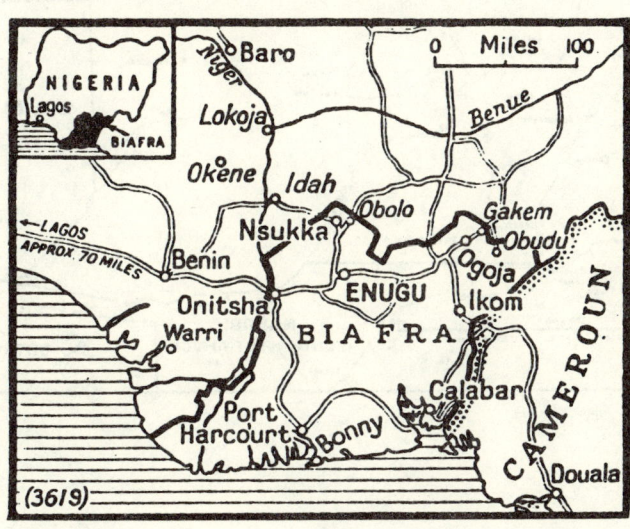

Angola

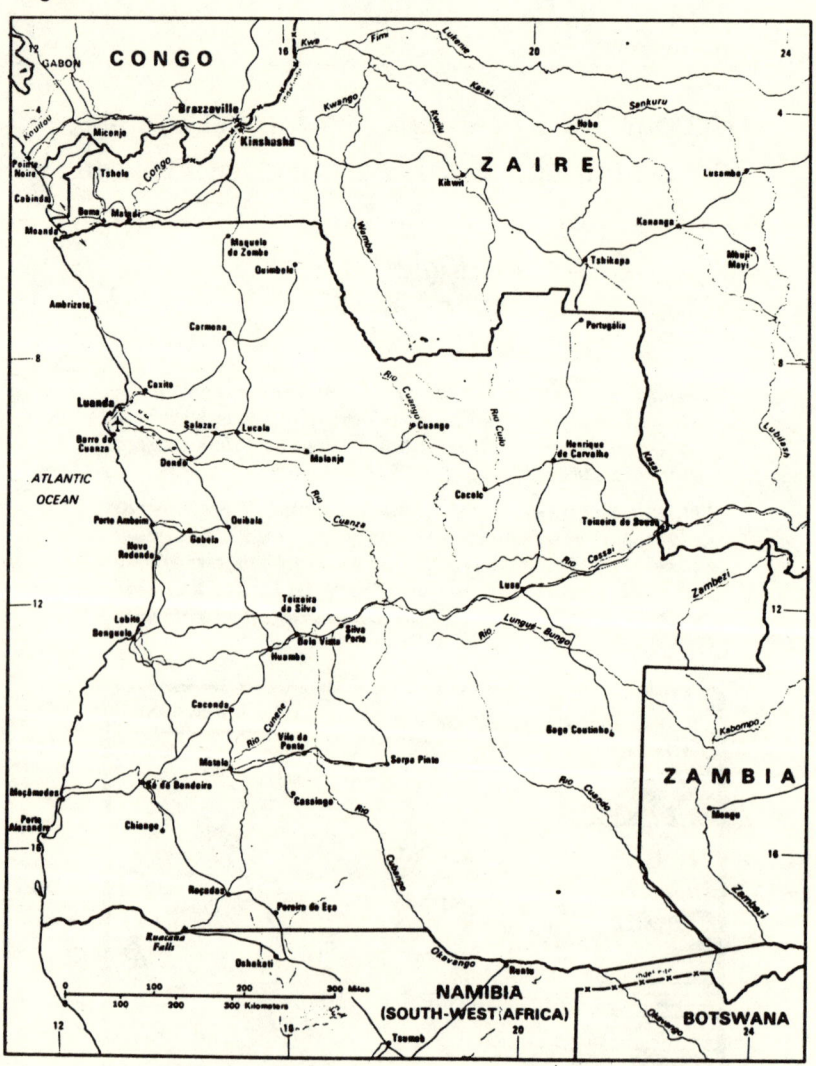

Africa

The beginning of Africa's third decade of continental diplomacy has coincided with growing institutional inertia and unresolved issues over Chad and Western Sahara that have cast a dark cloud over the continent's future. Notwithstanding the current paralysis, or perhaps because of it, scholarly interest in the study of African diplomacy remains undiminished; it may actually be growing. Moreover, a degree of sophistication and progress is clearly discernible despite the coexistence of many contending and sometimes conflicting approaches—orthodox, radical, and eclectic (DeLancey, 1981; Daddieh, 1983a).

Analysts in political economy correctly focus attention on the health of the political economy of particular states, the degree of extra-African interests in specific African issues, and the prevailing global politico-economic configuration, but they have not altogether abandoned orthodox explanations about ideological dispositions, national interests, or preoccupation with inherited issues of decolonization and national unity. Neither have they failed to take into account the interests and commitments of continental powers and personalities. The problem for Africa, as for the Arab world (Korany, 1983a), is that the regional system lacks a core or center. It functions in a leadership vacuum:

> The Organization of African Unity has survived many crises and accommodated many conflicting tensions between its members, conflicts that have often been exacerbated by the intervention of non-African nations, including the two superpowers. It has survived fundamental divisions over civil wars—four African countries recognised Biafra in 1968—but in 1972 something went wrong. The old glue did not stick any more; the centrifugal forces overcame the centripetal ones; and no elder statesman came forward to save the day. The African states not only seemed to lack confidence in their proved powers of healing and conversion, many of them appeared to lack interest in even trying to use them (de St. Jorre, 1972:676-677).

It is precisely this leadership role that states such as Ghana under Nkrumah, Senegal and Senghor, the Ivory Coast, Tanzania, Zambia and Egypt under Nasser have competed to fill with minimal success, intensifying the weaknesses in the economic bases of those states. Nigeria, with more bountiful natural resources, is now attempting to fulfill that mission with no less difficulty and some disillusionment (Shaw and Aluko [eds.], 1983). Apparent capability does not translate easily into usable power. Hence it is imperative to go beyond power politics to an examination of contradictions and coalitions within the political economy of peripheral social formations.

Although we believe that such a focus (on politico-economic processes) and mode of analysis (substructural rather than superstructural:

(Shaw, 1983b) holds greater promise for explanation and theorizing on African and Third World foreign policy, a sufficiently sustained paradigmatic shift has yet to occur. As Korany (1983a: 465) reminds us in a recent review article:

> current foreign policy theory has failed to raise the necessary questions and to provide proper guidelines for cumulative, empirically rigorous and conceptually relevant studies.

Furthermore, he maintains that, as a result of overemphasis on "psychological reductionism" as the most crucial issue for the Third World, "the process of converting inputs and outputs (the decision-making process)" lags furthest behind in analysis.

> Indeed, we have not yet started to ask the questions as to whether, how, and when such factors as domestic social structure, regime characteristics, trade patterns, treaty obligations, and membership in international organizations will influence the making of foreign policy (Korany, 1983b: 4).

The above remarks are blunt and challenging. They are welcome although we think Korany overstates his case, especially as it relates to recent developments in African foreign policy analysis (Shaw, 1983; Daddieh, forthcoming). In this article we make a modest attempt to respond to the challenge posed by Korany by reassessing our current understanding of the motivational bases of African foreign policy decision-making.

BIAFRA AND ANGOLA: A COMPARISON

African diplomacy has survived a number of crises in the OAU's turbulent twenty-year history but the Nigerian and Angolan civil wars were potentially the most divisive. Consequently, they provide ample opportunity for developing insights into the foreign policy process of African states. The two primary criteria—one political, one intellectual—for the choice of cases for study are thus not hard to state. First, because both of these cases had potentially important repercussions for the continent as a whole, few states could afford to be indifferent to their outcome. As Africa collectively participated in one form or another in resolving them, we are able to draw up a profile of decision-making on the continent. Second, sufficient time has elapsed since the two conflict episodes erupted that, while it has not receded from memory, the emotional residues surrounding the recognition decision have settled; furthermore, although decision-making in Africa is still personalized and secretive (Chazan and Shaw, 1982), enough is now known on major issues to attempt a reconstruction and explanation. To an extent, therefore, this is an exercise in revisionist history as well as in radical analysis.

Both cases also fit nicely into the two major clusters of crisis decision-making that are domestic (noninterventionist) and continental (interventionist). There are links between the two, of course, and Isawa Elaigwu (1977) performs a commendable service to the field with his essay exploring the linkages among domestic tensions and international alignments between Nigeria and Angola. Elaigwu saw these two cases as similar because both reflected the inability of the central governments to exert effective control over all parts of their countries; both posed challenges to state persistence. Moreover, in both cases it took a civil war to reestablish such control over the whole territory, however tenuous this may still be in the case of the MPLA:

> Just as Gowon's Lagos-based government lacked any effective authority over the former Eastern Region, so was the MPLA government ineffective in exercising control over FNLA and UNITA controlled areas of the north and the south. In Nigeria, it took a civil war to re-establish this control. In Angola, it is taking a civil war to establish an MPLA control over the whole country, for the first time (230).[1]

These similarities are, of course, not the only reasons why the two cases are comparable as well as generalizable. The differences between them bring into greater relief the preoccupations, motivational bases, and the problems of, as well as prospects for, implementing African diplomacy with effect. The first difference to note is that the mid-seventies Angolan imbroglio unfolded within a decade of the beginning of Biafra in 1966; second, the chief protagonist in the latter—the federal government in Lagos—had by then redeemed itself and become sufficiently "radicalized" (Akinyemi, 1978, and Ogunbadejo, 1980) to play an active role in determining the fate of rival claimants to power in Angola; third, Angola was a colony of Portugal that, along with South Africa, had been accused by Lagos of colluding with rebel forces in Biafra; and finally, and perhaps most decisively, Nigeria is situated in the West African subregion whereas Angola finds itself in the more geostrategic and volatile southern African subregion. The stakes were weighed more heavily in favor of Angola. While both countries—Nigeria and Angola—had abundant resources and were both potentially strong militarily, the latter's preeminence was easily recognized:

> Angola is a rich prize, probably the first prize in Africa. Its natural resources, including oil and other minerals, its abundance of water and

timber and its port commanding the approaches to the South Atlantic give it an economic and strategic potential greater than that of South Africa (*Sunday Telegraph*, cited in Elaigwu, 1977: 230).

The Benguela railroad, the control of the flow of trade to and from Zambia, Zaire, and elsewhere—the sort of control that creates transport dependence for several central African countries—coupled with exploitable vital resources (in short, strategic location), are a few of the special qualities that make a strong foothold in Angola a more lucrative and inviting temptation than one in Nigeria. Thus, external interests and actors were highly visible in the case of Angola and impinged heavily on the outcome. They appeared more marginal or inconsequential in the case of Biafra. At the same time, heavy extracontinental involvement reflected the volatility of the international environment within which contemporary international diplomacy has been conducted, as well as the permeability of the subsystemic environment within which African diplomacy has been and is pursued.

With such high stakes, there were always plenty of external associates to call upon to aid one or the other side; those associates could not resist the temptation. Meanwhile, extracontinental interests and pressures created frictions among African states with differing interests and perceptions; these differences were then exploited to create yet more friction and still more scope for external maneuver and influence. Furthermore, whereas the federal government in Nigeria enjoyed the benefit of six years of de jure legitimacy and international recognition prior to the declaration of secession, the situation in Angola was the opposite: the crisis there was over the right to control the state apparatus. The Biafran conflict broke out in an international climate of evolving detente. It is also fair to remark that this conflict raged at a time when the Western academics and statesmen alike were careful not to create the impression that they were interested in an imperialist repartition of Africa's most populous and potentially greatest power. Additionally, there was no ideological mystification of the issues involved—the federal as well as Biafran ideologies were compatible with each other, with most of Africa, and with the West; both were essentially capitalist.

By contrast, the conflict in Angola erupted in an atmosphere of strained East-West relations and mutual suspicion. The MPLA was said to be avowedly Communist and it was said in the U.S. State Department that if this party was allowed to control the emerging Angolan state, a domino effect could be expected throughout southern Africa. In the case of Biafra, the majority of states in the international political arena could, given the conducive climate and compatible interests, easily subscribe to the view that Biafra was an internal Nigerian affair or, at most, a continental African affair, and thereby decline to take sides (Stremlau, 1977). The strained detente, the lack of an established national government, the relative weakness of the movements vying for central political control, all made Angola fair game for extracontinental intervention and intrigue.

The heavy extracontinental involvement in Angola underscored the weak economic base on which Africa's comfortable consensual diplomacy had come to be anchored. Elaigwu (1977: 232) attempts valiantly but unconvincingly to make a virtue of this pervasive weakness by arguing that

> If in the Nigerian Civil War, the OAU stand prevented blatant external intervention, in the Angolan case, there was hardly an accepted OAU stand—beyond withdrawal of all foreign forces in Angola. The split in the OAU does not indicate a failure of that Organization. It does indicate that African states have attained such a level of political maturity that they can now agree to disagree. The "strictly cooperative" attitude among African states on issues indicated Africa's insecurity in relation to the outside world. The new trend, if channelled along constructive paths and limited to certain levels of hostility, may augur well for the future.

Given Africa's developmental crisis, the inability of continental powers to provide the system with an effective center, the permeability of the system, coupled with the concomitant pressures under which African diplomacy labors, we are considerably less sanguine than Elaigwu about the future of continental diplomacy. However, before we take a projective look into Africa's diplomatic future, we must concentrate the following analysis on Africa's response to the two specific crisis situations.

AFRICA ON BIAFRA: A HANDS-OFF POLICY

One of the OAU's most enduring articles of faith has been Article III of its Charter and similar sections emphasizing noninterference, sovereignty, and the inviolability of the inherited colonial boundaries. The majority of African states appeared, initially at least, to perceive events in Biafra as a challenge to Nigeria's territorial integrity with wider continental implications rather than just an assertion of Biafra's right to self-determination (Panter-Brick, 1968). The majority also shared the view that it was an internal Nigerian affair, although they were acutely aware that anything happening anywhere in Africa concerns the rest of the continent. This attitude, coupled with the possible repercussions of any outcome, prompted individual state efforts to conciliate the brothers. Such was the case with the initiative by Ghana's Aburi of January 4-5, 1967.

This initiative was motivated by a commonality of ruling-class interests—both military governments had stormed their way to power within the same three weeks; they shared a similar middle-class background and a conservative political bias (Hutchful, 1979, and Ninsin, 1983). Ghana's National Liberation Council (NLC) was also not unmindful of irredentist stirrings, particularly by the Ewe community. In arranging the talks, however, the "Bonapartist" regime appeared to be responding to popular opinion in Ghana that called for a ceasefire and for sense to be talked into the combatants. At the same time, the Ghanaian regime under the command of General Ankra saw in the Nigerian crisis an opportunity to pull off its first diplomatic coup as a way of enchancing its legitimacy, especially among the press, middle-class intellectuals, and the critical student movement.

The Ghanaian initiative points up characteristics of African decision-making in conflict situations that may be peculiarly African: (a) because of their weak economies, African states eschew firm commitments, preferring "pragmatism" on all but a few issues of principle (the decolonization of the white-ruled territories being the celebrated example). As Adda Bozeman (1976: 39) suggests:

> abrupt shifts, even total reversals of position, have been so common on the part of diplomatic establishments representing this particular region as to warrant the conclusion that pragmatism or opportunism rather than principle is the norm.

(b) African decision-making is both secretive and interpersonal, situational and behavioral. The continental situation provides ample opportunity for states and statesmen to hone their skills and reputations as mediators or to be helpful fixers by placing their good offices or bureaus at the disposal of feuding states to facilitate patient palavers (Bozeman, 1976: 38). It is in this context that Ankra of Ghana, Emperor Haile Selaissie of Ethiopia, Diallo Telli of the OAU Secretariat, and Humani Diori of Niger, all sought at various junctures of the conflict, to conciliate Biafra and the federal side. Similarly, in the Angolan case, a revived Nigeria came to be viewed as the leading supporter of the MPLA (hence the leading proponent of a more radical Africanist solution?). Senegal, on the other hand, came to be viewed as the leading exponent of the attempts to achieve a negotiated government of national unity (a nationalist-conservative solution?).

It is to be noted that whenever the OAU or individual member states have sought to mediate such conflicts they have done so on terms largely consistent with the shared political concerns as enshrined in the OAU constitution. This is clearly reflected in attitudes toward, and mediation efforts over, Biafra. Following the formation of the Consultative Committee at the Kinshasa summit in 1967, the OAU sought to bring the brothers together and to bring an end to the conflict, but on terms largely consistent with the federal Nigerian government's position.

The solid backing that Lagos received from the majority of African states has been characterized in the highly suggestive work of G. Aforka Nweke (1980) as the status quo position. The position adopted by the four states that recognized Biafra (Gabon, Ivory Coast, Tanzania, and Zambia) has been referred to as "revisionist", and that reflected in the attitudes of Botswana, Rwanda, Senegal, Sierra Leone, Tunisia, and Uganda have been referred to as "wavering".

By contrast with the earlier and later Congo crises, the lineup of supporters over Biafra and Angola produced some surprises, even some strange bedfellows. As Kaye Whiteman suggests:

> The Congo crises, broadly speaking, divided Africa into conservative and radical camps . . . But while a progressive and a conservative viewpoint were easy to discern in the Congo, Nigeria has held no such certainties for Africa. This has partly been because Nigeria's own politics contain so many contradictions, but also the world political situation—in particular the fragmentation of the cold-war power *blocs* which developed during the 1960s—has meant that, in the question's international aspect, ideology has been eclipsed by undiluted power politics. The undercover French intervention on the Biafran side is the best example of this, but it is hard to find much ideology in the alignment of Britain and the Soviet Union backing the Federal Government. Likewise in Africa, pragmatic conservative President Houphouet-Boigny and the radically-minded Nyerere and Kaunda are ranged together, pro-Tshombists and anti-Tshombists alike, as friends of Biafra (Whiteman, 1968: 449).

How can one explain these divergent African positions? It appears from the available evidence to date that the status quo advocates were strongly influenced by "the reflective attitude," a willingness to put themselves in Nigeria's position (Nweke, 1980: 199). Underpinning this empathy was the presumption that any encouragement given to Biafran independence would unleash centrifugal forces that might prove impossible to contain. As President Zinsou of Dahomey summed up: "If one admits the principle of secession, no one can say where it will stop, and a thousand reasons will be produced for areas to secede" (cited in Whiteman, 1968: 451, and Stremlau, 1977: 12).

While the secessionist concern exerted a powerful influence, it was hardly the primary consideration for most states. The policy of support for the federal government of Lagos hinged on other dispositions that were cultural and religious in nature. The material as well as diplomatic support given to Lagos by Algeria, Egypt, Libya, and Morocco reflected cultural and religious biases rather than a simple concern for African unity. According to Nweke (1980: 199-200), this religio-cultural disposition was consummated in President Boumedienne, who, at the Algiers OAU summit in September 1968, not only delivered a blistering attack on Biafran supporters but also barred Biafran delegates from entering Algeria.

This assessment is in conformity with the conclusion reached by Waugh and Cronje (1969), but the latter give far too much prominence to the religious dimensions of support for Lagos, more than is justified by the evidence. They posit that

> There is no particular political or ideological trend determining the African support which either side commands... The only bias in African attitude is religious. This may not be a religious war, but the Gowon government in Lagos came into power through the Moslem North, which has dominated the Nigerian political scene since long before independence. Nigeria therefore receives the automatic support of Islam. President Nasser in Cairo has supplied the Nigerian Air Force with Egyptian pilots, and countries with predominantly Moslem populations such as Guinea, Mali, the Sudan and Chad are solidly on the side of Lagos (Waugh and Cronje, 1969: 85).

They argue that President Senghor's dependence on the Moslem brotherhood explains his inability to come out openly in support of Biafra even though he accused Nigeria of genocide. Secretary-General of OAU Diallo Telli's religious bias is also presumed to have played a major role in hampering efforts by the OAU to resolve the conflict. The only anomaly in this rather neat religious line-up was President Bourguiba of Tunisia.

Even conceding that religion was a determining factor in the policy position of particular African states, the Senegalese case does caution against undue confidence in its explanatory utility. To the degree that Senghor was influenced by his dependence on the Moslem brotherhood, it is fair to suggest that he was influenced less by religion than by the economic power that the brotherhood presented. In that regard it can be said only that the Senghor regime, like all African regimes, knew very well on which side its bread was buttered: economic self-interest as well as regime preservation rather than religion explains Senegal's ambivalence.

This raises the issue of dependency that Nweke again identifies, and that in conjunction with the secessionist concern may explain much of the variance in support for both sides. Certainly, a number of African states were more constrained in their policy choices by (a) their geographical position as landlocked states and their proximity to Nigeria, and (b) the sorry state of their economies. These two factors ranked higher in determining political positions than either religion or the secessionist fears. For Chad, Mali, Niger, and Upper Volta, dependence on the goodwill of Nigeria for import-export trade was a powerful inducement to supporting Lagos. Nweke recalls that when Nigeria severed diplomatic links with France in 1961 over French nuclear testing in the Sahara, Nigeria's landlocked neighbors were terribly shaken as their economies almost ground to a halt. He suggests, therefore, that "in any conflict that threatened to engulf West Africa, Nigeria was the Achilles heel of her landlocked neighbors" (Nweke, 1980: 200).

Cameroon, on the other hand, was pro-Nigerian even though it was not unsympathetic toward Biafra. The trade between Ibo and Cameroon made continuing links between the two mutually beneficial. As a result, Cameroon did not observe the telecommunications blockade of Biafra by the federal government with any degree of seriousness. This was another clear case of economic self-interest of a regime moderating —this time a pro-Nigerian—sentiment. In a few cases, the same state held two positions simultaneously. Niger is illustrative of this dilemma, producing a desire by Diori's regime both to conciliate autonomist forces in Niger and to keep all channels of communications open with Nigeria in the form of roads and railways. This survival instinct made Diori reputedly "the most zealous peacemaker of all in the francophone heads of state" (Thompson, in Nweke, 1980: 200).

Underneath these outward policy manifestations, then, are the deep-seated interests which lie beyond contemporary diplomacy.

> It could be argued that Diori's behaviour was determined not so much by reasons of national interest as by his desire to play a major role in the Consultative Mission on Nigeria, and to identify with his Hausa ethnic group and co-religionists in Nigeria. But religious identity and solidarity served as both a cover and a means for reinforcing the legitimacy of this government, as well as for diverting the attention of the opposition at home (Nweke, 1980: 201).

Ethiopia's status quo stance was similarly induced by secessionist pressures from Eritrea, especially between 1965 and 1967. The Emperor had been buffeted by mounting demands for Eritrean autonomy, and later for independence, which, if met, would have denied Ethiopia her only outlet to the Red Sea. The Eritrean Liberation Front (ELF) elevated the stakes in early 1969 with land battles and a hijacking incident, designed to gain publicity abroad and to bring the Ethiopian economy to its knees. That such pressures and the responses they generate transcend mere personalities and ideological predilections is amply illustrated by Colonel Mengistu's subsequent pursuit of the struggle against the ELF.

> In these circumstances, it was unlikely the Ethiopian monarch would support secession in another African state. The emperor not only held firmly to the federal thesis of "one Nigeria," but also contributed more than any single member of the Consultative Commission [sic] in arranging for peace talks between the federal government and Biafra (Nweke, 1980: 201).

If Emperor Selassie's primary concern was with Eritrea and not Nigeria, Zaire, on the other hand, was not faced with any immediate secessionist threat. But memories of the Congo debacle were still fresh enough to induce a pro-Nigerian stance. In addition to trying to divert attention from domestic sources of discontent or mute criticisms at home, these states were conscious that support for the federal position, the likely winner, would be reciprocated at some future date when their own regimes might come under pressure from political dissidents.

To summarize, in the brothers' war the federal side was heavily favored by African decision-makers in part because of their collective aversion toward secession. As Whiteman (1968: 450) explains:

> The trump card of Nigerian diplomacy has been the reactionary associations of secession in Africa. No matter how much evidence can be produced of the genuine popular backing for secession in Biafra, Colonel Ojukwu and his colleagues cannot escape the Tshombe shadow.

Thus, from the Biafran point of view, most of the African states were not impartial arbiters in the conflict. No matter how they may have felt in private, many of the leaders were constrained by national interests and the preservation of their own power—that is, they were careful not to send the wrong signals to their political opponents by extending diplomatic support to Biafra. The international climate sustained this majority position. To the extent that religio-cultural affinities were salient, their influence on policy decisions has to be situated within and mitigated by the context of national socio-economic and political pressures.

Economic prospects and political survival were not the only moderating influences on policy decisions. For instance, the strident tone of the Algiers resolution was not unconnected with the prospects of imminent military defeat of Biafra. The Algiers conference coincided with the Nigerian army's final offensive—the so-called "final push"—that scored such impressive successes as the capture of Aba on September 5th, the day the OAU Foreign Ministers' conference opened (Whiteman, 1968: 451). Even Waugh and Cronje (1969: 89) recognized this influence. Modifying their earlier overemphasis on the religious dimension in the light of this mitigating factor, they wrote:

> In retrospect the Algiers vote was influenced by the military situation: delegates were told that the defeat of Biafra was only a matter of days, and that a cease-fire call would come too late. In fact, the Nigerians had made determined efforts to bring Biafra to the verge of defeat whenever international pressures forced them to consider a political rather than a military solution.

As was the case with the fall of Aba and Owerri during the Foreign Ministers' Conference, so too was the case with the fall of Port Harcourt that preceded the Kampala Conference; the federal strategy confirmed the interrelatedness of battlefield and conference hall. During the third meeting of the Consultative Committee that took place in April 1969 in Monrovia, the Nigerians were again on the verge of capturing Umuahia, which was a temporary capital for the Biafrans for some months. It is hard to escape the conclusion that although pro-Ibo sympathies were aroused by the bloodshed, African states had an even greater psychological incentive to be on the winning side, particularly if it dissuaded political dissidents and thereby reinforced territorial integration. Like the recognition of the MPLA, as we shall see shortly, the overwhelming support for the federal side was reflective of a pervasive perception that Biafra would not succeed as a viable proposition. If John Stremlau (1977: 62-64) is correct, the African states were not the only ones whose cautious response reflected this calculation; the United States "wavered," presumably because it, too, was unsure of Biafra's chances of success. And Ojukwu showed political insight into the subtleties of decision-making among African states when he reportedly told Stremlau (1977: 67) that

> he did not expect immediate diplomatic recognition, given the little that Biafra had to offer any prospective ally, but that this would follow eventually should Biafra prove to be a viable proposition—a situation that would necessarily include retention of control over the oil fields in the Rivers area.

Moreover, the acute embarrassment caused by a Radio Biafra newscaster's announcement on the very day of secession that Ghana, Togo, the Gambia, Ethiopia and Israel had all extended diplomatic recognition to the new republic and that more recognition could be expected shortly, damaged the chances of revisionist policies. Ojukwu was said to be furious about the announcement. As soon as the federal government learned of the announcement it demanded that the identified governments publicly repudiate the Biafran claims and pledge their support for Nigeria. The five quickly complied (Stremlau, 1977: 64).

Notwithstanding such calculations and pressures to conform, Botswana, Dahomey, Rwanda, Senegal, Sierra Leone, Tunisia, and Uganda showed a tendency to waver in the course of the war. While their sympathies appeared to lie with Biafra, they initiated no sustained diplomatic efforts to serve the cause of Biafra; nor did they themselves recognize her. As Nweke (1980: 206) argues, this set of countries found the interplay of secessionist and dependency factors, as well as the clash between national interests and leadership preferences, impossible to reconcile. Dr. Zinsou, for instance, was not in favor of secession but he was equally against the invasion of Biafra. He told President de Gaulle that he thought a solution could be found in a political confederation that would give "as much independence to Biafra as possible while retaining direct links with Lagos" (*West Africa,* 1968: 1163, and Nweke, 1980: 206). Ambiguities in this Dahomean position were further revealed through a pair of rhetorical questions that Zinsou posed: "Can one say that the boundaries of colonisation were so well made as to be irreversible, and in respect for them should thousands die? If four million Rhodesians can make a state, why not eight million Ibos of the same race and culture?" Such rhetorical formulations undermined Zinsou's professed neutrality; he was never taken seriously by either Lagos or the OAU Consultative Committee. But Dahomey's policy did not transcend these expressed doubts.

Senegal and Tunisia also expressed concern over the war; both openly condemned it as "genocidal". Senghor made it known that his country opposed secession for "political and 'African' reasons" but he also chastized the intransigence of Lagos in insisting on a solution by force. In a federation, presumably, a self-governing state can always opt out. Nweke (1980: 208) suggests that Senghor's qualified approval of secession was a defensive reflex prompted by his own country's secession from the Mali Federation in 1960. Moreover, as we argued earlier, Senegal's ethnic cleavages and the interplay of religious and economic factors imposed severe constraints on the regime's ability to intervene in Nigeria. Tunisia, like Senegal, voted for the profederal resolution at the Algiers summit, even though it had earlier introduced a proposal at the foreign ministers' conference to amend the agenda to broaden the discussion on Biafra. Chief Awolowo later told a press conference that the profederal votes of Tunisia and Senegal did not make them any more committed to Lagos than the four Biafran recognizers (*West Africa*, September 21, 1968: 1091; Nweke, 1980: 208).

Sierra Leone's wavering policy may have reflected her experience with a series of military coups and President Stevens' hostility toward military regimes. The arrogance displayed by General Gowon over the peace negotiations may have offended Sierra Leone, causing her to abstain from voting in support of Lagos at the Addis summit in 1969. These attitudes were no doubt reinforced by the successful lobbying efforts of an able Biafran diplomat, Francis Nwokedi, whose wife happened to be Sierra Leonean (Nweke, 1980: 208-209).

In the end, just two francophone states in West Africa (the Ivory Coast and Gabon) and two front line states (Tanzania and Zambia) recognized Biafra. By their own accounts, they were all deeply moved by the suffering in Biafra. As Houphouet-Boigny asserts (1968: 10-13; also Baker, 1970: 5-8), his recognition was a humanitarian gesture because Biafra was "a human problem, a human tragedy." Houphouet vowed to plead the cause of Biafra in international fora and he began, quite naturally, by bringing de Gaulle to Biafra's side (Bach, 1980: 259-272). The Ivorian role went well beyond diplomatic recognition and the provision of homes for refugee children. There is reason to believe that French and later South African and/or Portuguese arms were funnelled through the Ivory Coast and Gabon. It has been suggested (Bon and Mingst, 1980: 13) that

> Biafra to France meant two things: (1) the possible break-up of the country most likely to erode French influence in West Africa—Nigeria—and therefore a chance "to knock the Anglo-Saxons"; (2) oil, and Biafra sought to purchase French support by promising potential oil reserves.

If the overwhelming size of Nigeria posed a potential threat to the hegemonic aspirations of France in the subregion, it was no less worrisome to the subimperial designs of the Ivorian leadership, particularly when such designs had strong implications for Ivorian growth prospects. A reunited and resurgent Nigeria was likely to serve as a powerful attraction to investments and labor, thereby exerting an influence on its smaller francophone neighbors. But Ivorian prosperity depended on cheap migrant labor and foreign (still mainly French) investments that could not withstand competition from Nigeria. An independent Biafra with strong links to the Ivory Coast would undoubtedly scale Nigeria down to a manageable size, so the thinking went. If such links could be sweetened with a concessionary sulphur-free oil deal, the Ivory Coast's revisionist policy would have been so much more meaningful. However, there is as yet no evidence to suggest that any such deal was struck. In any event, Houphouet had an additional reason for his unflinching support for Biafra. His celebrated hostility toward Communism (see Daddieh, forthcoming) made him quite uneasy over Nigeria's flirtation with the Soviets. Nigeria could provide a base from which to export their revolution elsewhere in Africa. Having got rid of Nkrumah and the Soviet influence next door, the Ivorian leadership was in no mood to tolerate the apparent new coziness between Moscow and Lagos.

Like Houphouet, Kaunda was influenced by "humanist" considerations (Anglin and Shaw, 1979). Zambia provided a variety of support to Biafra, although Kaunda's precipitous departure from Algiers to attend a prior engagement in Paris hurt his principled position as well as his defense of Biafra (Whiteman, 1968: 452). But even those four revisionist states did not necessarily intend their recognition to be construed as an approval of secessions. As Anglin (1971, 1980) suggests, Zambian recognition was a symbolic, humanitarian gesture, not an approval of secession. Such nuances were beside the point in a situation in which recognition counted a great deal. It legitimized the demands of competing sides: this fact was well understood within the diplomatic circles of the two sides.

Tanzania was also concerned about the extent of "that cruel war". Thus, her recognition was essentially humanitarian as well. However, in all four cases there were moral and philosophical underpinnings for the revisionist policy. The Tanzanians insisted that, by opting for the wanton destruction of Biafran lives and property, the Nigerian state had abdicated its most elementary duty on the basis of which a people surrenders its right and power of self-defense to the government of the state under which it lives.

> In the light of these circumstances, Tanzania feels obliged to recognize the setback of African unity which has occurred.
>
> We therefore recognize the state of Biafra as an independent sovereign entity and as a member of the community of nations. Only by this act of recognition can we remain true to our conviction that the purpose of society, and of all political organizations, is the service of man.

It is quite evident from the foregoing assessment and the statement with which we opened this essay that for both Tanzania and the other three African recognizers (revisionists) the central thrust in the policy decision related to the principle of self-determination. One was either a serious advocate of the principle, in which case he or she would be compelled to support Biafra's bid for statehood, or one was a detractor. For this set of countries as well as for one Africanist (Post, 1968), at least, Biafra had a case, perhaps even a special case. It is equally obvious that the rest of Africa and another Africanist (Panter-Brick, 1968) disagreed.

AFRICA ON ANGOLA: A HANDS-ON APPROACH

Barely six years later, Angola presented a different set of constraints and opportunities for African diplomacy. In contrast to Nigeria, none of the religio-cultural influences on African decision-makers was relevant. Moreover, there was no confusion between self-determination and respect for the territorial integrity of a member state. Interference and interventions were endemic to the Angolan situation from the onset. Given the heavy infusion of external military personnel and hardware, many African states retreated behind rhetorical condemnations of the dangerous precedent being established; some arranged meetings designed to bring the factions together in a coalition government, while a few acted as conduits for external associates.

In January 1976, the OAU was evenly split between those favoring recognition of the MPLA and those favoring a Government of National Unity, with Ethiopia and Uganda adopting a neutral position. This line-up is significant for a number of reasons: first, all former Portuguese territories favored recognition of the MPLA; it is safe to assume that they were influenced by shared ideological preferences and the prospects of close collaboration with the MPLA. Second, three of the four revisionists in the case of Biafra now favored national unity. It is worth noting, however, that none of the countries presumably favored the FNLA-UNITA coalition to form the government. The 22 states that supported a Government of National Unity did so because they did not want the OAU to play a divisive role in Angola.

The initial response to the crisis in Angola was consistent with the spirit of the policy toward Biafra, which was to avoid entanglement in the civil war. President Idi Amin, as Chairperson of the OAU, appealed to member states to refrain from recognizing either faction so as to give the various efforts at reconciliation time to yield results. Although Nigeria, Tanzania, and Zambia, among others, sought unsuccessfully to achieve a rapprochement, it is significant that the African states initially complied with OAU policy by declining to choose sides until the situation clarified (Anglin and Shaw, 1979).

The OAU position proved untenable as soon as South African involvement on the side of the FNLA-UNITA coalition was exposed. If the trump card of Nigerian diplomacy had been the reactionary associations of secession in Africa, then the South African invasion in collusion with FNLA-UNITA was no less decisive in shifting African opinion in favor of the MPLA. Support from the Central Intelligence Agency (CIA) proved equally embarassing. The Angolan case involved a struggle to control an emerging state and not a case of secession. The invasion from the south, in collaboration with the FNLA-UNITA forces and U.S. connections, destroyed any credibility the leadership might have had in African decision-making circles. Rather than autonomous statesmen committed to safeguarding African interests, they were seen as the Trojan horses of imperialists in Africa.

No less damaging was their association with the Front for the Liberation of Cabinda Enclave (FLEC) that, like Biafra, was supported by France. These combined interests in opposition to the MPLA revived memories; if not of imperialist exploitation and repartition designs, then at least of imperialist hostility toward African commitment to the total eradication of racism in all its guises from the continent. This explains why Zambian support for UNITA was attacked with such vehemence. FLEC, the CIA, and South Africa proved to be an albatross around the neck of the FNLA-UNITA coalition; they were unhelpful as far as the diplomatic aspect of the battle for control of the state was concerned. In any event, the prize was lucrative enough to be worth the gamble. As the Nigerian Federal Commissioner for Industry, Colonel Wushishi, commented in a speech in Lagos on January 27, 1976:

> Angola should not, under normal circumstances, be of strategic importance to Africa more or less than any other African country but for certain exceptional considerations ... By virtue of her navigable rivers and traditional slave trade routes, including the Benguela Railway into the hinterland, she is able to control the flow of trade from certain central African countries such as Zaire, Zambia and Rhodesia to the sea. Furthermore, Angola occupies a very strategic position on the South Atlantic sea route to and from the Cape of Good Hope which is a vital link between the highly industrialized countries in Europe and their markets in Africa and Asia. The riches of Angola—diamonds, petroleum, copper and coffee to name a few, have been of special interest to West European countries which exploited the territory during colonial administration (in Elaigwu, 1977: 230).

A reunited and reinvigorated Nigeria was the architect of the diplomatic drive towards winning recognition for the MPLA, whereas Senegal sponsored the resolution designed to encourage the diplomatic palavers aimed at achieving consensus on a coalition government of National Unity. However, prior to Nigeria's announced recognition of the MPLA on November 25, 1975, she had indeed been one of the staunchest advocates of the OAU position on reconciliation, even after it had become clear that the policy was untenable. On November 8, 1975 the External Affairs Commissioner, Joseph Garba, called for the postponement of Angolan independence by three weeks to allow more time for working out the modalities of a government of national unity (Sotumbi, 1981: 2). Thus the Nigerian recognition of the MPLA, consistent as it was with the federal government's experience over Biafra, was stunning and took many observers by surprise. Sotumbi has suggested that the recognition was the new leadership's way of announcing its arrival on the world scene. More important, this decision was taken against the backdrop of "petro-naira", financial prosperity, and a growing confidence by the leadership in Nigeria's ability to influence relations with African states now that the financial constraints on policy goals had been removed. If the announcement itself was long in coming, it was because a number of interests were exerting influence on Nigerian policy and pulling it in different directions. Most of these pressures had to be accomodated before the new post-Gowon policy could be unveiled.

The Nigerian policy was constrained by the fact, first, that public opinion had not been sufficiently molded to receive any policy shift. The élite press—which was a good barometer of what the attentive public would accept—was by and large still wedded to the OAU, which Nigeria's policy on national unity reflected. Second, for bureaucratic reasons, officials at the Ministry of External Affairs were opposed to the recognition of the MPLA. Third, Nigeria's own internal political matrix of class, ethnicity and geography may have influenced this regime's preference for a government of national unity (Sotumbi, 1981: 9-10).

Meanwhile, a new factor intervened to mediate the attitude of the Nigerian foreign policy élite toward the issue of Angola's national unity. This new factor was the revelation of the open and direct military invasion of southern Angola by South Africa in alliance with UNITA-FNLA forces, a much greater presence than that of the minority regimes on the side of Biafra. As a result of this new factor,

> the Nigerian government not only recognized the MPLA government which had been set up in Luanda, but threw its diplomatic and financial assistance behind it. A cash donation of ₦ [naira] 13.5 million was given to the Angolan Prime Minister, Lopo do Mascimento, in Lagos while high-level Nigerian delegations criss-crossed African capitals, not only explaining the Nigerian position but also trying to drum up support for the MPLA government (Akinyemi, 1978: 111-112).

Akinyemi (1978: 113) contends that "the Angolan crisis, largely through the involvement of South Arica, presented Nigeria with an opportunity to consolidate the concept of national interest in a way that no Nigerian government had done before." Apparently, the Nigerian foreign policy élite perceived South Africa to be the agressor and the MPLA to be right in resisting it. More important, it was believed that both the FNLA and UNITA were instrumental in promoting South African aggression. It was held that if South Africa were to succeed in installing a satellite government in Angola, it would ultimately attempt to control governments in Zaire, Mozambique, and even Nigeria, a reverse "domino" effect (Sotumbi, 1981: 17-18).

This deduction was made possible and plausible by the bitter memories of the war in Biafra. It was believed in Lagos that the first bomb dropped on Lagos by "Biafra" was made in then-Rhodesia; that South Africa, Rhodesia and Portugal had made deliberate efforts to balkanize Nigeria. Thus, the continued existence of the minority and colonial regimes in southern Africa posed a fundamental threat to the security of Nigeria itself. The invasion of Guinea in November 1970 under circumstances that implicated Portugal tended to reinforce this view in Lagos. Polhemus (1977: 490), as further evidence of this élite perception, cites Gowon's 1971 statement that

> Besides the vivid affront which they [South Africa, Rhodesia and Portugal] constitute to our conscience, the threat they pose to our political independence and security is as real as it is intolerable.

As for political associates and military collaborators, the war in Biafra may have produced a small crop of strange bedfellows, but the Angolan imbroglio produced a bumper harvest of even stranger ones. It witnessed Zaire and Zambia in the same camp with the FNLA-UNITA factions; the latter were being actively provisioned and supported by South Africa and the United States (Azevedo, 1977; Ebinger, 1976; El-Khawas, 1976; Anglin and Shaw, 1979). Of course the motivations underpinning the position adopted by African states, particularly Zaire and Zambia in 1976 in contrast to their divergent stances over Biafra in 1969, derived from sources that are well known. El-Khawas (1976: 60) provided a first approximation of these motivations for Zaire and Zambia when he posits that:

> Their interest derives not only from their desire to have a friendly government next door and secure borders, but also from a need to have continuing access to Angola's transportation network and energy resources.

Zaire (the main force behind the formation of an anti-MPLA coalition inside Angola) feared MPLA retaliation because of her longstanding support for the rival FNLA. Mobutu was not about to be squeezed between two leftist governments, one in Angola and one in the Congo.

Zambia's initial hostility toward the MPLA was conditioned, on the other hand, by her concern over the Benguela Railway. Zambia, like Zaire, was anxious to ensure the minimal disruption possible so as to contain the damage already inflicted on the Zambian economy by the sharp decline in the price of copper on the world market (Anglin and Shaw, 1979). Thus geographical proximity and economic dependence on rail services for Zambia's life-blood, copper, were cardinal influences on Zambian foreign policy toward Angola. Such calculations of the national interest have a tendency to push the larger southern African subregional struggle to the background. Critics of Zambia were quite disillusioned by support they perceived for the reactionary, puppet factions, suggesting that she had betrayed the struggle and deserted to the enemy camp. For some critics the Zambian policy was a clear indication that Kaunda's radicalism ("humanism" too?) wears rather thin. However, as El Khawas (1976: 61) again explained:

> both leaders have a priority to their countries' economic needs and proved to be relatively insensitive to other factors in determining whether and how to intervene in Angola. Both wished to ensure the establishment of a non-communist government that would allow them access to Angola's transit facilities. In doing so, however, they reinforced the existing rivalries between Angolan factions by giving exclusive support to the Western-backed movements, the FNLA-UNITA group.

As in all decisions, and not just African, interpersonal factors played a role in suggesting which side would best safeguard Zambian and Zairois national interest and was therefore a prime candidate for support. Kaunda enjoyed a better personal rapport with Savimbi whom he, along with Nyerere and Machel, regarded as the ablest and most charismatic of the party leaders. Neto seemed a difficult character to deal with (Anglin and Shaw, 1979: 322). Mobutu, on the other hand, was brother-in-law to Roberto of FNLA. Thus the same interpersonal influences on the wavering policy of Sierra Leone and the committed revisionism of the Ivory Coast were made salient yet again. In the case of Sierra Leone, it was the impressive diplomatic efforts of Biafra's Francis Nwokedi, facilitated by his marriage to a Sierra Leonean, which created ambiguities. Similarly, Houphouet was so impressed by the strength of character of Ojukwu, his charisma, that he took to him as an old man to his grandson. The FLS leaders were no less partial to such interpersonal and interfamilial influences.

The outcome of this struggle for control of the Angolan state is well-known. Following the withdrawal of South African forces and the defeat of the rival FNLA-UNITA faction by the MPLA with the helpful intervention of Cuban forces and Soviet materiel the OAU finally recognized the MPLA as the sole legitimate government of Angola and a member state of that organization. Angola, along with Nigeria and the FLS, has become a pivotal partner in the liberation of Namibia.

CONCLUSIONS

Several lessons can be drawn from these two cases of recognition. First, they show that African foreign policy is fluid or elastic rather than static. The old preoccupations of African diplomacy regarding continental unity, noninterference, conflict-resolution by peaceful means, and mediation no doubt remain salient. They are, however, intersected or moderated by a variety of other concerns that include regime or party and national interests, ideological solidarity, the support or acquiescence of bureaucrats who have to implement the policies and, occasionally, the personal preferences of the decision-makers. African foreign policy is no longer the preserve, if ever it was, of presidents alone (Chazan and Shaw, 1982).

These cases also make it clear that given their weak economies, domestic and external pressures exerted upon them, and the tenuousness of their own bases of legitimacy, many of the regimes in Africa are reluctant to get entangled in affairs beyond their borders let along take bold initiatives, unless it can be demonstrated that such affairs and their resolutions will have a profound impact on their own states. There is a growing isolationist impulse—another form of self-reliance?—in contemporary Africa as elsewhere in the world system. We also observe that African states agonize over having to choose between competing claimants to power. However, if a crisis proves too nagging and if the contending parties show resolve, African states will get involved, willy-nilly, in mediation attempts (e.g., Chad and the Western Sahara in the 1980s). As Biafra shows, it is not a foregone conclusion that incumbent governments will always succeed in galvanizing continental support by raising the issue of territorial integrity, especially if the contenders show resolve, demonstrate that they are a going concern, and, more important, that they will have something to offer supporters in their hour of victory.

In this regard, the recent resurgence of UNITA military activity in southern Angola must be of serious concern to the MPLA government. This resurgence reflects the fact that intra-African conflicts have a certain permanence about them: most defeated factions see their defeat as a temporary setback; they rejoin the struggle at different levels and in different times (the Congo crisis, Shaba I and II, Morocco-Algeria reincarnated in struggle over Western Sahara, Chad and numerous attempted and successful coups reflect this behavior). This condition puts a premium on efficiency norms in politics (Ake, 1976) and on dependence on external props. Thus, while African states seek to avoid their own as well as superpower entanglements, all indications are that disengagement is no longer tenable. For the foreseeable future, the MPLA's external props will remain; and if the UNITA military campaign increases, it is possible that the debate over support for the incumbent government of Angola may be rejoined.

However, contenders must be aware of one danger. The trump card in Nigeria's diplomacy was African hostility towards secession; the secessionist aspirations of FLEC did not help the FNLA-UNITA cause. Until a new continental consensus emerges on inherited boundaries, any attempts to redefine borders will be resisted. The struggle for control can only be directed against the existing state rather than aimed at creating a new one. Finally, as FNLA-UNITA found out, simply accepting external associates, even superpower ones, is not necessarily an asset but can even prove to be an embarrassing liability. On questions of decolonization and secession, South African support can be rather costly.

Furthermore, as the economic climate has deteriorated it has caused fluctuations in the historical fortunes and reputations of several African states and leaders. Few if any can now play the role of successful mediators. Thus the African system continues to lack a core. The recent dramatic opening to Israel by Liberia and Zaire and the continuing and improving links between Israel and the Ivory Coast reflect emerging revisions.

These diplomatic points also indicate important analytic factors. African foreign policy is no longer susceptible, if it ever was so, to a simplistic form of analysis: the factors—internal and external—have become too complex and contradictory for orthodox assumptions to remain valid. Instead, in attempting to come to terms with ambiguities and antagonisms, the field has moved beyond orthodoxy towards either more pluralist approaches or political economy. The formation and interaction of apparently unlikely coalitions as well as contradictions both within and between states—as in the two historic cases examined above—constitute one area for further analysis and explanation. Decision-making or external affairs has rarely been the sole prerogative of any one person in Africa or elsewhere; and, given current changes and conjunctures, it is becoming even less so. Crises on the continent involve a variety of issues and interests; they can be neither resolved nor understood without some basic—i.e., "radical"—investigation and recommendation.

BIBLIOGRAPHICAL NOTE

By the end of the 1970s, the academic as well as popular literature on African international relations had grown considerably. A gradual but perceptible shift in both the focus and mode of analysis could be detected taking shape. This inching toward sophistication was not unrelated to the crisis of confidence—intellectual as well as personal, professional, and political—induced by the current world recession and inflation. It was a global conjuncture whose continental manifestations have included economic stagnation and political decay, even repression, external penetration, and cooptation of African decision-making (Libby, 1976), political interest—student and worker riots in Ghana, Ivory Coast, Zambia—coupled with numerous abortive and a few successful coups (Daddieh, forthcoming; Kraus, 1983; Shaw, 1982; Ninsin, 1983; Chazan, 1983; and Mortimer, 1983). In short, incumbent regimes have found it increasingly difficult to meet the basic aspirations of their people (Eicher, 1982; Ajayi, 1982; Leys, 1982). As a result, they have become simultaneously more susceptible to external pressures and more open to domestic challenges to their rule. The mood, as John de St. Jorre (1982: 675) asserts, may be both melancholy and conflictual:

> African states have lost confidence in their ability to regulate their interterritorial conflicts as well as in their capacity to develop their economies and cope with growing socioeconomic problems. They have lost a measure of faith in the ability of the West, particularly the United States, to help them finish the work of decolonization and bring stability to the southern end of the continent.

While the developmental crisis is pervasive and the concomitant mood is pessimistic, suggesting the "need for fresh approaches and such indications are being noticed" (Ajayi, 1982), the new departure—that of political economy—has not been sufficiently sustained as yet. This promising and timely—in terms both of the discipline as a whole and of African studies in particular—approach relates fortunes and needs to policy orientations and results. It reflects the view that the constraints as well as the opportunities resulting from the positions occupied by particular African and Third World states in the evolving world capitalist system (that according to Wallerstein [1974], is increasingly stratified) are peculiarly salient for understanding the shifts and reverses in foreign policy.

NOTE

1. UNITA is the acronym for the National Union for the Total Independence of Angola; FNLA is the acronym for the Front for the National Liberation of Angola.

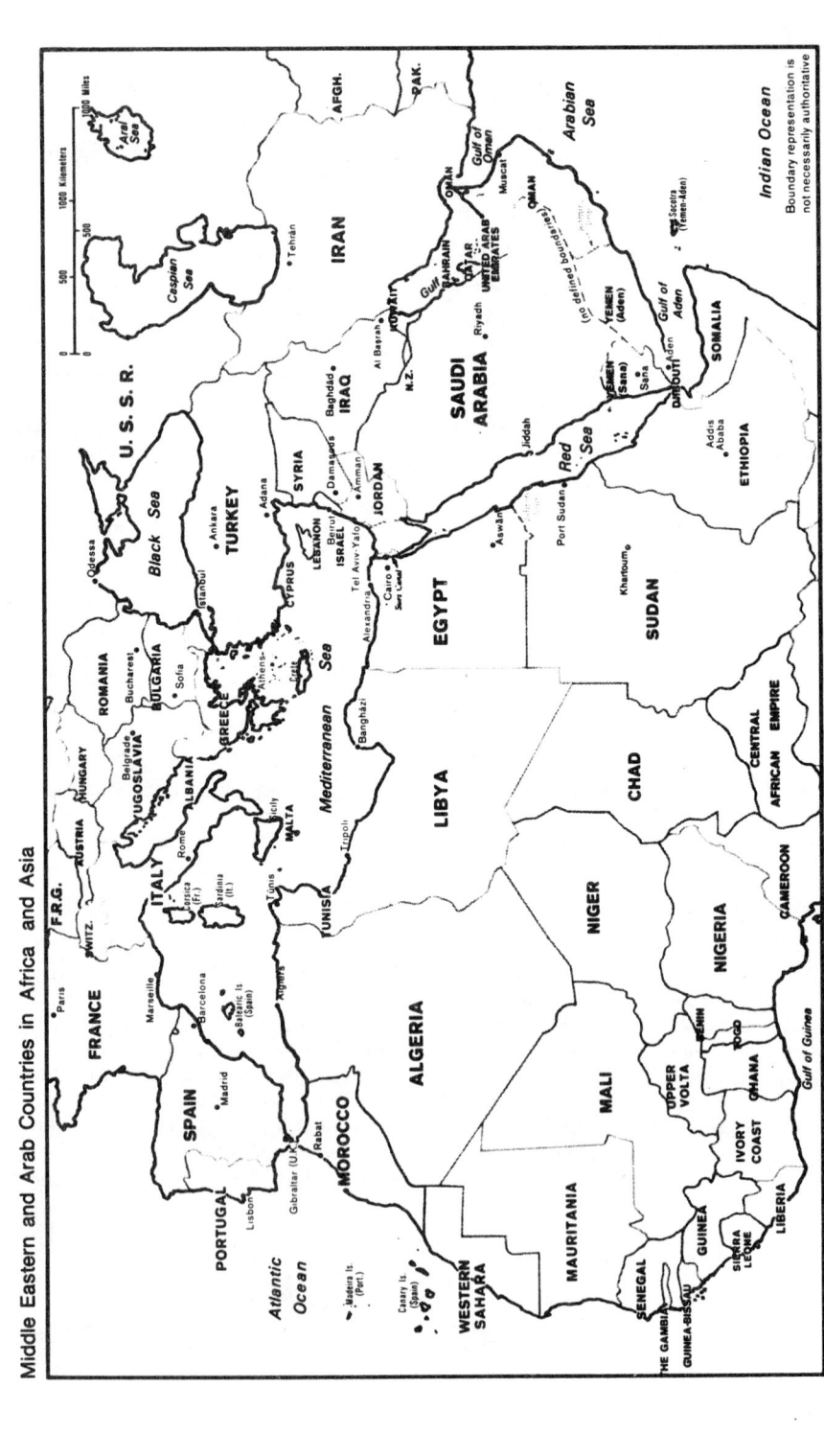
Middle Eastern and Arab Countries in Africa and Asia

4

THE GLORY THAT WAS?

The Pan-Arab, Pan-Islamic Alliance Decisions, October 1973

Bahgat Korany

At 2 p.m. on October 6, 1973, Middle Eastern time, human waves of Egyptian and Syrian Armed Forces stormed over the Suez Canal and the Golan Heights beyond the 1967 cease-fire lines with Israel. The fifth Arab-Israeli war (since the 1969-1970 Attrition War is considered the fourth) had started. Given Israel's military superiority over her Arab adversaries, the world watched the implementation of this "irrational" decision in complete amazement. The decision's "suicidal" aspect seemed confirmed when Israel's Chief of Staff declared that his army would chase the attacking forces back to their initial bases to "crush their bones."

The first days of the war saw impressive Arab advances and the demise of the "invincible" Barlev Line. Despite Israel's subsequent military successes, the effect of the Arab surprise attack was to undermine Israel's concept of military security and to have wide-ranging political effects at both the regional and global levels. From the military viewpoint, for instance, the losses in tanks during the 15 days of the war are estimated at 3000.[1] By comparison, the estimate of losses in the biggest tank confrontation in World War II, which lasted for six months between Rommel and Montgomery in the North African desert, is no more than 650 tanks (Heikal, 1975: 264). From the political viewpoint, President Sadat's 1977 Jerusalem visit and the 1979 peace treaty with Israel would not be conceivable, it is believed, without this war. In this sense, the October attack was dubbed the "war to end all wars" and the "war for peace decision." Moreover, this war heralded Egypt's foreign policy change from a pro-Soviet posture to an increasing alignment with the USA, culminating in the present Pax Americana in the region.

In addition to its military and political repercussions, the October war decision triggered another decision cluster of wider impact on the global economy: the Arab decision to impose an oil embargo. The oil embargo included, in fact, several decisions:

(a) The announcement on October 17, 1973 by the oil ministers of the Organization of Arab Petroleum Exporting Countries of a monthly 5% cut in the flow of oil to the USA and other countries supporting Israel against the Arabs;

(b) Saudi Arabia's decision (announced on October 18) to cut oil production by 10 % at the time the USA especially was pressing oil-producing countries to increase their production to meet the demand of an increasingly oil-thirsty world; and

(c) Saudi Arabia's decision (announced on October 20) to stop all oil exports to the USA following President Nixon's demand to Congress for $2.2 billion in emergency security assistance to Israel (announced October 19) and the continuation of a massive U.S. airlift (beginning October 13) to compensate Israel's war losses.

Two countries were crucial for all these decision clusters: Saudi Arabia and Egypt. Saudi Arabia has usually represented pan-Islamic orthodoxy, whereas Egypt represented secular pan-Arabism. Their basic social structures differ: bedouin-based versus peasant-based. Whereas Saudi Arabia remained "uncontaminated" by colonialism and maintained its traditional structures intact, Egypt was directly integrated in the world system as early as Napoleon's 1798 expedition and, later, through the British occupation from 1882 to 1956. At least until 1972, Egypt had conducted her regional and international political strategy in conjunction with the Soviet Union, whereas Saudi Arabia had allied herself with the "free world" against "atheist" Communism. Whereas Saudi Arabia's population has been traditionally just less than one-fifth of Egypt's, her per capita income has continued rising in the last decade until it reached, in 1980, 15 times that of Egypt.

These countries represented divergent leadership poles in the Islamic-Arab world, even before the rise of oil power or Nasserism. Indeed, these divergent leadership claims transformed the Arab cold war into a hot one around the mountains of Yemen from 1962 to 1967. The 1970s, however, saw an increasing rapprochement between the two countries. In fact, both the October war decision and the oil embargo were a reflection of the rising Egyptian-Saudi axis.

Thus, at a time when the war between pan-Arab Iraq and Iran's Islamic republic has been raging for more than three years, concerned observers might like to know how only ten years ago both pan-Islamism and pan-Arabism were in alliance and managed to coordinate their moves to achieve successful decisions.

This analysis is organized in three main parts: the context of the decision, decision-planning and participants, and thirdly decision formulation and implementation. The conclusion spells out some differences and similarities between the two decision sets. If a general proposition can be ascertained at this stage of the analysis, it is the slight weight of personality factors and the rising pressures of regional geopolitical factors (i.e., the intransigence of the adversary and the need to maintain the legitimacy bases of the two regimes).

The data for the analysis are based on an extensive survey of newspaper and documentary material, political memoirs, participants' analyses and different yearbooks. Data gaps—a traditional obstacle for any analyst of Third World political decisions—have been greatly reduced in the case of the war decision because of material gained through interviews, underlining the usefulness of interviews as a technique of analysis for the study of Third World decisions.

THE DECISION CONTEXT

Most decision analyses are exceedingly synchronic. In the case of the 1973 decisions, one cannot escape the weight of historical factors, whether related to the belief in "one Arab nation from the Atlantic Ocean to the Arab Gulf," or the establishment of the state of Israel as an "imperialist base" in the area. Without going so far back as to trace historical forces shaping the decision context, it is certain that the regional and national repercussions of the 1967 Arab defeat crystallized these historical factors and shaped the frame of reference of the different 1973 decisions. Because Egypt of the 1960s presented itself as the leader and protector of pan-Arabism, it was this country's credibility, more than that of any other state, that was undermined by the defeat.

EGYPT

On November 23, 1967, Nasser admitted that his country's direct losses—at the hands of a state with one-tenth Egypt's population—were 11,500 killed and 5,500 captured, 80% of the Egyptian armor and 286 of the country's 340 combat aircraft destroyed. The chaotic collision between two divisions of the Egyptian army in their disorganized race to withdraw to the mountain passes showed that the army as a military corps had disappeared. And there was no diplomatic victory (as in the 1956 Suez war, for instance) to compensate for this military wipe-out.

> The pre-war picture of Israel as a beleaguered fortress . . . had earned the Israelis wide international sympathy. . . . By the discrepancies between their threats and their performance, the Arabs had invited the world's derision. This had been skillfully encouraged by Israeli psychological warfare and propaganda which stressed the cowardice rather than the lack of skills of the Arabs and took every opportunity of showing the Arab and especially the Egyptian armies in a humiliating light—for example, by photographing Egyptian prisoners stripped to their underwear or in other unheroic situations (Stephens 1971: 497, 504).

The speeches of the time are crammed with the themes of "ordeal," "cruelty of our situation," "our great pains," "the greatest test and crisis of our modern history." Nasser's drawn and haggard features, his half choking and uncharacteristically hesitant voice, symbolized the state of nervous and physical collapse of post-1967 Egypt. To describe this situation, Nasser used some telling images. "After this great catastrophe," he said in November 1967, "we were like a man who went out in the street to be hit by a tram or a car and lay both motionless and senseless on the ground." Five months later, he described himself then as "a man walking in a desert surrounded by moving sands not knowing whether, if he moved, he would be swallowed up by the sands or would find the right path" (speech of April 25, 1968).

The country's independence and basic foreign policy strategy were strained. When President Podgorny came to Egypt immediately after the defeat to see what had happened, Nasser offered to hand over Egypt's entire air defence to the USSR. The presence of some 21,000 Soviet experts shed doubts on the country's nonalignment and its leading role in the movement (Korany, 1976: 312-313). A main Egyptian political participant of the period has said that "the Russian experts had automatic access to the authorities in Egypt, and this caused a good deal of resentment in the higher levels of the Egyptian bureaucracy" (Heikal, 1978: 212). Moreover,

> there were the quarrels between General Mohamed Sadiq, the Minister of War, and senior military men; there was the demand by Admiral Gorshikov for special facilities for Russian warships . . . there was the Russian attempt virtually to take over Cairo West airport to the exclusion of all Egyptian authorities, and their self-isolation in Cairo, where they had bought up a lot of property in the centre of the city for the exclusive occupation of the experts and diplomats and their families (Heikal, 1978: 238).

If we add to these immediate contextual factors, structural ones resulting from underdevelopment, we can see the weight of the factors shaping the decision-makers' frame of reference. For in addition to the societal disorganization and conflict flowing from social change, Egypt was poor. The resultant gap between rising demands and insufficient disposable resources heightened social conflict. The pie was no longer the same size but appeared to shrink, and different social groups were increasingly impatient and self-seeking. The regime's crisis was correspondingly intense.

Less bound by a certain type of Arab nationalist behavior than his predecessor, and confronted with Egypt's weak capabilities in relation to Israel, Sadat tried to get out of the crisis by political means. He aimed to mend fences with the United States. At the time of Nasser's funeral, Sadat met very quietly with E. Richardson, American Secretary of Health, Education and Welfare. Early in 1971, in his interview with *Newsweek's* A. de Borchgrave, Sadat said for the first time that he would be ready to establish peace and recognize Israel. Not only did Sadat refuse to give in to the hawks and break the ceasefire, but on February 4, 1971, he proposed a partial settlement and the opening of the Suez Canal. In May, he held talks in Cairo with William Rogers, the first U.S. Secretary of State to visit Egypt since May, 1953. Contacts continued and culminated in the sending to Washington of Hafez

Ismail, Sadat's national security advisor (who would work opposite Kissinger) in February, 1973. After a public meeting with Nixon at the White House and three secret ones with Kissinger, Egypt was asked to offer "something concrete" in exchange for some Israeli withdrawal.

> Ismail's meeting with Kissinger ... failed to produce any results. It was impossible ... to make a move if we ourselves did not take military action to break the deadlock. The drift of what Kissinger said to Ismail was that the U.S. regrettably could do nothing to help—as long as we were the defeated party and Israel maintained her superiority (Sadat, 1978: 238).

When Mrs. Meir visited Washington less than a week after Ismail's meeting, she left with Nixon's promise to send Israel an additional 48 phantom jets over the next four years.

Apparently this presidential decision (revealed in mid-March) convinced the new Egyptian leadership that the impassse would continue unless the situation on the military front changed (Kalb and Kalb, 1974: 511). The repeated street demonstrations, dismissal of journalists, arrest of intellectuals, publication and popularization of Heikal's "no war-no peace" articles, reflected that Egyptian public opinion was tired of the stagnation, and that it was urgent for Sadat to plan effectively for a military confrontation. Roughly at this time (early April 1973), he told A. de Borchgrave that "the time has come for a shock .... Everything in this country is now being mobilized in earnest for the resumption of the battle—which is now inevitable. ... One has to fight in order to be able to talk."

In retrospect, Sadat had to shift from moderation and political means of conflict resolution to the belief that one has to fight in order to be able to talk. If his subsequent behavior toward Israel, right up until his assassination, is any indicator of a basic attitude, Sadat's October war decision seems to be out of character. As I argue elsewhere in this issue, the psychological approach does not really come to grips with the problem. Moreover, it seems that it was the operational environment's potency that pushed toward war. Israel's ex-chief of the Intelligence Service confirms this view:

> Throughout this period, Sadat's personal position was becoming weaker and weaker. He had become a laughing stock in his own country with the passing of 1971, the 'Year of Decision' in which no decision was made. His specious excuses about the India-Pakistan War and other explanations for his failure to go to war were the subject of much biting humour among the wits of Cairo. His image was that of a foolish man and he headed a

hesitant Egyptian society which was to a great degree demoralized and in which the credibility of the government was very low. The impression gained abroad was of a regime desperately preoccupied in an endeavour to survive from month to month (Herzog, 1975: 14-23).

Dayan agrees:

> Change by political means seemed unattainable after the fruitless attempts by H. Ismail to secure Nixon's support.... The pity is that the United States failed to engage in intensive diplomatic activity during the decisive years of 1972-1973 (Dayan, 1977: 749).

In the same month that witnessed H. Ismail's unsuccessful visit to the United States (February 1973), planning for war became operational, as evidenced by the order to prepare the Gamassy military document.

SAUDI ARABIA

Saudi Arabia, though also underdeveloped, Islamic, and Arab, had a decision context quite different from Egypt's. Despite her underdevelopment, Saudi Arabia was not poor. Even before the 1973 oil boom, her annual revenue from the daily oil production of eight million barrels was $4.4 billion. Most importantly, she did not have Egypt's crippling gap between increasing population and limited resources.

Saudi Arabia prides herself on being the birth place of both Arab culture and Islam and the protector of their purity. Since she is the guardian of Islam's two holiest cities, Mecca and Medina, it is toward Saudi Arabia that Moslems all over the world turn five times a day for their prayers. and aspire to visit this country at least once during their lifetime to carry out the pilgrimage and "wash away their sins." The country's association with Islam thus confers on her leadership a very specific responsibility. The Saudi leaders were incited to deploy all possible efforts to liberate the third holiest town in Islam: Jerusalem. Since the Egyptian pole was in decline, Saudi Arabia could not, so to speak, pass the buck.

The post-Six-Day-War Khartoum Arab summit conference (August 1967) indicated the rise of Saudi leadership. Riyadh came to the rescue of Egypt's crumbling economy by offering £100 million a year to compensate Egypt for her losses. One of the most important consequences of this subsidy was that Nasser's Egypt became financially dependent on her erstwhile rival. Egypt's withdrawal from Yemen as Saudi Arabia had long demanded, and Nasser's preoccupation with problems nearer to the home front (rebuilding of the army, consolidation of the regime legitimacy) fostered the rise of Saudi regional leadership.

With Nasser's death and Sadat's arrival in 1970, Saudi and Egyptian leadership positions in the Arab system (Korany, 1983a and b: Noble, 1984) changed even further. After a cold peace in the 1967-1970 period, it was a drive toward close cooperation that, on the eve of the October war, ended in a Cairo-Riyadh axis based on mutual convenience.

> An Egypt under relentlessly increasing economic strain henceforth expected substantial and continuing access to the growing riches of the oil states. In exchange, a Saudi regime acutely conscious of its multifaceted vulnerability, and for years under ideological, political and even military attack by the 'radical-revolutionary' camp now looked forward to, indeed demanded, relief from such pressures. It expected from Cairo, the erstwhile leader of the adversary camp, abandonment of revolutionary confrontation, supra-national appeals, unduly close ties to the Communist world, the promotion of socialism within the Arab World, and other such policies and practices subversive of the *status quo* (Jabber, 1982: 430).

Having assumed a leadership role in the Arab system, Saudi Arabia could no longer practice fence-sitting. She had to be in the forefront of pan-Arab action. This necessity was accentuated when her partner, Egypt, was fully involved in the defense of the Arab course, and such rivals for Islamic leadership—say, Kadhafi's Libya—were working so hard to undermine the royal family's legitimacy. More than a month *before* the oil embargo *The Economist* put it nicely:

> The Saudis are discovering the perils of Arab leadership. Never before have they taken the lead in an Arab nationalist cause. Now they are finding that any Arab leader who gives a decisive lead has to keep moving forward briskly if he is not to be trampled down by his enthusiastic following. (September, 1973: 36)

Because of the Saudi pattern of state formation, these pressures were intimately linked to the regime's legitimacy. Islam and Arab culture played the important role in the rise and maintenance of the Saudi state from its inception in the middle of the eighteenth century (Helmes, 1981: 76-126; Lackner, 1978: 14-31; Rentz, 1980: 15-34) through the alliance between *deen and donia* (religious and political authority), *ulama and umara* (religious scholars and princes), between Sheikh Abdel-Wahab and Al-Saud families. Through the formidable army of militant Moslem brothers *(Al-Ikhwan)* and in the name of Islam, Al-Saud imposed his rule on the different warring tribes in the peninsula's segmented society.

As a result, Islam acquired a primary status in both domestic and foreign policies of the kingdom.

In addition to the traditional religious elements who favor a militant Islamic policy toward the question of Jerusalem and the whole issue of Zionism, the technocrats favored the same militancy but not for the same reasons. Since they are usually nationalist on foreign policy issues, they tended to insist on an even-handed U.S. foreign policy in the Arab-Israeli conflict. Moreover, many of them thought that Saudi Arabia should not go on increasing her oil production and depleting her main resource unless Saudi Arabia was properly rewarded. If not, she should produce only to the limit of her economy's absorptive capacity and, due to world inflationary pressures, the stored petrol would increase in monetary value.

The technocrats influence and the appeal of their views have been gaining momentum. For instance, their resistance to waste and undisciplined consumerism appeals to many members of the religious élite. Moreover, other direct participation in decision-making has also been increasing since the establishment of the first Council of Ministers in 1953. When fighting erupted within the royal family between King Saud and his brother Faisal in 1958 to 1960, Saud, to regain his influence, used the technocrats' support and established a cabinet where they made up the majority. But this move was short-lived and merely tactical on Saud's part.

However, their participation in government continued and, with the rush to development (El-Mallakh, 1982) that began in the late sixties, their presence in decision-making bodies was accelerated. For instance, in 1965 the Saudi Council of Ministers was composed of 14 ministers: 5 princes, 3 representatives of the Al-Sheikh family, and 6 technocrats. After the shuffle of 1975, the number of cabinet members rose to 25. The representatives of the Al-Sheikh family remained at 3, whereas the number of princes rose to 8, and that of technocrats to 14. Their support was thus essential for King Faisal to protect his own position at home against those Saudis who do not like to see their country used as a guard force for U.S. interest (e.g., the attempted coup in 1969 by Saudi air force officers; explosions at one of Aramco's largest refineries on August 5th and 16th, 1973: *The Economist*, September 1, 1973: 16; Lackner, 1978: 89-109). As Faisal told his American television audience almost six weeks before the actual decision: "We are now under attack from the Arabs themselves because of our friendship with the USA, and we are accused of being in collusion with "Zionism and American imperialism' against the Arabs" (*New York Times*, September 10, 1973). Oil executives close to Aramco confirmed this national-regional pressure, saying that the king was finding it increasingly hard to resist radicals in the Arab world and inside his own country who pushed him to demand correction of U.S. policies (*New York Times*, September 10, 1973).

Though he is not the militant nationalist his predecessor Abdullah Tariki was (Duguid, 1970: 195-220), Minister of Petroleum and Mineral Resources Ahmed Zaki Yamani is a good sample of this technocratic group. The son of an eminent religious judge, the 55-year old Yamani received his LL.D. from the University of Cairo when he was only 19. He went to the U.S. in the mid-1950s and studied comparative law at New York University and Harvard. Back in Saudi Arabia, Yamani went into government service. In 1958 he was appointed legal advisor to the nation's Council of Ministers, and by 1962 was Minister of Oil. The only book he published is entitled, interestingly, *Islamic Law and Contemporary Issues*. Despite his moderation, he could understand and communicate the technocrats' demands. His influence was the more felt since he was deeply trusted by Faisal and was in constant contact with Aramco (*Time*, December 17, 1973: 44; *Le Monde*, November 28, 1973: 3). He is bound to be the important participant in the decison's implementation, if not in its planning.

DECISION PLANNING AND PARTICIPANTS

> In February 1973, I asked the Chief of Operations (General Gamassy) for a research paper selecting—on the basis of recent advances in modern technology—the best "D" day. To respect secrecy, only one copy of the research paper was available. It was also hand-written. It studied natural phenomena, different political and military aspects, climate change, star movements and new technological developments. It was a document of high scientific and technical standards which concluded by specifying three day clusters as the most suitable for an attack: the second half of May, September, and first half of October. (Sadat in Sabri, 1974: 22-23)

Contrary to the psychologistic literature's overall characterization of the decision-making pattern in Third World countries as based on the leader's whims and moods (Thompson, 1967: 415-21), the October war decision was based on long-term and minute planning, systematic information-gathering and analysis, and detailed discussion and bargaining among the different participants.

WAR PLANS

If not at the top political level, at least within the army ranks, general thinking about preparing for another war started, according to one participant, right after the 1967 defeat (Heikal, 1975: 2). Specifics in planning changed of course with the passage of time: both in form (from defensive to offensive) and in partners (from Libya, Egypt and Syria, to only Egypt and Syria—since Libya had a different concept of the attack). It was also accepted that planning for war necessitated modification in the army's composition and structure, and precise knowledge about the adversary.

By many accounts the Egyptian army of the 1970s was quite a different one from that of 1967. Professionalization was sytematically promoted among the leadership, and the centers of power were pursued and dispersed. As to the rank and file, a great emphasis was put on the level of education. Thus, in the process of rebuilding the army after the defeat, Nasser ordered that any tank commander or officer responsible for electronic equipment must be a graduate of either an engineering or a technical school (Heikal, 1975: 35). Consequently, of the 800,000 Egyptians under arms in 1973, no less than 110,000 were graduates of universities or institutes of higher education. Egypt had "begun to match Israel in the quality of its troops, while having of course far greater potential in quantity" (Heikal, 1975: 35-36). Moreover, training was pushed to the extreme. As the Chief of Staff admits: "By 1970 pilot exhaustion had pushed training accidents to an alarming rate. We eased off the training pressure. But that merely meant training would take longer" (Shazli, 1980: 17,19). Similarly, reconstruction continued unabated at the top. From autumn 1968, the General Headquarters of the Egyptian Armed Forces began annual strategic exercises among all services (including Air Force Headquarters, Naval Headquarters, and special forces Headquarters) and under conditions approaching as closely as possible the expected war environment. The result was that the gulf between planning and capabilities, enormous in 1968, shrank with the passage of time until, in October 1973, they were identical (Heikal, 1975: 17-18).

It was after the 1967 defeat too that a Center for Strategic Studies was established as a think tank and attached to Al-Ahram, where Nasser's confidant (Heikal) was editor-in chief. The Center's directorship was confided to Hatem Sadek, Nasser's son-in-law, to insure that red tape or a "narrow concept of security" would not prevent its researchers (among whom were top military personnel, many university professors, as well as Nasser's oldest daughter, Hoda) from synthesizing conflict theories and analyzing needed data. Thus they hoped to prevent a repeat of the 1967 debacle.

The result of all these efforts at planning and information processing was that the military ended by producing two plans for the crossing of the Canal: (a) the High Minarets, Egypt's first realistic plan to capture 6 to 8 miles in Sinai and dig in there under the proper air protection provided by SAM batteries: and (b) Operation 41, which aimed to seize the strategic passes in the middle of Sinai, 30 to 40 miles east of the Canal.

Both of the plans were ready by September 1971, but neither was backed by the military capabilities to carry it out. The military High Command decided that only Operation 41 was to be revealed to the Soviets to get the needed military equipment. Yet even the biggest arms deal ever made with the Soviet Union, reached during Sadat's visit there in October 1971, did not meet all the needs of Operation 41. Operation 41 was slightly modified and renamed Granite Two.

At the beginning of 1972 General A. Ismaïl (then head of the Intelligence Service) prepared a political-strategic estimate of the Middle East situation. The document was drafted for the President and only the most senior levels were familiar with its contents. It reiterated the gap separating Egypt from Israel and warned against the consequences of any Egyptian attack. When Ismaïl was appointed minister of war in October 1972 to replace Sadek, Granite Two was definitely discarded and the "High Minarets" (the plan for very limited attack) was developed into the final offensive plan: coded Badr. Even the President, who initially favored the capturing of the passes, had to comply with the wishes of the top military command and entrust them, in writing, with the final decision concerning the goals to be attained by the operation. At the same time, a version of Granite Two to capture the passes was still to be debated to pacify the Syrians (Shazli, 1980: 38). On January 31, 1973, Egypt and Syria set up a unified command for their armed forces. At that time the army was in a position to mount the attack, and it coincided with the failure of the Washington negotiations between Ismaïl and Kissinger.

An attack in May, 1973 was intentionally planned to coincide with the Summit Meeting between Nixon and Brezhnev in Washington. In the event the Israelis sensed danger and quickly mobilized to counter an attack. Finally May was discarded for "political reasons," according to Sadat. Thus when the Syrian Minister of Defence, accompanied by the top five most senior officers of the Syrian army, arrived in Alexandria in August 22, 1973, their objective was to decide with their Egyptian counterparts on the specific day—and hour—of the attack.

OIL EMBARGO

What is striking about the oil embargo decision is the change in public attitudes of Saudi leadership, especially King Faisal's and consequently Sheikh A. Z. Yamani's. All along, the King had believed that oil was a commodity to procure money to buy weapons rather than being a weapon in itself. This was the logic used during the 1967 Arab Summit in Khartoum following the Arab defeat, and subsidies were paid to Egypt and Jordan to prove that the flow of oil—rather than its stoppage—could help the Arab cause. In 1970, Faisal was still saying that to stop pumping oil was out of the question (*New York Times*, May 16, 1973). As late as April 1973, Yamani expressed the same view in an address to the Middle East Institute in Washington (Heikal, 1975: 271-272).

By the spring of 1973, oil policy was increasingly central to Saudi policy. The oil glut of the 1960s and early 1970s was at an end and oil companies were pressuring oil-producers, notably oil giants such as Saudi Arabia, to increase their production. Thus by May 1973, a high-level ministerial committee, chaired by the present King Fahd (who was then Minister of the Interior) was reviewing all aspects of Saudi Arabia's oil policy, including "desirable levels of production and the political aspects of satisfying Western oil demands" (*New York Times*, August 20, 1973: 39-41). Different factors interacted to favor a policy change toward the use of oil as a politico-economic weapon. These factors included the perceived complete U.S. support of Israel even when the latter was unreasonable; mounting domestic and Arab pressures on the kingdom to use its privileged position with the USA to try to warn Washington of the consequences of its pro-Israeli policy; the Al-Saud's concern about the maintenance and credibility of their regional leadership and of their internal legitimacy; and, of course, the favorable global context of the end of the oil glut.

Thus by the summer, messages from Yamani and the King's entourage indicated the possibility of using oil in the battle, but not the exact form of this use (*Nouvel observateur*, September 10-16, 1973:

30-31). No longer was the battle of oil to be fought only on two fronts—prices and participation—but a third one was to be added: the level of production.

During a secret visit to Saudi Arabia at the end of August, Sadat (keeping Quaddafi waiting for him in Cairo) informed the King of the decision to go to war. When they discussed the role of oil in the impending battle, Faisal was open to the possibility of its use but suggested two conditions: (1) no union between Egypt and Libya; (2) a conciliatory gesture toward King Hussein of Jordan and an attempt to integrate him in the Arab family (Sheehan, 1973-1974: 52-58). Then the King added a third condition: "give us time. We do not want to use our oil as a weapon in a battle which only goes on for two or three days and then stops. We want to see a battle which goes on for long enough time for the world public opinion to be mobilized" (Heikal, 1975: 275).

But though the King seemed to have joined the radical camp in the family and gave in to domestic and regional pressures for a Saudi active role, he still did not want to alienate the USA and the kingdom's moderate elements. This explains the contradictory signals that kept coming from Saudi Arabia reflecting the wavering within the decision-making group concerning a definitive oil policy. Thus in the same day (August 30, 1973), two statements came from Saudi Arabia. In a television interview, Faisal said that his country was "deeply concerned that if the U.S. does not change its policy in the Middle East and continues to side with Zionism, then ... such course of action will affect our relations with our American friends because it will place us in an untenable position in the Arab World" (*Facts on File*, September 2-3, 1973: 737). On the same day the Beirut weekly *Al-Hawadess* carried statements by Faisal and his son Prince Saud, then undersecretary of the Petroleum Ministry, warning against slogans "which deliberately intend to push the Arabs to gamble with their strongest weapon" (oil). The King wondered that "no one is asking where we would get the money we need if we cut off the oil, not only for supporting our country, but also for providing assistance to our brothers on the front lines" against Israel, (*Facts on File*, September 2-3, 1973: 737).

Yet in a declaration published three days later (*Newsweek*, September 3, 1973), Faisal alternated and went a tiny step in the direction of the radical camp: "the U.S.," he said, "must refrain from giving unlimited aid to Israel ... If no American response is forthcoming, one of our conditions for increasing our (oil) production will not have been satisfied."

Thus by September 1973, the Saudis advised the Americans either to lean on Israel to secure the full implementation of the 1967 U.N. Resolution 242, or face the consequences of a diminshed oil supply: from 8 million barrels a day to 7 million (*The Economist*, September 22, 1973: 64). It is important to notice the moderation of Saudi position: there was no demand to stop arms supplies to Israel or to insist on other U.N. resolutions, and the ticking of this time bomb (oil reduction) was kept secret by both the Americans and the Saudis themselves.

DECISION FORMULATION AND IMPLEMENTATION

THE EGYPTIAN-SYRIAN DECISION

Alternative dates were put forward by the military planners: September 7 to 11, and October 5 to 10. Since the military commanders had asked for a countdown of twenty days, they knew when they met in late August that the September date was ruled out, and the offensive had to be an October war. October was deemed to be the most suitable month for the following reasons (from my interviews in the Nasser Academy: February-March 1981):

(a) Favorable atmospheric conditions on both the Egyptian and Syrian fronts.
(b) The nights were long (and thus favorable for establishing bridges across the Canal).
(c) Israeli elections were to take place on October 28 and most Israelis would be occupied with them long before the specific election day.

As for the specific day of the offensive, the following factors carried the weight:

(a) October 6 was not only a Saturday, a Sabbath, but it was also Yom Kippur, holy feast for the Jews.
(b) The first half of the night would have moonlight to help establish bridges across the Canal.
(c) On that day, the water level in the Canal was most convenient for the crossing.

Not all aspects of decison-making were easy sailing between the Egyptians and Syrians. For instance, the exact hour of the attack represented a problem (Heikal, 1975: 3-4). Since the Egyptians were to cross the Suez Canal from west to east, they wanted to attack in the late afternoon to have the sun behind them and in the eyes of the Israelis. This "H" hour would give them some hours of daylight for the crossing, 6 hours of moonlight to complete the bridges across the Canal, and a further 6 hours of total darkness in which the armour could be brought to the East Bank. The Syrians however, were attacking from east to west, and were eager—exactly as the Egyptians—to have the sun in their back and in the adversary's eyes. They thus lobbied to attack in the first light of day. Several compromises were proposed by the Egyptians: The Syrians could attack at dawn on October 6th and the Egyptians would follow in the afternoon, but the Syrians declined this offer since it would leave them a few hours alone in face of the Israeli army. When the Egyptians suggested that they start first on the afternoon of October 6, allowing the Syrians to follow on the morning of October 7, the Syrians again objected—this time on political grounds: such a timing would make the Syrians look as if they were lagging behind. In any case, both proposals suffered from a major fault: they diminished the effect of surprise on two fronts. The matter was thus referred to the Syrian President Assad for a solution and a compromise was struck. Both would attack at the beginning of the afternoon, at 2 o'clock, and thus the crucial effect of surprise was kept. Here the "bureaucratic politics" emphasis on bargaining among participants, and the emphasis on decisions as an outcome, is applicable.

That model's emphasis on the plurality of participants is relevant in other instances of the decision-making process in Egypt. Between September 30 (Sadat in Sabri, 1974: 25-27) and October 2 (Heikal, 1975: 16-17) two high-level meetings were held. The first was a meeting of the National Security Council—the political body that included the President, the two Vice-Presidents, two assistants to the president, the Vice-Prime-Ministers, the Minister of War, the Director-General of Intelligence, and the Director-General of Military Intelligence. Some ministers connected with the war effort were also invited to attend this meeting. The participants were informed of the objective of a limited attack, and they discussed plans for political coordination as well as possible scenarios of the effects of the war.

This meeting was immediately followed by one of the War Council headed by the President and comprising only the military: the Minister of War, the Chief of Staff, the Director of Operations, the Chiefs of the Air Force and Navy, and the heads of all service departments—twenty senior officers in all. During this meeting, which lasted for ten hours, the code name Sparkle was chosen for the attack and the President signed its order.

As can be seen from the minute planning and discussion efforts, the decision was based on coordination and deception. Its successful implementation depended on three elements:

(a) The simultaneous attack on two fronts to prevent the limited Israeli forces from concentrating their fire power on one side or managing to end the war by a blitzkrieg. The most important aim was to keep the war going as long as possible to exhaust the enemy, both its armed forces and its economic capacity. Since Israel could not continue a war without mobilization, and since mobilization leads to a standstill in the country, a long war could lead to economic paralysis.

(b) This aspect of coordination is related to the political front, especially at the regional level. The coordination goal was to capitalize on all Arab resources without ideological discrimination or communication breakdown with any Arab country:

> My clear and declared policy was that Egypt could not distinguish one Arab country from another on the basis of so-called progressive and reactionary or republican and monarchical systems. We should be committed to one thing only—our Arab character, pure and simple" (Sadat, 1978: 239).

In effect, however, the emphasis was put on countries with the most needed of world resources, oil, and whose impact on the global level could be directly felt.

THE SAUDI ARABIAN DECISION

Even though it was Saudi Arabia who finally made the difference, the participants in the final formulation of the decision were not limited to Saudis or, for that matter, to oil producing countries.

The Framework of Options Set in Cairo

Parallel to the military preparations for the war, a task force in the Egyptian Ministry of Foreign Affairs was studying possible courses of action to profit to the maximum from the oil weapon. And either by chance or by prior planning, in the spring of 1973 the Al-Ahram Center for Political and Strategic Studies had asked Dr. Mustafa Khalil (a former deputy prime minister for Industry and Mineral Resources and later prime minister) to prepare a study of the energy crisis in the United States and its implications for the Arab states. This report was handed over less than a week before the start of hostilities in October and was immediately shown to the President.

On the second day of the war, the President asked Sayed Mareï, his special assistant and chairman of the Committee of Policy Coordination with Arab Governments, to go immediately to the petrol-producing countries and to discuss how petrol could be used in the service of the Arab cause. It was logical that Dr. Khalil be included in the delegation (Mareï, 1979: 724-755).

Khalil's three-file data-based study formed the framework of the discussion on how oil could best be used to further the objectives of the battle. It raised some crucial questions: for instance, is it more effective to stop oil production altogether, or simply to reduce the amount produced; should the oil weapon be applied indiscriminately, or to reward or punish countries according to the evolution of their attitude toward the Arab cause? These were the questions Mareï put to Sadat before taking off to the oil producing countries. Sadat was emphatic: put the options before them and let them choose. There was, however, the warning not to reach the point of no return with the USA, and this appealed quite well to the Saudi leadership.

With this prerequisite in mind, Mareï and Khalil met on October 8 in a tête-à-tête at Mareï's house for five full hours to elaborate strategy and coordinate moves during the discussion in the Gulf countries. The following morning, they met again to discuss Khalil's more manageable thirteen-page summary of his three-file study. This meeting took place in the Foreign Ministry and was enlarged to include Dr. Mohmoud Fawzi, the Vice-President and respected politician in both the Nasser and Sadat eras, and Mohamed H. Heikal, the influential editor-in-chief of Al-Ahram. Different options were again debated and the decision was reached not to use oil as a weapon to threaten all countries but to use it as an economic resource and a strategic commodity in the service of Arab objectives (Mareï, 1979: 729-734). As an economic resource, the Arabs have the right to regulate the volume of their oil production as the USA does her petrol and other natural resources. But oil is also a strategic commodity, in the sense that the Arab world can barter it for another strategic commodity, such as arms. Similarly, if a country withholds from the Arabs a strategic commodity or provides it to their enemy, the Arabs can withhold their oil from that country. As a result, two points were emphasized in this rationale for the use of oil in the battle: (a) its use was to be discriminatory: to reward friends and punish enemies; and (b) the objective was not to paralyze Western economies but mainly to defend Arab interests by giving a warning rather than turning off the tap altogether.

TABLE 4.1

Percentage Share of Saudi Arabia in Crude Oil Production of the Middle East, the OPEC Countries, and the World
(Saudi Arabia's production as percentage of respective totals)

	Middle East[a]	OPEC[b]	World Total Excluding Sino-Soviet Area	World Total Including Sino-Soviet Area
1960	24.8	15.1	7.5	6.3
1965	26.3	15.4	8.9	7.3
1970	27.3	16.2	10.0	8.3
1971	29.3	18.8	11.9	9.9
1972	33.4	22.2	14.3	11.9
1973	36.0	24.5	16.3	13.5
1974	38.9	27.6	18.6	15.1
1975	36.3	26.1	17.1	13.4
1976	38.3	27.5	18.1	14.4
1977	41.2	29.2	19.0	15.0
1978	39.3	27.7	17.8	13.8
1979[c]	44.5	31.0	19.6	15.1

SOURCES: International Monetary Fund, Saudi Arabia—An Economic and Financial Survey March 26, 1976: 1); British Petroleum Company, Ltd, BP Statistical Review of the World Oil Industry (1976: 6) and (1977: 6); Oil and Gas Journal, December 25, 1979; 102-103); Ministry of Petroleum and Mineral Resources, Economics Department, Petroleum Statistical Bulletin (1979: 21), as in R. Mallakh: Rush to Development. London: Croom Helm.
a. Excluding North African countries.
b. Includes the 13 members of OPEC at the end of 1975.
c. Provisional.

These different elements were written down, and Heikal—at the end of this second five-hour meeting—took the document to Sadat. A telephone conversation between Mareï and Sadat reaffirmed the President's preference: explain what Egypt and Syria had done until then, specify options and their different evaluations, and leave the form of the final decision to each Arab country. The final decision had to specify that the Arab countries "do not aim to destroy anybody, and this is why reduction of production is preferred to complete cut-off. The exact percentage of this reduction is left to each individual country" (Mareï, 1979 734).

TABLE 4.2
Saudi Arabia: Oil Revenue (US $ millions)*

Year		Index (1970 = 100)
1960	333.7	31.10
1965	664.1	54.70
1970	1,214.0	100.00
1971	1,884.9	155.26
1972	2,744.6	226.08
1973	4,340.0	357.50
1974	22,573.5	1,859.43
1975	25,676.2	2,115.01
1976	30,754.9	2,533.35
1977	36,540.1	3,009.89
1978	32,233.8	2,655.17
1979	48,443.1	3,990.37

SOURCES: SAMA, Annual Reports (1969: 84) (1977: 140), and (1979: 138); Ministry of Petroleum and Mineral Resources, Economics Department, Petroleum Statistical Bulletin (1979: 44), as in R. El-Mallagh (1982) *Rush to Development*. London: Croom Helm.
*including the value of royalty oil payments in kind and Saudi Arabian government's share in the Abu Sa'fah oilfield.

The Meeting with King Faisal

The four-man Egyptian delegation left on October 10, and was received by King Faisal a few hours after their arrival. In addition to the King, the Saudi side included his adviser, Rashad Pharaon, and his brother, Nawaf Ibn Abdel-Aziz, who was then his special advisor on Gulf Affairs. The Egyptians led the discussions by providing information to the King and answering his questions. Perceptively, Sadat had sent one of his generals, Saad El-Qadi, with maps to explain the details of the Canal crossing and the mastery of the Barlev Line, as well as the evolution of the situation on the Egyptian and Syrian battlefields. When the discussion moved to energy questions, Mustafa Khalil, using his recent data, talked extensively. The King listened more than he talked. The meeting lasted from mid-afternoon to dusk, finishing half-an-hour short of the Ramadan breakfast (the Moslems' fasting month).

Immediately after the Saudi-Egyptian meeting, an emergency session of the Saudi cabinet was held. To the convened ministers the King presented the situation as analyzed by the Egyptians, and discussed the different options and scenarios involved in the use of the oil weapon. The cabinet approved the Egyptian point of view "one hundred percent" (Mareï, 1979: 741).

The influence of the Egyptian viewpoint was apparent even outside official meetings. During their stay, the members of the Egyptian delegation were constantly surrounded by members of the Saudi royal family or high Saudi officials. Both groups listened to Cairo Radio assiduously and monitored news agencies and dispatches. This camaraderie was interrupted, however, when the Egyptian delegation was summoned unexpectedly to meet with Faisal once the cabinet meeting was over.

In this second meeting with the King, the composition of the two delegations did not change. Faisal talked a bit more this time. He wanted to know the Egyptian view on the role of the USA in the crisis and what Saudi oil could do. The Egyptian chief delegate Mareï then spoke, and it is worthwhile to quote in detail the relevant part of his analysis:

> Egypt knows that your Majesty met on the third of May—that is more than five months ago—with the Director of Aramco resident in Saudi Arabia, and later in the month with the Directors of the four oil companies owning the shares of Aramco. Egypt also knows that in this meeting you told them that time is running out, and that you would not run the risk of Saudi Arabia being ostracized in the Arab World because of U.S. failure to show support for the Arab cause... You then asked the Americans to make up their mind, and quickly, about where their vital interests lie, otherwise they might lose everything.... Despite this early warning, the USA persisted in her pro-Israeli behavior. This is why we have now to be more forthcoming and warn the USA that Arab oil might be cut off from this country. We should then follow this warning by a concrete action: reduce oil production in such a percentage as to make the warning credible and to show that we mean business. This is what we propose concerning oil. As far as political contacts are concerned, we suggest that you write directly to President Nixon to explain to him the situation and inform him of the possible Arab reaction (Mareï, 1979: 742).

The King then asked whether a reduction of oil production by 10% would be enough to give credibility to the warning. The Egyptian delegation answered positively and suggested that the initial reduction could be as little as 5%, to be increased to 10% if the warning was not heeded and the change in Washington's pro-Israeli posture was not forthcoming.

The King then instructed his entourage that the Saudi foreign minister Omar El-Saqqaff, who was then heading the Saudi delegation to the U.N. regular session, should immediately meet with the heads of

Source: Middle East Oil & Gas, Exxon Background Series, Dec. 1984, p. 4.

delegations of other oil-producing countries, and ask for an urgent meeting with President Nixon. Interestingly enough, the King then asked the Egyptian chief delegate to dictate to the King's advisor Rashad Pharaon the contents of the cable to be sent to New York and to "put in it what Egypt wants" (Mareï, 1979:743).

Then the King returned to what Egypt suggested about warning President Nixon beforehand. Since the U.S. Ambassador to Saudi Arabia was still absent in the United States, the charge d'affaires was summoned for an urgent meeting with the King.

Convening the Special OAPEC Meeting

The official declaration of the Oil-Embargo decision came from OAPEC in its meeting of October 17, in Kuwait. It was Egypt that summoned this meeting. But given the Saudi-Egyptian axis, Riyadh's support was crucial in both convening the meeting so promptly and in succeeding in taking the "right" decision. In fact, Egypt decided to go along with the summoning of the OAPEC meeting only when it could see that Saudi support for the use of the oil weapon was unwavering and forthcoming. Indeed, King Faisal decided to contact other oil-exporting countries so that the Egyptian demand would be acted upon very favorably.

> Where are you going after Saudi Arabia? [Faisal asked]. To Kuwait... and other Gulf countries, [Mareï answered]. If God wishes, [Faisal said], you will find everything ready for you in each country you visit... And when you summon the special meeting of the oil ministers of OAPEC and suggest the reduction of oil flow by 5%, Saudi Arabia will be backing you fully... And whatever the OAPEC decision, Saudi Arabia herself will reduce production by 10% (Mareï, 1979: 744-45).

In their meetings in Kuwait (October 11), in Qatar (October 12), in Bahrain (October 12), in Abu Dhabi (October 14), in Oman (October 15), the members of the Egyptian delegation found that their task was half-completed due to prior Saudi groundwork. "Wherever we went," Marei remarked, "we found that the Saudis had already been working actively. As a result different national leaders were ready to give full support" (Mareï, 1979: 749).

CONCLUSION

The two decision clusters differed in some important respects. Variations in data availability apart, one decision cluster (the Egyptian-Syrian attack) had been minutely planned for a long time, was executed in complete secrecy among a handful of the very top leadership in Egypt and Syria and, consequently, succeeded in attaining the maximum effect of surprise. The other decision cluster (the Oil Embargo) was decided upon relatively late in the preparations for the battle, after differences within the Saudi leadership toward this issue had been ironed out. By the spring of 1973, King Faisal changed his mind and came to believe in the use of oil as a weapon. The King's change of mind, however, was much less of a decision to be carried out literally and immediately than a deterrence mechanism to avoid, in fact, the real use of the oil weapon. This is why the King himself and other Saudi officials issued warnings to the USA through various channels (e.g., through the oil companies). If there was any element of surprise about the use of the oil weapon, it stemmed from the incapacity of USA and other countries to believe that Saudi Arabia could radicalize her foreign policy decisions and go so far against the USA. Saudi Arabia's pro-Westernism had been taken too much for granted.

But both Saudi Arabia and Egypt—and this brings us to the similarities—were under immense national and regional pressure to do something to get out of the rotting no war-no peace situation. Because of this geopolitical context, the objectives of the two decision clusters were the same: to make things move by focusing world attention on the intolerable situation prevailing in the Middle East since the 1967 war, and by encouraging an even handed U.S. policy in the region. The two prime movers, Egypt and Saudi Arabia, were careful not to reach the point of no return with the USA, and indeed made many prior contacts with that country to avoid being pressured to take these painful decisions. Geopolitical factors as well as the leadership's belief systems or worldviews determined both the decisions and their limited impact. For instance, since neither of the two leaderships was ready to weaken U.S. influence and/or consolidate Soviet influence in the region, the impact of both decision clusters was halted once U.S. mediation was forthcoming (Kissinger, 1982: 891-895). Thus, in addition to Egypt's unilateral ceasefire decision without even consulting with her Syrian partner, the oil embargo was finally lifted before its declared objectives were attained (Israeli withdrawal to the 1967 lines). In this sense, these decisions were crucial in indicating subsequent Arab orientation in the global system and the increasing Pax Americana in regional and even national affairs. This Pax Americana is confirmed whether we think of Sadat's 1977 visit to Jerusalem and the 1978 Camp David Accords, or the USA's multifaceted involvement in the Lebanese crisis, involvement ranging from arranging the ceasefire and the departure of the Palestinians following the Israeli invasion, to the increasing participation of U.S. Marines in the "Lebanese civil war".

APPENDIX

A Sample of Decisions, Candidates for Analysis: 1970-1983

There is not a dearth of decisions to analyze in the Arab-Islamic region. A sample for the period 1980-1983 includes the following (even though all these decisions are concerned with "high politics," another predominant category is added in brackets).

Year	#	Decision
1970	1.	Syria's decision not to intervene in the war between the Jordanian army and the Palestinians (military).
	2.	Mini-Arab summit in Cairo to stop the civil war in Jordan (diplomatic).
1971	3.	Algeria's decision to nationalize French oil installations (economic).
1972	4.	Egypt's decision to ask the 20,000 Soviet advisers to leave (political).
1973	5.	The Egyptian-Syrian decision to launch the October War (military).
	6.	The Oil Embargo (economic).

1974	7.	Summit Arab League Conference decision to designate the PLO as the single representative of the Palestinian people (diplomatic).
	8.	Syria's decision to sign the disengagement agreement with Israel (military).
	9.	Decision by OPEC to lift the oil embargo (economic).
1975	10.	Morocco's Green March (diplomatic).
	11.	Egypt's second disengagement agreement with Israel (diplomatic).
1976	12.	Riyadh Tripartite meeting for Egyptian-Syriam reconciliation following Egypt's second Disengagement Agreement, and Syria's sending its army in Lebanon (diplomatic).
1977	13.	President Sadat's decision to visit Jerusalem (diplomatic).
1978	14.	The making of the Camp David Accords (diplomatic).
1979	15.	Arab decision to transfer Arab League headquarters from Cairo to Tunis and to suspend Egypt's membership (diplomatic).
1980	16.	Iranian decision to occupy the American Embassy and take some of its personnel as hostages (diplomatic).
	17.	Sets of decisions in the context of the Iran-Iraq Gulf War (military).
	18.	Algeria's decision to mediate USA-Iran agreement to end the hostage crisis (diplomatic).
1981	19.	Libya's decision to intervene militarily in Chad's civil war (military).
1982	20.	PLO decision to leave Lebanon following Israeli invasion (military).
1983	21.	Lebanon's decision to sign the agreement with Israel for the withdrawal of foreign troops from the country (diplomatic).

BIBLIOGRAPHICAL NOTE

Until at least 1975, the systematic analysis of foreign policy of Arab-Islamic countries was rare in quantity and modest in quality. Thus the search in English and French standard bibliographical sources on five powers of this area (Algeria, Egypt, Iran, Iraq, and Saudi Arabia) resulted in tracing 78 items (56 articles, 9 books and 13 Ph.D. dissertations) for the decade 1965-1978—or 8 items per year. No analysis applying foreign policy decision theory was found. Writing in 1977, Dawisha reached the same conclusion: "the systematic analysis of foreign policy in the Middle East is an underdeveloped area of study" (Dawisha 1977: 70).

I have surveyed the recent quantitative and qualitative trends elsewhere and—given space limitations—the reader can look at these references (Korany 1978a, b, 1982b, 1983c). Suffice it to say that in an inventory of the literature published between 1965 and 1981 on 22 Arab countries, the total number of articles was 297, of which 124 articles dealt with the dynamics of the Arab system itself, leaving 173 articles dealing with the foreign policy proper of one or another Arab country (Korany and Dessouki, Westview 1984). Yet the distribution of these studies is very uneven with some countries very "underpublished" (Jordan, Morocco, Sudan), some not having even one single published study on their foreign policy (Lebanon).

But the extreme newness of publishing on the foreign policies of Arab-Islamic countries should be emphasized. Thus as recently as 1975, no book in English, French, or Arabic was published on Egypt's foreign policy—an "overpublished" country according to our categorization. As for the other overpublished country, Saudi Arabia, two of her scholars surveyed 120 books and 5500 articles in eleven U. S. scholarly journals to find out that by the mid-1970s, regarding the country's politics and society as a whole there was a "scholarly aridity comparable to Al-Rub Al-Khali, that vast empty quarter of Arabian

Desert rarely traversed by man" (Braibanti and Al-Farsy, 1977). This situation seems to be changing, however, given the increasing publication of Ph.D. dissertations on these countries' foreign policy by young and innovative scholars very well-versed in interdisciplinary conceptualization and recent techniques of analysis.

NOTE

1. Because of the technological intensiveness of this war, both sides poured into the battlefield a total of 5000 tanks and 2000 aircraft. Losses were one aircraft per hour, more than one tank every 15 minutes and, in the three-week period of the war, amounted to 555 aircraft, 2700 tanks, and 16 ships. The immediate financial cost of the war was between $8 and $10 billion. *SIPRI Yearbook 1974:* 5-9, 151, 152.

5

THE PRIMACY OF POLITICS

Comparing the Foreign Policies of Cuba and Mexico

Jorge I. Domínguez
Juan Lindau

The foreign policies of Latin American states changed in the 1970s in response to a new set of circumstances. First, the relative decline in the economic and political power of the United States in the international system was especially significant because the United States had been so important in Latin America. Latin American governments became less fearful of U.S. opposition or retaliation if they took foreign policy initiatives that the United States might have opposed in the past, and they became convinced that their economic prosperity and their security required them to diversify their international links (for discussion see Hoffmann, 1978).

Second, the considerable economic growth of most Latin American countries from the late 1950s to the late 1970s enabled them to acquire the economic, political, and at times military, means to project power beyond their borders.[1] Latin American countries could trade a greater volume and greater variety of products, especially with industrialized

Central America and the Caribbean

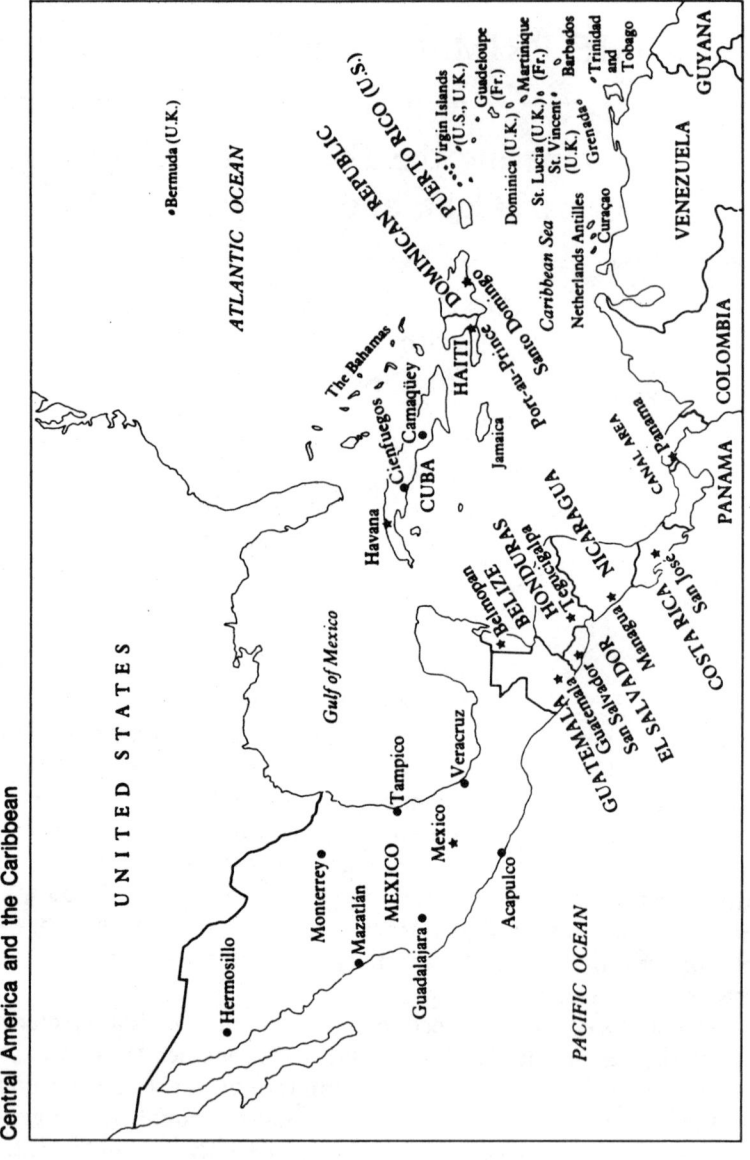

countries; some of their firms multinationalized; and their armies became engaged in wars against each other (Peru-Ecuador in 1981), against the United Kingdom (Argentina in 1982), or against transcontinental enemies, as in the case of Cuba in Africa.

Third, governments built up a diplomatic staff and formulated policies to project power, even if only through political symbols, beyond their boundaries. Most of the major Latin American states became very active in international organizations during the 1970s.

Notwithstanding these changes, the foreign policies of Latin American governments have remained conditioned by three structural constraints. The first is the persisting hierarchy of the international system. Apart from the revolutionary victories in Nicaragua and Grenada in 1979—the first such changes in two decades—no Latin American state broke with its previous superpower patron, the United States or the Soviet Union respectively. Another consequence of the international hierarchy is that, despite some rhetorical activity in international organizations, most Latin American foreign policy activism was concentrated within the international subsystems of the western hemisphere (for a general discussion, see Domínguez, 1971: 175-208). The main exceptions were Cuba and, less dramatically, Brazil.

The second structural constraint is that Latin American countries were, at most, marginally industrial. Typically, their economies remained underdeveloped. Their international activities exhibited features that marked their foreign policies as characteristic of those of underdeveloped countries, even when they played a leading international role.

The third structural constraint does not impede foreign policy activism but it does impart to it a certain character: internal decisonmaking has tended to be highly centralized politically. In many Latin American countries with authoritarian political systems, patterns of centralization are plain (for a general discussion see Collier, 1979, and Malloy, 1977). But even in countries with formal parliaments, or with active political contestation, foreign policy decision-making is more centralized than other decision domains.

The foreign policies of Latin American states, under these constraints, have come to have varied effects. These are exemplified in Table 1. This table notes cases where these foreign policies have mattered for military, political, and economic issue areas. The economic issue area includes matters related to the ownership or production of

TABLE 5.1
Examples of Latin American Foreign Policy Decisions, 1970-1982

International System	Military	Political	Economic
A. Direct Effects On:			
Structure	Cuba Sends Troops to Africa	Venezuela and Mexico in North-South negotiations	Venezuela and Ecuador join 1973-1974 oil price increase
Regimes	Brazil sells weapons to Iraq and Libya	Cuba leads Non-Aligned Movement	Governments must decide whether to accept new GATT Tokyo Round codes
B. Indirect Consequences	—	Violations of human rights in Chile becomes major international issue	Expropriations of foreign-owned oil or mining firms in Peru, Chile, Venezuela
International Subsystem			
A. Direct Effects On:			
Structure	Argentine request for Rio Treaty support against United Kingdom Falklands-Malvinas	Mexican activism in Central America	Brazilian neomercantilism toward Uruguay, Paraguay and Bolivia
Regimes	Brazil and Argentina reach enduring nuclear energy agreement	Founding of Sistema Economico Latino-Americano includes Cuba, excludes U.S.	Chile withdraws from Andean Pact perceived as too statist
B. Indirect Consequences	El Salvador's civil war draws in policies of its neighbors	Illegal international outmigration and conflicts at border	Honduras' closure of Pan American Common Market

resources; the military issue area denotes the actual or potential use of force or arms transfers; and the political issue area refers to allocations of power, or negotiations among governments, and nonmilitary border disputes. We also divided the cases into those that affected international system as a whole and those that affected the western hemisphere subsystem only. For each level, we note examples that affect the structure of the system or subsystem, namely, the basic distribution of power and resources; or that affect international regimes, namely, the norms, rules, and institutions that govern particular issue areas; or, last, certain actions taken by states at home that have important though indirect international consequences.

It is clear from Table 1 that the foreign policies of Latin American states are quite varied and, in some instances, quite influential. To be sure, the success of Latin American foreign policies in some of these cases is quite limited; and the categories could be refined even further. But what should be clear is that these countries now have complex and wide-ranging foreign policies that feature both conflict and collaboration over many different issues at various levels of the international system and relevant subsystems. They are no longer simple, passive, or parochial.

We have chosen to examine two clusters of decisions to illustrate, and to qualify, these preliminary observations. We analyze Cuba's decisions to send conventional troops to fight in African wars and Mexico's decisions to become actively involved, politically and economically, in Central American affairs. These decisions launched new foreign policies in the mid-1970s. They both responded to the relative decline of the power of the United States as well as to the relative increase in the relevant capabilities of Mexico and Cuba (economic for Mexico, military for Cuba). Presidents José López Portillo and Fidel Castro built up their foreign policy personnel and policies for these initiatives. Both decisions have a high political rather than economic purpose, and both challenged the U.S. government. One affected the structure of the international system as a new military power when it crossed the seas, while the other was limited to a change in a subsystem's structure of power.

We will also endeavor to show that both sets of decisions illustrate very high political centralization and that they provide evidence of the effect of underdevelopment on foreign policy implementation. Governments widened the scope of relations with the pertinent superpower without violating the perceived boundaries set by the hegemonial superpower. An important difference—and a reason for the selection, too—is that the Mexican policies were consistent with a focus on subsystem behavior while the Cuban policies broke away beyond the western hemisphere. In short, these cases are perhaps more dramatic than others in the region, but they are consistent with the broadly observable patterns that permitted and constrained the new international activism by many governments. Each case is structured around a set of questions to facilitate their comparison. We will attempt in our conclusions to draw some generalizations that emerge from the cases.

THE OVERSEAS DEPLOYMENT OF CUBAN COMBAT FORCES

In late 1975, the Cuban revolutionary government deployed a large conventional military combat force across the Atlantic ocean to Angola to help the forces of the Popular Movement for the Liberation of Angola (MPLA) defeat their internal enemies and the invading South African armies. The Cuban armies reached up to 36,000 troops at the peak of the 1975-1976 war (Castro, 1979). Beginning in December 1977, Cuba sent an army of about 15,000 to help Ethiopia defeat Somalia's invasion.[2] We argue that a highly centralized Cuban foreign policymaking apparatus made autonomous strategic decisions that responded both to a changed international context and to the particulars of each case. Constraints appeared mostly in the choice of policy instruments.

These were, of course, not the first times that Cuba had sent military personnel overseas. But the scale of the action was utterly unprecedented (for a general discussion, see Domínguez, 1978a). There have been many wars among less-developed countries, but these have occurred ordinarily between neighbors. Cuba's successful conduct of a big power's foreign policy would thus appear to put it in a different category from most other less-developed countries. We argue, however, that Cuba retains some features in common with other less-developed countries even as it acts like a major power.

AUTONOMOUS STRATEGIC CHOICES

The internal and international contexts in 1975 were propitious for the intervention in Angola. In the wake of the fall of Saigon, the United States was not likely to commit its forces to prevent a victory for the MPLA in Angola, especially if that meant an alliance with South Africa as it invaded Angola. Within Cuba, the economy had just witnessed the single best five-year period of growth since the revolution came to power in January, 1959 (Mesa Lago, 1981: Ch. 3). Moreover, the same years had witnessed an impressive professionalization of the Cuban armed forces that enabled them for the first time to conduct the type of war they would face in Angola (Domínguez, 1978b: Ch. 9). The Cuban government had also developed a far-reaching international diplomatic network that would provide political support for the Cuban decision; Cuba had much support among many African governments in helping to repel the South African invasion in Angola (see, for example, LeoGrande, 1982b).

In late 1977, circumstances were less favorable. Cuba's economic performance in 1976-1977 was poor (Mesa Lago, 1981: Ch. 3); moreover, Cuba remained burdened by a continuing large military commitment to Angola. On the other hand, Cuba's armies were more experienced. The Carter administration had seemed willing to accept Cuba's continued presence in Angola so that it was possible it might react passively to a Cuban entry in the war in the Horn of Africa. Given that Cuba would defend existing borders at the request of the Ethiopian government against the Somalian invasion, support—or at least acquiescence—might be garnered from other African countries, helping to contain U.S. opposition as well. Cuba's general influence in the Non-Aligned Movement had also continued to increase.

The Cuban political system is highly centralized, especially for the making of foreign policy. The Cuban National Assembly—the country's parliament—receives reports on international affairs and on military topics, but it does not really debate them. This is in contrast to a more active role that the assembly plays in other less important legislation, such as a new traffic code or the design of environmental protection legislation (Domínguez, 1982b: 33-38).

Decisions on major foreign policy issues remain the special prerogative of Fidel Castro, President of the Councils of State and of Ministers, and Commander in Chief of the Armed Forces. President Castro tends to consult his close associates on the making of major decisions. In the case of Angola, Fidel Castro and the party's Political Bureau and Cabinet made the decision (*Granma Weekly Review,* March 28, 1976: 3). The National Assembly did not yet exist. The party's Central Committee was in the throes of major restructuring in preparation for the First Party Congress that would be held in December 1975—well after the decision to commit troops was made. In the case of Ethiopia, the formal decision was made by the party's Political Bureau (*Granma Weekly Review,* March 26, 1978: 4-5). The party's Central Committee, the National Assembly, or its Council of State, apparently did not play a role. In the semi-official history of the war in Angola, Fidel Castro's personal role is clear: "Fidel Castro himself was keeping up to date on the smallest details of the war," in every facet of decision-making (García Márquez, 1977a).

Therefore, explanations drawing on factors internal to Cuba are not very helpful. Cuba would commit troops overseas under two very different sets of internal economic conditions in 1975 and 1977. The Cuban political system was stable and the regime was consolidated. It is unlikely that President Castro had to take either decision to satisfy some internal constituency. Instead, international strategic factors set the context for each decision.

The details of each decision also illustrate their strategic nature. The timing of Cuba's decision to enter the Angolan war was shaped by the Angolan political and military calendar. As Angolan independence neared, the struggle among groups within that country sharpened. There was a nearly classic process of escalation. Cuba and South Africa would be key players. The MPLA requested Cuban assistance in the spring 1975, and it was given. Cuban advisors were in Angola by August 1975, led by Major Raúl Díaz Arguelles (Marcum, 1978: 272-273; and García Márquez, 1977c: 6). In the meantime, summer war games held in Cuba were the most complex ever. From August 20 to September 5, all of Cuba's top military commanders were relieved of their routine posts; they would take charge of the war effort (Domínguez, 1978b: 345-355). In late September, the first ships sailed from Cuba carrying no fewer than 480 soldiers, along with other Cuban personnel. These arrived in Angola between October 4 and 11.[3] South African military units had begun to move gradually into Angola in June, after the beginning of the Cuban aid. The Cuban reinforcement by the late summer of 1975 was a response to the increasing South African penetration of Angola (Marcum, 1978: 272-273). The major South African attack in mid-October, in turn, was a response to the previous increase of Cuban military presence in Angola.[15] Cuba's massive subsequent intervention in early November, days before Angola's independence on November 11, was a response to the South African action. This pattern of statecraft rests wholly on an autonomous politico-military logic.

The details of the decision to fight on Ethiopia's side against Somalia also emphasize strategic aspects. President Castro had attempted to mediate in person in March 1977, to no avail (*Granma Weekly Review*, March 27, 1977: 4). The Cuban justification for entry into the war emphasized the defense of Ethiopia's territory and borders. The Cuban response, as in the Angolan case, escalated gradually. Some Cuban personnel had arrived by July 1977. The first combat troops consisted of several hundred tank, artillery, and aviation specialists, who began arriving in mid-December 1977, and who would operate this equipment for Ethiopia. The subsequent introduction of Cuban infantry troops was explained as needed to improve military coordination, given the language barriers between Cuban artillery and Ethiopian infantry (*Granma Weekly Review*, March 26, 1978: 4; *Granma*, July 22, 1977: 3).

In short, the Cuban government responded to a set of politico-military circumstances, in the world as a whole and in the countries in question, with the full, though gradually escalating, commitment of combat forces. The decisive instruments were military: instructors and combat troops. Political and diplomatic support for Cuban allies was, of course, also very important. Carefully calibrated decisions on military escalation were made easier by the highly centralized nature of the Cuban political system. The goals of Cuban policy were plain: to support revolutionary movements, such as the MPLA, and revolutionary regimes, such as Ethiopia's, that were willing to be responsive to Cuban goals for enhancing its own political influence (for a discussion of goals, see Domínguez 1978a:83-90). Revolutionary regimes such as Somalia's that were unwilling to accept Cuban political leadership were rejected.[4] This combination of political and revolutionary objectives characterizes Cuban foreign policy and has enabled its leaders to make choices. These decisions were possible because the survival of the Cuban regime was no longer credibly threatened by the United States and because the Soviet Union provided crucial support for the Cuban government.

DEPENDENCE AND UNDERDEVELOPMENT

The importance of the Soviet Union for Cuban decision-making illustrates the constraints on the Cuban government's choice of policy instruments. The Cuban revolution could not have survived without considerable Soviet economic, political, and military support. In the 1975-1977 period, Cuban dependence on the USSR deepened. We will illustrate it only very briefly.[5]

In 1975, on the eve of the Angolan decision, the Soviet Union paid 482 pesos per metric ton of Cuban crude sugar, only slightly above the average price of 458, and well below the surprisingly high price paid by Japan at 613 pesos. In that year, the USSR supplied 58.4% of Cuban crude sugar earnings, and crude sugar accounted for 89.4% of all Cuban export earnings. In 1977, on the eve of the Ethiopian decision, the USSR paid 490 pesos per metric ton of Cuban crude sugar, well above the average price of 387, and much, much higher than the price paid by Japan at 126 pesos. In 1977, the USSR suplied 77.0% of Cuban crude sugar earnings, and crude sugar accounted for 85.3% of Cuban export earnings. In short, while Cuban dependence on sugar was basically unchanged, Cuban dependence on the Soviet Union rose dramatically.

In 1975, the Soviet Union charged Cuba 39 pesos per metric ton of petroleum. Prices charged to Cuba by other oil suppliers averaged 276 pesos. In 1977, the respective prices were 51 and 225 pesos. Despite these trends favorable to Cuban autonomy, however, the USSR supplied 99.8% of Cuba's petroleum imports both years so that, in effect, the level of Cuban dependence on this measure remained constant.

In 1975, the Soviet Union did not provide net subsidies to Cuba through the price of sugar. Average prices paid by the Soviet Union to Cuba were either consistent with average world market prices or even below (Japan typically paid prevailing world market prices). In 1977, the Soviet Union provided massive sugar price subsidies along with continuing high petroleum subsidies. Excluding all other rather substantial subsidies provided by the Soviet Union to Cuba, the combined crude sugar and crude oil Soviet subsidies in 1977 were equal to 20.4% of Cuba's gross social product (GSP).[6]

Cuba's decisions to send troops to Angola and to Ethiopia were principally its own. Cuba is not a proxy for, or a puppet of the USSR. There is no evidence that Cuban foreign policy is overtly "mercenary," supplying Cuban troops in exchange for Soviet economic support. And yet, both sides are surely conscious of Cuba's dependence and of the deepening of its dependence from 1975 to 1977. Cuba should be expected to have been more responsive to Soviet interests and to have accepted Soviet leadership more readily in the making of the Ethiopian decision in 1977.

In the Angolan case, Cuba probably acted on its own. Cuba had been supporting the MPLA since the mid-1960s; it had been reliable and steadfast. In mid-1975, when the Soviet Union turned down the MPLA request for Soviet military personnel, Cuba committed its own forces. To minimize the Soviet exposure or involvement in the earliest stages, Cuban troops were transported in prerevolutionary Bristol Britannia aircraft (not in Soviet-supplied Cuban planes) and on Cuban merchant marine ships. Soviet assistance to the MPLA and its Cuban allies came directly to Angola only when it was clear that the United States would not intervene. On the ground, the Cuban forces fought along with the MPLA, with no apparent involvement by Soviet personnel.[7]

In the Ethiopian case, there was much closer and much earlier coordination between Cuba and the Soviet Union. Soviet generals commanded the allied forces that defeated Somalia in the Ogaden. The Soviet Union became a closer ally of the Ethiopian government than did Cuba, because Cuba differed from Ethiopia on its preferences for a solution of the Eritrean rebellion within Ethiopia—Cuba had been a strong supporter of the Eritrean rebellion in earlier years (LeoGrande, 1982a: 36-40, 47). While Cuba responded, in the Ethiopian case, to its own perception of its interests—as evidenced by President Castro's personal mediation—the Soviet factor weighs more heavily in Cuba's Ethiopian decision consistent with the deepened dependence across economic and military issues. There was an increased correspondence between deepened economic dependence and deepened military collaboration.

Thus even in the display of its impressive military might, Cuba's persisting underdevelopment and dependence were manifested. Cuba decided on its own, but it could only do so in the clear expectation of Soviet support. It had to be responsive to Soviet interests in two respects. In Angola, responsiveness meant eschewing Soviet-supplied transports in order to spare the Soviet Union from too much U.S. criticism, and engaging, instead, in the heroic feat of transporting Cuban troops in aircraft that risked runing out of fuel before they got to Africa's Atlantic coast. In Ethiopia, it meant committing troops perhaps beyond what prudence and Cuba's own resources might have counseled.

This paradox of assertion and weakness is also evident in Cuba's trade with Angola and Ethiopia. As seen from Table 2, such trade is trivial. Precise data are not yet available; Cuba includes Angola and Ethiopia in the "other African" category that contributed under 1% of Cuban exports and imports (except for 1980 exports). The table also shows that modest crude sugar exports to Angola were sold consistently

TABLE 5.2
Cuba's Trade with Angola and Ethiopia

Trade	1976	1977	1978	1979	1980
Trade with Other African Countries					
Exports as % of total exports	0.8	0.9	0.9	0.7	2.2
Imports as % of total exports	0.6	0.5	0.1	0.2	0.1
Cuban Exports to Angola					
Crude sugar as % of total value of crude sugar	0.3	0.3	0.2	0.2	0.9
Crude sugar as % of total volume of crude sugar	0.6	0.8	0.9	0.7	1.1
Canned fish as % of total value of canned fish	—	64.2	93.7	85.3	87.7
Canned fish as % of total volume of canned fish	—	59.0	93.4	86.6	85.7
Value of crude sugar + canned fish as % of total exports[a]	0.2	0.3	0.3	0.3	0.8

SOURCE: Computed from Comité Estatal de Estadísticas, (1980: Ch. 10).
a. The value of Cuban exports (in thousands of pesos) of crude sugar and canned fish to Angola was as follows:

1976	1977	1978	1979	1980
6153	9978	9425	9463	33181

below the average sugar prices received by Cuba. While Angola takes almost all of Cuba's canned fish production, the combined total value of crude sugar and canned fish exports—the only items for which there is detailed data on Cuban trade with either Ethiopia or Angola—remains quite small. At best, the 1980 sugar export data suggest that Angola might grow as a customer of Cuban sugar, so long as its international and internal wars continue to disrupt Angola's own sugar production, and that it could become a customer for Cuban nonsugar products and services. Among the latter, the most promising so far have been construction contracts. Angola pays a Cuban state enterprise for construction work done by Cubans in Angola (*Granma Weekly Review*, February 27, 1983: 9). There is, however, no parallel between the trade and military relations: Cuba's underdeveloped economy could not build a trade link to match the politico-military relationship.

These overseas wars have established Cuba as major factor in international relations, especially in Africa. Cuba gained political influence and prestige; it helped to consolidate two revolutionary regimes with which it cooperates closely. Nevertheless, Cuba has also experienced certain costs. As one of us has written, "Cuba has found it difficult to maintain coherence among its closest friends in Africa, Asia and Latin America as new issues have arisen. Cuban influence over host countries has been negligible in a number of important instances, while the demands of these clients continue to mount. Cuba has been embroiled in internal politics where its own prestige has suffered, and its ambassadors have had to be recalled home. Cuba has incurred the costs of casualties, high military budgets, and direct and indirect economic costs. These, in turn, have led to a political malaise as the 1980s open that has even truncated the careers of many top government leaders" (Domínguez, 1982a: 132).[8] The costs of the military budget alone doubled during the period of the wars. Beyond Africa, Cuba's participation in these wars ended the two best possibilities for reconciliation with the United States and, in 1978, opened a period of severe hostilities between the United States and Cuba under the late Carter and Reagan administrations. It is unclear whether Cuban leaders were aware in advance of most of these costs.

The Cuban leadership, therefore, chose a foreign policy autonomous from both internal constraints and the superpowers, but its choice of policy instruments was greatly constrained by persistent dependence and underdevelopment. Policies were made more conscious of benefits than of costs, even though the latter may linger longer than the former.

MEXICO'S POLICY TOWARD CENTRAL AMERICA

The change in Mexico's policy toward Central America dates from early 1979. Prior to that time, Mexico's dealings with the countries in the area (with the possible exception of neighboring Guatemala) had been limited to the maintenance of normal diplomatic contacts and little else. Trade with the region, though balanced in favor of Mexico, was—and is—of such small volume as to be a factor of little importance.[9]

The alteration in Mexican policy largely consisted of the decision to play a much more active role in the region. Underlying this decision, in part, was the decline in U.S. hegemony evident during the Carter administration. The partial withdrawal of U.S. power created a much more fluid international situation that opened opportunities for other regional actors to assume more prominent positions. This development coincided with the discovery of huge new oil reserves in Mexico that substantially increased the Mexican government's capacity to act internationally.

A third conjunctural factor should be noted. The intensification of strife in the region in 1979 (particularly of the Nicaraguan civil war) that prompted Mexico to act, occurred at a time when the Mexican government was able to turn its attention outwards. Mexican president, José López Portillo, had come to power in December 1976, in the midst of a profound economic crisis. For the succeeding two years, his administration focused on resolving the Mexican economic crisis, and then on expanding the economy. By mid-1979, with the economy booming, the government could increase its foreign activity. In May, Cuban President Fidel Castro visited Mexico for the first time in over twenty years. Next came Costa Rica's President, Rodrigo Carazo Odio. During the state banquet in his honor, López Portillo announced the withdrawal of Mexican recognition of the Somoza regime in Nicaragua. Shortly thereafter, in June, Mexico led the successful opposition in the Organization of American States (OAS) to a United States proposal that would have led to collective intervention in Nicaragua (*Latin America Political Report,* June 29, 1979: 193).

THE DECISION-MAKING APPARATUS

Policy toward Central America, and particularly the decision to assume a more active role there, has rested almost entirely with the Mexican president. The Mexican polity is characterized by the centralization of power. Power is almost entirely concentrated in the hands of the president, who governs for a six year non renewable term. [10] This concentration and centralization of power results in a number of domestic foreign policy actors. Interest groups have little direct impact on the formulation of much of Mexico's foreign policy. These groups have some impact on the formulation of economic policy (and particularly domestic economic policy), but they have a negligible effect on most purely political foreign policy decisions.[11] On the other hand, because of the relatively noncoercive nature of the political system, the Mexican president, despite his great power, must balance and consider domestic pressures and interests, though to a significantly smaller extent than would be the case in a more pluralistic polity. Mexican policy toward Central America clearly evidences the government's desire to placate certain domestic interests. Nonetheless, because of the centralization of power, short-run domestic considerations play at best a secondary role in determining foreign policy. This centralization of power also contributes to the consistency of Mexican foreign policy.

The Mexican Congress, as well, does not play a role in the formulation of foreign policy. This Congress has been controlled by the governing party, the PRI or Partido Revolucionario Institucional (Party of the Institutionalized Revolution). The PRI has held power for over 50 years. All senators and about three-quarters of the deputies are PRI members. The party, in turn, depends overwhelmingly on the power of the president. The Congress, as a result, serves as a forum to ratify presidential initiatives in a largely pro forma fashion.

The Foreign Ministry, PEMEX (the state oil monopoly), and the Armed Forces, among others, may play a consultative role in the formulation of policy. PEMEX's role is focused on oil and gas policy; the military play a role on policy toward Guatemala. The Foreign Ministry, in particular, has the most significant role. Its ability to perform this function has increased steadily over the years with its growing professionalization. This professionalization has been given an important spur by the decision to assume an active role in Central America. Indeed, the adoption of a high profile position on Central America in 1979 was accompanied by the replacement of the Foreign Minister, Santiago Roel, a man with little professional foreign policy background, during a cabinet shakeup. In contrast, his successor, Jorge Castañeda, and Mexico's current Foreign Minister, Bernardo Sepulveda, are both professionals of considerable standing. Professionalization has occurred as well at lower levels of the Mexican diplomatic corps. Little is known, however, about the deliberative process that precedes the formulation of policy or about the exact weight of different bureaucratic actors, but it is clear that the president plays an overwhelmingly central role in policy making.

THE DETERMINANTS OF MEXICAN POLICY

The position elaborated by Mexico toward Central America reflects a fairly long-term determinant of Mexican foreign policy. It has been a practice of the Mexican government to use foreign policy as a means to coopt and preempt the left. As Olga Pellicer (1981: 91) notes,

> Left-leaning diplomacy helps to maintain Mexican political stability. It strengthens the government's hand in its dealings with the country's opposition whose demands are occasionally pre-empted by government action.

Though evident prior to the 1970s, particularly in some of the policies during the presidency of Adolfo López Mateos (1968-1974), this approach became most pronounced during the presidency of Luis Echeverría (1970-1976). The Position of the López Portillo administration toward Central America, and toward a number of other issues as well, also represented, in part, an attempt to coopt and preempt the left. In this regard, Mexican foreign policy has been very consistent throughout the 1970s.

This use of foreign policy is also illustrative of a distinct approach to managing social change derived from Mexican domestic politics. It has been the practice of Mexican political élites to coopt domestic opposition whenever possible and to resort to repression only when absolutely necessary.[12] In part, the regime carries out this process of cooptation by conceding some change and appearing to grant more.

Mexican policy toward Nicaragua, El Salvador and Guatemala—all in upheaval since the late 1970s—in part evidences this same belief that inflexible opposition to social change is more apt to inflame things than quiet them. This is not to say that the Mexican government is opposed to social change in Central America. Rather, it believes that social change is necessary and inevitable, but wishes to contain that change within limits that do not threaten it. Viewed in this way, Mexico's approach to the region is much more conservative than it appears at first sight. The substantive long-term goal of Mexican policy, then, is stability based on social change. Short-run tactical considerations are at times juxtaposed against this longer term goal. This distinction can be illustrated, for example, by Mexico's relatively early support for the Sandinista rebels in Nicaragua and its reluctance, on the other hand, to opppose the Guatemalan government. As one moves geographically closer to Mexico along the Central American isthmus, the Mexican government's support for the forces of social change wanes; Mexican policy becomes much more equivocal.

In some of its determinants, then, Mexican policy in Central America is not new. What is new is both the type of instruments that are being used to pursue the government's goals and the scale of its activities. For the first time Mexico has committed significant material resources to the pursuit of a foreign policy goal. The San José oil facility agreement signed by Mexico and Venezuela in San José, Costa Rica on August 3, 1980 embodies this policy. Mexico and Venezuela undertook to fulfill all the imported oil requirements of all Central American and several Caribbean countries on subsidized terms.[13] The beneficiaries of

TABLE 5.3
Mexican Trade with the Central American Common Market

	Exports		Imports	
Year	Thousand Dollars	% of Total	Thousand Dollars	% of Total
1975	81,600	2.85	19,400	.29
1976	76,400	2.30	26,600	.44
1977	100,800	2.70	17,000	.31
1978	143,000	2.30	10,100	.12
1979	137,000	1.55	13,000	.10
1980	229,000	1.49	32,000	.17

SOURCE: Computed from *Anuario Estadistico de los Estados Unidos Mexicanos* (Secretaria de Programación y Presupuestó, 1979 and 1980).

this assistance are required to pay only 70% of the cost upon receipt of the oil. The balance is paid through long-term credits at below-market interest rates (López Portillo, 1980: 1023).

This new capacity to commit material resources has undoubtedly increased Mexico's leverage in the region. On the other hand, several structural constraints remain that limit the role that Mexico can play. In the first place, the persistent fragility of the Mexican economy makes long-term foreign commitments that require the continuing infusion of resources particularly difficult to sustain. A second constraint faced by Mexico is the fact that in many ways Mexico and the Central American countries have "parallel" economies.[14] Since Mexico and Central America both produce many of the same labor intensive, low-technology goods and primary products, Central American exports encounter many high tariffs designed to protect the Mexican domestic market. As a result, there are strong structural impediments to the development of closer and weightier trade. The lack of trade can be seen in Table 3.

The continuing absence of really significant trade relations constrains the type of assistance that Mexico can provide. This, of course, will continue to limit the amount of power and leverage that Mexico has in the area.

Since Somoza's overthrow, Mexico has supported the Sandinista regime. The Mexican government has been at odds, virtually from the outset, with the United States over how to diagnose the ideological makeup and objectives of the Sandinista govenment. Convinced of the legitimacy of the Sandinistas and of the widespread support that they enjoy, Mexico has granted Nicaragua substantial economic and technical assistance beyond the concessionary oil prices. Mexico helped Nicaragua reschedule its debt and provided assistance in agriculture, industry, mining, energy, education, and health. The volume of this support was such that, through early 1981, Mexico had provided 16% of Nicaragua's foreign assistance, more than twice what was coming from any other Latin American country (Williams, 1981: 9). Politically as well, Mexico has supported the Sandinistas in international organizations.

Mexican policy toward El Salvador and Guatemala has been more equivocal. This is, in part, because the situation in both countries still lacks definition. The fact that the U.S.-backed governments of both countries may remain in power for some time has forced Mexico to keep some channels open to both regimes, regardless of how unpalatable it may find them. At the same time, the Mexican government has been critical of both regimes, though much more active and visible in its criticism of the Salvadoran government than it has been of Guatemala.

In the case of El Salvador, as well as opposing U.S. intervention, Mexico has argued that all political forces must be included in negotiations aimed at resolving the internal crisis. In the Mexican government's view, the continuing exclusion of the left makes a viable political solution impossible. This was not the position of the Mexican government from the very beginning. Especially at the outset of the conflict in El Salvador, there was the widespread view in Mexico that the extremism of the opposition forces on the left made support for them difficult (Pellicer, 1981: 90). Since then, the behavior of the government forces has brought about a change of attitude in Mexico. The exclusion of the left prompted the Mexican government to make some pronouncements and cosponsor initiatives that were sharply critical of both the Christian Democratic-military regime headed by José Napoleón Duarte and of the regime that came to power following the March, 1982 elections. For example, Mexican Foreign Minister Jorge Castañeda has "deplored the constant, massive, and flagrant violation of human rights in El Salvador and taken notice of the growing incapacity of the authorities to stop the violence" (Williams, 1981: 10).

Of course, Mexico's view of the crisis in El Salvador is not unlike that of several European governments. Illustrative of this congruence is the joint statement on El Salvador issued by Mexico and France in August, 1981; both countries recognized the Salvadoran opposition front, the FDR (Democratic Revolutionary Front), and the guerrilla coalition, the FMLN (Farabundo Martí National Liberation Front) as "representative political forces." In a speech delivered on September 22, 1981 in the United Nations, Foreign Minister Castañeda commented about this statement:

> Recently together with the Government of France, we called on the international commmunity to help achieve a political solution to the civil war that is racking that country. But we imbue the term "political solution" with the only content which, in our opinion can make it just, viable and lasting. The term means negotiation between the conflicting parties. For this reason, we recognized the organizations which the Salvadoran opposition has engendered, that is, the FMLN-FDR, as representative political forces with a legitimate right to participate in any negotiations (Castañeda, 1981:430).

At the same time that Mexico was issuing these pronouncements, it kept channels open to the Salvadoran government. Though Mexico brought its ambassador home from El Salvador in 1980, it did not withdraw recognition of the government. More important, Mexico continued to provide El Salvador with 7500 barrels of oil per day at subsidized prices.

Other factors have prompted Mexico to be more cautious in its dealings with Guatemala. Because of its size and proximity, Guatemala poses the most formidable regional challenge to Mexican policymakers. The duration and intensity of civil strife in Guatemala has resulted in the elimination of most moderate political forces in that country. It has helped, as well, to generate perhaps the most radical guerrilla movement in the region. The intensification of the conflict in the early 1980s has presented potential dangers for Mexico, especially the possibility that the conflict would spread across the border. Already, the Guatemalan army has made several incursions into Mexican territory in pursuit of guerrillas. The growing number of refugees from the war gathering along the Mexican side of the border aggravates the situation. Mexican policy toward Guatemala is therefore dominated by national security considerations. Mexico has carried out an unprecedented military build-up in the southern part of the country. These security considerations also explain in part the Mexican government's response to the intensification of the Guatemalan internal war. Despite continuing reports of the genocidal practices of the Guatemalan army against the indigenous population, Mexico has not adopted the same high-profile, condemnatory response that events in El Salvador have prompted. It has shown its displeasure, however, by cooling its formal relations with Guatemala and yet, the Mexican mililtary retains close and cooperative relations with their counterparts in Guatemala, even including the coordinated pursuit of guerrillas along both sides of the border (*Latin America Political Report*, January 26, 1979: 32).

COSTS AND BENEFITS

Overall it is difficult to evaluate the effects of Mexican policy in Central America within Mexico. Whatever the government has gained in support from the left it has probably lost from the right.

Internationally, the results have been more clear cut. Policy toward Central America has probably resulted in a net increase in the international prestige of the Mexican regime. Mexico's substantial congruence of opinion over this region with some European governments strengthened its relations with them. The high-profile approach adopted by Mexico has also solidified the country's position as a leading spokesman of the Third World and it has enabled Mexico to become a genuine regional power. Mexico's approach to the region has also contributed to the improvement of its relationship with Cuba over the short run. Mexico and Cuba differ over the desirable long-term future of the region. They differ as well in the type of instruments that they are using to pursue their goals. They have, however, coincided on some short-run developments.

On the other hand, Mexico's relationship with the United States has undoubtedly suffered. Both countries have fundamentally different views of the sources of conflict in Central America. They differ even more over ways to resolve the problem and on the utility of different solutions. These differences have become most evident in the loud rhetorical recriminations over the issue. It would probably be a mistake on these grounds to infer that the relationship has been fundamentally damaged. Strident rhetoric is nothing new in the history of relations between the two countries; on the contrary, it is one of its more enduring characteristics.

Mexico's relationship with Venezuela has blown hot and cold over the region. Though largely congruent over policies toward most countries, they differed sharply over the legitimacy of the Duarte regime in El Salvador. This difference cooled their relations for a time. Since the election that resulted in Duarte's removal from office, Mexican and

Venezuelan approaches to El Salvador have coincided more. Venezuela has also remained more lukewarm in its support of the Sandinista regime in Nicaragua than Mexico. This has also provoked some differences between the two countries.

Another cost has been the abandonment of one of the central tenets of Mexican foreign policy, namely the opposition to foreign intervention. Along with the principle of self-determination, nonintervention has long formed the cornerstone of Mexican foreign policy. A strict adherence to these two principles over the years has given Mexican policy much of its moral force. In its dealing with Central America, Mexico for the first time has itself engaged in clearly interventionist policies. The most salient example of this is the Franco-Mexican initiative on El Salvador, which constitutes a clear intervention in Salvadoran domestic politics. It may be possible to hypothesize that an ineluctable component of power, and the activism it breeds, is interventionism. Perhaps as power grows so does the tendency to intervene.

The greatest cost is economic; it is likely to grow with time. The granting of foreign assistance represents quite a cost to an underdeveloped country like Mexico even in the best of times. At a time of nearly complete financial collapse such as Mexico suffered in 1982, it represents a very substantial burden. On July 27, 1983, Mexico and Venezuela announced their decision to renew the San José facility for an additional year, albeit under somewhat less generous terms. The new agreement reduces the amount of payment that can be withheld for a five-year grace period from 30% to 20%. The interest charged on the loans that cover this unpaid balance have also been raised from 6% to 8%. If the 20% balance is used for certain purposes, particularly to develop alternate energy sources, the term of credit is increased to twenty years at an interest rate of 6% a year. Under the previous agreement, however, the interest charged if the 30% credit was used for these purposes was only 2% a year over the 20 years. On the other hand, an additional nation, Belize, has been made a recipient of this assistance. Nonetheless, these changes represent substantial reductions in the amount of aid that Mexico is providing. Given the importance that Mexico accords to its policy toward Central America, this illustrates the constraints imposed by the country's difficult economic circumstances. These economic costs were not foreseen when policy toward the region was first formulated. As a result, the Mexican government was unaware of, and consequently failed to calculate a number of the costs that have accompanied its policy.

CONCLUSIONS

These paired case studies support several propositions that may be relevant for other cases also marked by their high political content and defiance of the U.S. government. Under these circumstances, governments behave as "unified rational actors" (Allison, 1971) responding to strategic threats and opportunities. Bureaucratic political bargaining within the government does not play a major role, as most such players defer to the presidency in matters of high politics. The presidency in each country is, by far, the most potent factor shaping Cuban and Mexican foreign policy decision-making. There is, however, a difference between Mexico and Cuba. The more centralized and authoritarian the political system, the less likely foreign policy decisions will need to satisfy internal political needs. There is much evidence that Mexico's Central American policy serves long-term internal political needs; there is no such evidence for Cuba's overseas wars.

Both Cuba and Mexico show considerable continuity with certain aspects of past policies. Mexico has always sought to restrain U.S. intervention in Central America or the Caribbean. Cuba has supported revolutionary movements and regimes throughout the world since its own revolution came to power. But both governments changed their policies in the mid- and late 1970s. Mexico moved away from a passive foreign policy that was marked by nonintervention, and designed a complex policy to serve its new definition of interests to its south. Cuba dramatically increased the scale of its global foreign policy commitments by deploying large transoceanic armies to serve the needs of its emerging big power foreign policy.

Both Cuba and Mexico could act when they did because the United States was no longer such a constraint on their international actions and was itself more constrained in the wake of the Vietnam war defeat. Cuba and Mexico were not simply after international prestige, however. They acted to serve a new and expanded definition of their national interests responding to events in Central America and Africa. Both countries built up a large diplomatic network to serve their newly activist policies.

Both Cuba and Mexico acted first after their economies improved markedly (Cuban economic recovery in the early 1970s and Mexico's discovery of oil in the mid-1970s) but both retained their newly activist foreign policy even after their economic fortunes deteriorated (Cuba's entry into the Ethiopian war despite no real economic growth per capita in 1976-1977 and Mexico's persistence after the decline in oil prices began in 1981). Their new foreign policies, in short, were made possible initially by economic growth but were eventually conducted rather independently of their internal economic circumstances.

Perhaps because we chose policies whose purposes were military or political, we should not be surprised that the economic content is so modest. And we need to stress that Mexico and Cuba would like stronger trade ties with Central American and African countries, respectively. That they do not have them reflects the persistent underdevelopment of their economies. Economic gains have been negligible or nonexistent from the policies examined. On the contrary, Mexico and Cuba incur economic costs from the pursuit of their strategic goals.

Mexico retained greater independence from its politically closer superpower, the United States, than did Cuba with regard to the Soviet Union. While Mexico was somewhat constrained by the need to take into account U.S. policies, Cuba was doubly constrained by having to take into account the needs of both the United States and the USSR. Cuba's choice of policy instruments, moreover, was constrained not only by its persisting underdevelopment (as was Mexico) but also by specific features of its relationship with the Soviet Union. This suggests the propositon that the United States is a difficult but ineffective enemy of underdeveloped countries when they differ over issues of the type discussed, while the Soviet Union is a difficult but effective ally.

Both countries have retained their new policies even when problems arose, demonstrating a perhaps surprising steadfastness. Their foreign policies may be less volatile and fickle than that of industrialized countries. Cuban troops remain in Angola and Ethiopia, and Mexican oil subsidies are still being provided to the weakened Central American economies. Mexico and Cuba continue to defy U. S. preferences in both regions. Contrary to Mexican and Cuban policies before 1975, real resources, not just political rhetoric, have been and remain committed.

Neither country has given evidence of being much aware of possible costs when the initial decisions were made, and both countries have given evidence of a surprising willingness—at their peril—to ignore economic costs as they have resulted from these policies.

Cuba and Mexico emerged in the mid- and late 1970s as far more active in international affairs than ever before. Mexico became an important regional power and Cuba a global one. They came to think of themselves as important for the affairs of others. They now have become so. They made decisions that responded principally to an autonomous definition of national interests based on strategic choices. They have been both constrained by the persisting underdevelopment of their economies and, in the Cuban case, by the ties that bind it to a superpower. The international system's hierarchy, therefore, has been shaken but not altered fundamentally. There are more international actors—including Cuba and Mexico—but the theater, the plot, and the script have not changed.

BIBLIOGRAPHICAL NOTE

The study of Latin American foreign policy-making is a slowly growing field. Its growth is both stimulated and constrained by the persisting greater attention to U. S. foreign policy toward Latin America, or to the subject of Inter-American relations (Domínguez 1978c). Nevertheless, studies of the foreign policies of Latin American states have been appearing with greater frequency and higher quality. Many appear especially in journals published in Latin American countries on international topics, such as *Foro internacional, Estudios internacionales,* or *Estrategia,* and less frequently, in journals published outside the region. A helpful annotated bibliography of books and articles published in the late 1970s on the international relations of Latin America was edited by Dolores Moyano Martin (1979). The Departamento de Asuntos Culturales of the Organization of American States has also been publishing, and updating, a good bibliography on the same subject since 1975 (1982).

There is a good edited collection (Davis and Wilson, 1975) on the foreign policies of these countries but the coverage of recent years is meager. There is also a good edited collection on contemporary topics in the foreign policies of these countries (Ferris and Lincoln, 1981) but it doesn't place these topics in the larger context of each foreign policy. There are now some excellent books on some major Latin American countries, such as Mexico (Ojeda, 1976), Brazil (Schneider, 1976), or Venezuela (Bond, 1977). And there are, of course, many articles and book chapters on topics in the foreign policies of the various countries. But, perhaps surprisingly, there are still no general, analytical books on the foreign policies of such countries as Colombia or Peru.

Most analytical research on the foreign policies of these countries has focused on their relations with the United States, or on other substantive aspects of the content of their foreign policy. There is much less work on the process of foreign policy-making: design, negotiation, and implementation; the role of various individuals and government or private agencies; or generally on the politics of foreign policy. The research agenda, therefore, remains inviting, though difficult, for many scholars.

NOTES

1. For statistical data, see Inter-American Development Bank (1982:400). The gross domestic product in 1980 dollars of all Latin American countries increased by 306% from $169.9 billion in 1960 to $519.5 billion in 1980. The GDP per capita in 1980 dollars for all these countries grew 182% from $824 to $1507 in those twenty years. Mexico grew faster, and Cuba slower, than those averages.

2. For the timing of the first arrivals, *Granma Weekly Review*, March 26, 1978: 4-5. See various estimates in Nelson P. Valdés (1982: 72).

3. President Castro has acknowledged the arrival of weaponry and of Cuban military personnel "at the beginning of October at the request of the MPLA." He argues, however, that no Cuban regular military unit had been sent to Angola in order to participate directly in the war. (*Granma* April 20, 1976). For geater detail, see García Márquez (1977c: 6-15).

4. There should be no doubt that President Castro (1977) had thought well of the top Somali leader on the eve of going to war with him. He said of Somali President Siad Barre that "not only did he consolidate Somali independence but he also channeled it toward the revolutionary and socialist paths. . . . he has developed a revolutionary consciousness in the Somali people and he has organized a vanguard party to lead the revolution in Somalia."

5. The computations that follow are based on Comité Estatal de Estadísticas, 1978: 169, 181, 191; and 1980:172, 184, 194.

6. Sugar subsidies were calculated as the difference between what the USSR would have paid if it had used prices paid by Japan compared to what it did pay. Oil subsidies were calculated as the difference between what Cuba would have paid if it had used the prices paid to other countries compared to what it did pay. GSP data from Comité Estatal de Estadísticas: 50.

7. For a good discussion of the Soviet-Cuban-MPLA triangle, see LeoGrande (1982a: 22-26). For Cuba's transatlantic transportation of troops, García Márquez (1977b).

8. See also Roca (1982).

9. For current Mexican trade statistics see *Comercio Exterior* (published monthly by the Banco Nacional de Comercio Exterior, Mexico D.F.).

10. During the late 1950s and early 1960s there was some debate over the extent of the Mexican President's power. Vernon (1963), for example, argued that the Mexican President is hemmed in by competing pressures and is far less powerful than he appears to be. Since then, there has been a growing consensus on the authoritarian nature of the political system and concomitantly on the great power of the President. Some of the studies that propound this view are Purcell (1975) and Hansen (1971).

11. For a good discussion of interest groups in Mexico see Purcell (1975).

12. A substantial body of literature has described this characteristic of the Mexican political system. An oft-cited source on this topic is Anderson and Cockcroft (1969: 366-89).

13. The countries that are receiving this assistance are: Barbados, Costa Rica, the Dominican Republic, El Salvador, Guatemala, Haiti, Honduras, Jamaica, Nicaragua and Panama.

14. The authors are indebted to René Herrera for suggesting this concept. For a fuller discussion of the problems posed by the existence of parallel economies see Herrera (forthcoming).

6

DECISION-MAKING IN A NONSTATE ACTOR—OPEC

Bahgat Korany and Selma Akbik

INTRODUCTION

The analysis of international relations has been dominated by the state-centric frame of reference. For Hans Morgenthau (1967), international relations are interstate relations; Raymond Aron (1962) limited international action to two agents: the soldier and the diplomat (i.e., the official representatives par excellence of nation-states). Decision-making theory—even though it emphasized its break with traditional perspectives and its integration within the scientific-behavioral approach—did little to break with the state-centric frame of reference. With rare exceptions (Cox & Jacobson, 1972; Lister, 1984), the basic studies of decision-making, from Snyder et al. (1962) and Brecher (1969, 1974, 1980) to Allison (1969, 1971), Steinbruner (1974), and Alexander George (1980), all centered on the state and its representatives.

Yet one of the most important characteristics of international relations in the last century and a half has been the exponential growth in the number of intergovernmental organizations (IGOs), from just one in the period 1830–1834 to 292 in 1965, an increase of just less than 300 percent. The number of members, too, has increased, and even more dramatically: from 5 to 6,432, an increase of 1,284.5 percent (Feld and Jordan, 1983: 16). Part of this increase in IGOs and their memberships is related to the rise of the Third World. For instance, in 1934 African and Asian nations constituted 9 (or 15 percent) of the 58 members of the League of Nations. Thirty years later, they accounted for 72 (or 56 percent) of the 147 members of the UN.

The Third World was soon to establish its own intergovernmental institutions. Some are purely regional in character (e.g., the Arab League, founded in 1945, and the Organization of African Unity, founded in 1963). Others aim to group all Third World countries and to be globally oriented

The OPEC Countries

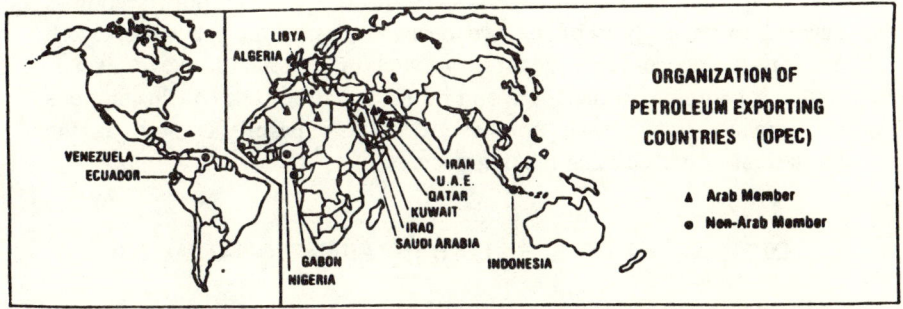

(e.g., the Nonaligned group [1961] and Group of 77 [1967]). Still others, although their membership constitutes only a minority of the Third World and although their objectives seem limited, could hardly be more influential as actors in world politics and the world economy. The Organization of Petroleum Exporting Countries (OPEC) is a prime example of this category.

But, paradoxically, the decisions of OPEC since its establishment in September 1960 have been shaped by global systemic factors. In the face of this dominant system, OPEC's thirteen member states have, individually and collectively, reacted by varying their oil prices and/or output. Two decisions of the 1980s are analyzed here to illustrate OPEC's decision-making process and the factors shaping it. The first decision—fixing a price ceiling of $32 per barrel—was taken at the Fifty-seventh Ordinary Meeting of the OPEC Conference in Algiers on June 9-11, 1980. The second decision, taken at the Sixty-third Extraordinary Meeting of the OPEC Conference and convened in OPEC headquarters in Vienna on March 19-20, 1982, concerned the level of production and fixed an output ceiling of 18 million barrels per day (bpd). World market conditions, though very different in each case, provoked individual reactions by member states, and OPEC had to intervene to impose a minimum of coordination in the adaptation of oil prices and/or output to market fluctuations. Given the diverse sociopolitical conditions and the varying absorptive capacities of the economies of the thirteen member states, both decisions were reached only after heated debates.

This chapter is divided into three parts. The first deals with OPEC as an influential international actor. The second analyzes two sets of factors shaping OPEC's decision-making process: on the one hand, those coming from the global system (e.g., multinational companies, world market fluctuations), and on the other, those factors internal to the organization, such as the formal (e.g., membership categories) and the informal power structure (e.g., the Saudi role as a "swing" producer, or "balancer," given that Saudi Arabia's share of OPEC production rose from 25 percent in 1973 to 45 percent in 1981) (Kanovsky, 1981: 392). The third section is devoted to an analysis of the two decisions, using the same framework and organizing concepts as those applied in Chapter 4: the decisions' contexts, planning, formulation, and implementation. The conclusion pulls the threads together and emphasizes OPEC's payoffs as well as the limitations of its decision-making process.

OPEC AS AN INFLUENTIAL INTERNATIONAL ACTOR

In brief, OPEC's influence is based on three related elements. First is the concentration among its thirteen members of oil resources (production and reserves) in an energy-hungry world. According to data compiled by Sid-Ahmed (1980: 132-136, 540-541), OPEC accounted for 56 percent of the world's oil production and 87 percent of the world's oil exports, and according to the 1974 figures supplied by the Bank of England, OPEC countries accounted for some 90 percent of the world's petroleum exports. As for OPEC's share of the world's oil reserves, 65 percent of the total world reserves of crude were in OPEC member countries (Ajomo, 1977: 40, 54, 58).

Second, the accelerated increases in oil prices in the 1970s led to the accumulation of huge quantities of petrodollars in the hands of these developing countries, whose economies had, after all, a very limited absorptive capacity. The result has been the flooding of the world economy with petrodollars (see Table 6.1). The presence of this "money to grab" encouraged many developed-country governments and multinational companies to rush exports to the oil-producing countries consisting of development equipment, weapons, and luxury goods, thereby "recycling" petrodollars. For instance, in the twelve-year period 1969-1981, total Saudi and Iranian defense expenditures were $110,537 million and $75,555 million respectively, the major part of which went to arms imports. U.S. arms transfers alone to these two countries for the nine-year period 1970-1979 totaled $63,059 million (Cordesman, 1984: 160-161). Thus the rate of growth of the economies of many developed countries and the survival of entire sectors of society depended on transactions with OPEC countries. Moreover, OPEC's importing of labor has made its members direct key countries of employment (Peterson, 1983: 199), having already been creators of employment in developed countries.

Third, these "liquidity surplus effects" were bound to spill over into political influence at the world level. Thus, as far back as 1975, OPEC member countries were accorded 15 percent voting rights in the World

TABLE 6.1 OPEC Member Countries' Oil Revenues, in millions of U.S. dollars (1961-1980)

	1961	1962	1963	1964	1965	1966	1967	1968	1969	1970
Algeria	28.0	45.0	52.0	60.0	76.0	128.0	199.1	251.8	266.7	271.9
Ecuador	-	-	-	-	-	-	-	-	-	-
Gabon	.4	.4	.4	.6	.8	.8	2.5	3.5	4.0	4.3
Indonesia	96.2*	96.3*	102.0*	97.0*	97.9*	97.4*	109.0*	133.1	201.8	254.3
Islamic Rep. of Iran	291.2	342.3	380.0	482.2	514.1	608.2	751.6	853.4	922.8	1109.3
Iraq	265.4	266.3	308.0	353.1	367.9	394.2	364.4	487.9	479.0	521.0
Kuwait	461.4	480.3	521.4	566.4	598.2	637.8	714.7	701.8	759.1	820.7
S.P. Libyan A.J.	3.0	39.8	107.8	210.6	351.1	522.8	625.0	1001.8	1175.2	1351.3
Nigeria	18.7	23.8	16.5	20.3	36.3	57.5	59.6	45.7	89.5	247.0
Qatar	54.3	56.6	60.5	63.8	69.2	90.7	105.4	111.8	117.6	122.4
Saudi Arabia	377.6	409.7	455.2	523.2	664.1	789.9	903.6	926.4	949.2	1214.0
United Arab Emirates	-	2.0	6.4	12.3	33.3	99.7	109.6	153.4	190.8	233.0
Venezuela	842.7	962.8	994.4	1080.3	1097.1	1074.8	1213.3	1223.0	1228.6	1376.8
Total OPEC	2439.4	2725.4	3004.6	3469.8	3906.0	4501.8	5157.8	5903.6	6384.3	7526.0

	1971	1972	1973	1974	1975	1976	1977	1978	1979	1980
Algeria	321.0	613.3	987.7	3299.2	3261.8	3699.0	4253.7	4589.1	7513.0R	10787.0
Ecuador	-	29.7	128.8	413.9	292.8	532.7	499.3	500.0	800.0	1200.0
Gabon	9.4	18.1	29.4	172.7	483.5*	800.0	600.0	600.0	900.0	1600.0
Indonesia	336.2	505.8	687.7	1364.3	3233.1	4465.7	4692.3	5200.0	8100.0R	10500.0
Islamic Rep. of Iran	1851.1	2396.0	4599.2	17821.8	18433.2	22042.9	21210.2	19300.0	20500.0	11600.0
Iraq	840.0	575.0	1843.0	5700.0	7500.0	8500.0	9631.0	10200.0	21291.0R	25981.0
Kuwait	954.3	1403.7	1734.7	6542.6	6393.1	6869.5	7515.7	7699.5	16863.0R	18016.0
S.P. Libyan A.J.	1674.2	1562.6	2222.9	5999.0	5101.0	7500.0	8850.0	8400.0	15223.0R	22527.0
Nigeria	846.8	1117.2	2048.0	6654.2	7422.1	7715.0	9600.0	7900.0	15900.0R	20000.0
Qatar	199.6	255.2	463.1	1849.0	1684.9	2091.9	1994.0	2200.0	3642.0R	5377.0
Saudi Arabia	1884.9	2744.6	4340.0	22573.5	25675.8	30754.9	36538.4R	32233.8	57522.0R	102212.0
United Arab Emirates	431.0	551.0	900.0	5536.0	6000.0	7000.0R	9030.0R	8200.0R	12862.0R	19344.0
Venezuela	1674.7	1901.6	3028.7	9270.6	6968.0	7712.8R	8106.2R	7319.0R	11647.1	14881.1
Total OPEC	11023.2	13673.8	22813.2	87196.8	92449.3	107884.8	122520.8	114341.4	192763.1	264025.1

* = Estimated

R = Revised

Source: OPEC, Annual Statistical Bulletin 1980, p. xlix, as cited in Al-Sowayegh, 1984:47.

Bank and 10 percent in the International Monetary Fund (IMF), compared with their previous 5 percent voting rights in each body (Ajomo 1977: 57), and before the end of the 1970s Saudi Arabia was included in the very exclusive club of the IMF board of directors. In addition, OPEC members had become involved in capital transfers to other developing countries, and their official aid contributions were generally far greater, as percentages of their GNP, than those of developed countries, as Table 6.2 shows.

All such facets of monetary and political influence notwithstanding, these countries are still part and parcel of the Third World and all are characterized by its subordination to, and dependence on, the vagaries of the world system. Consequently, external factors are the primary, if not the only, determinants of their decision-making. This brings us to the analysis of the decision-making process proper.

THE OPEC DECISION-MAKING PROCESS

THE PRIMACY OF THE EXTERNAL FACTOR

Weak or strong, OPEC is controlled almost entirely by external forces. The only variation in outside influence is the change in the external partner. In the early stages of its existence, when OPEC was still weak, the dominant partner consisted of the multinational oil companies, whether U.S., British, or Dutch—the so-called Seven Sisters (Exxon, Texaco, Socal, Gulf, Mobil, British Petroleum, and Shell) (Sampson, 1976). But when OPEC started to cut its financial teeth and succeeded in its drive for "participation" (i.e., as a partner in ownership) and "nationalization" (i.e., complete ownership by the national government), the dominant external partner became the vacillating world capitalist economy, itself dominated by a handful of developed countries. Let us now consider each of the two situations facing OPEC: domination by the multinationals when OPEC was weak, and domination by the world market when it was strong.

OPEC and the Multinational Companies

The ownership of the major oil companies is indicated in Figure 6.1; their actual impact on the world market is detailed in Table 6.3. As late as 1977, the Seven Sisters were responsible for 77.1 percent of OPEC oil production (Sampson, 1976: 241)—in effect, a complete domination of almost all stages of operation from the production of crude oil to its refinement and distribution. This domination by the multinational companies has been such as to foil any nationalist attempt at change (such as Mossadeq's effort in Iran in the early 1950s) and, instead, to impose

FIGURE 6.1: The Network of Ownership of Major Oil Companies in the Gulf Prior to 1974

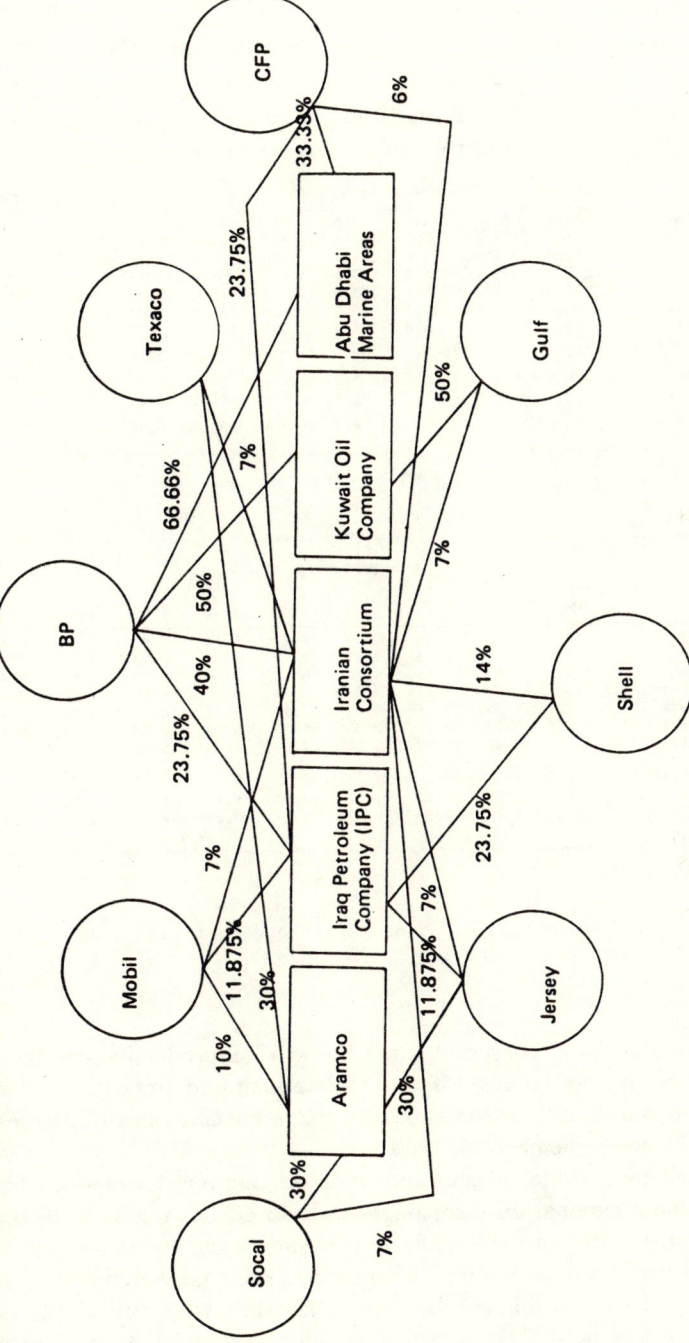

Source: Edith T. Penrose, *The Large International Firm in Developing Countries* (M.I.T. Press, Cambridge, Mass., 1968), p. 151.

TABLE 6.2 OPEC Official Development Disbursements (1973-1981)

Donor Country	Total ODA Disbursements (in $ US millions)								
	1973	1974	1975	1976	1977	1978	1979	1980	1981
Algeria	25.4	46.9	40.7	53.6	46.7	43.1	272	83	65
Iran	1.9	408.9	593.1	752.6	251.2	213.2	25	3	150
Iraq	11.9	422.9	218.4	231.7	56.0	144.2	1115	1062	143
Kuwait	345.2	622.5	976.3	615.3	1433.0	856.4	1055	1188	685
Libya	214.6	147.0	261.1	93.6	109.6	141.5	105	281	105
Nigeria	4.7	15.3	13.9	82.9	64.4	38.0	30	42	149
Qatar	93.7	185.2	338.9	195.0	194.3	100.8	277	319	175
Saudi Arabia	304.9	1029.1	1997.4	2407.1	2400.8	1455.3	2298	3040	5798
UAE	288.6	510.6	1046.1	1060.2	1229.4	616.5	1115	1062	799
Venezuela	17.7	58.8	31.0	102.8	51.5	94.6	83	130	62
Total	1307.8	3466.6	5516.9	5594.7	5846.9	3703.6	6106	6977	7836

	ODA as a percentage of GNP								
	1973	1974	1975	1976	1977	1978	1979	1980	1981
Algeria	0.29	0.37	0.28	0.33	0.24	0.18	0.87	0.21	0.10
Iran	0.01	0.88	1.13	1.13	0.30	0.26	0.03	0.01	-
Iraq	0.21	3.98	1.65	1.44	0.29	0.66	2.53	2.12	0.37
Kuwait	5.72	5.72	8.12	4.36	10.09	4.54	5.89	4.80	1.98
Libya	3.32	1.23	2.31	0.63	0.62	0.77	0.45	0.92	0.37
Nigeria	0.04	0.07	0.05	0.25	0.16	0.08	0.04	0.05	0.17
Qatar	15.62	9.26	15.62	7.95	7.83	3.48	5.89	4.80	2.64
Saudi Arabia	4.04	4.46	5.40	5.73	4.30	2.32	3.01	2.60	4.77
UAE	15.96	7.57	14.12	11.02	10.67	5.37	5.87	3.96	2.88
Venezuela	0.11	0.20	0.11	0.33	6.14	0.23	0.17	0.23	0.10

Source: Annual Development Assistance Committee 1974-1982, as cited in Hunter, 1984:168.

unilateral decisions concerning the volume of oil production and the level of prices. It was because of one such attempt to impose a unilateral decision that the oil companies became the *immediate* cause of the creation of OPEC on September 14, 1960.

Faced by a world oil glut and price discounting, Exxon—the biggest of the multinational oil companies—announced on August 8, 1960, that the posted prices in the Middle East would be cut by an average of 10 cents a barrel. Given the interdependence among the Seven Sisters, other companies were to follow suit. Thus, a few days later, British Petroleum cut its prices by 4.5 cents, "and the other companies hovered between

TABLE 6.3 Oil Output of Major Oil Companies in the Gulf, in millions of metric tons (1971)

Gulf OPEC Countries	Esso	Shell	BP	Gulf	Texaco	Socal	Mobil	CFP	Other	Total
Iran	14.5	29.1	83.8	14.5	14.5	14.5	14.5	12.5	26.3	227.0
Saudi Arabia	66.6	--	--	--	66.6	66.6	22.2	--	--	222.0
Kuwait	--	--	72.5	72.5	--	--	--	--	--	145.0
Iraq	9.8	19.7	19.7	--	--	--	9.8	19.7	4.3	83.0
Abu Dhabi	3.3	6.5	17.8	--	--	--	3.3	12.2	1.4	44.6
Neutral Zone	--	--	--	--	--	--	--	--	26.4	26.4
Qatar	1.1	12.5	2.4	--	--	--	1.1	2.4	0.5	20.0
Total	95.2	67.8	196.2	87.0	81.1	81.1	50.8	46.8	58.9	764.9

Source: OPEC, Annual Statistics Bulletin, 1972.

different prices until they were all down, and all level. . . . All hell *did* break loose" (Sampson, 1976: 188-189). The hell breaking loose, according to Sampson and many others (Servan-Schreiber, 1980; *Les Sept Crises, 1973-1983*), was the creation of OPEC and its effects on the global system. But behind the image of OPEC as a "Frankensteinian" monster lies the fact that the very creation of OPEC was brought about by a decision made by one multinational company.

True, the Arab oil producers were concerned about controlling oil and its use since the 1948 Palestine War, when the Arab League prevailed over the government of Iraq and the Iraq Petroleum Company to force the suspension of shipments through the pipeline to the Haifa refinery. It also tried to put pressure on companies marketing in Israel to withdraw their business with that country. In 1951, some Arab countries suggested the formation of a joint body to control the supply of oil, and the Arab League established an Oil Experts Committee. In 1954, the League set up a permanent Petroleum Department within the League's Secretariat (Ajomo, 1977: 38). But the Arabs realized that the diktat of the multinational oil companies concerned all oil producers: Arabs, non-Arab Middle Easterners (i.e., the Iranians), and Latin Americans. The companies' diktat was ever-present; they would use virtually any pretext to impose complete compliance by the oil producers. As Howard Page, the director of the eight-company consortium in the Middle East (the so-called Iranian Consortium), put it: "Sometimes they made it easy to cut down by breaking an agreement, as in Iraq; then we could tell 'em to go to hell."

This imposition of compliance (proceeding from the oil companies' diktat of "cooperate or else" cemented personal ties between countries and people of different languages and even cultures—as, for example, the bonds created between the scholarly oil minister of Venezuela, Perez Alfonso, and the American-educated nationalist oil minister of Saudi Arabia, Abdallah El-Tariki. It was on the occasion of one such diktat— the first price reduction in 1959—that the initial Arab Petroleum Congress was convened in Cairo and observers from Venezuela and Iran were invited to attend. According to Alfonso, this congress "constituted the first seed of the creation of OPEC."

The second price reduction in 1960 intensified the sense of threat on the part of oil-producing countries. Iraq, for instance, was engaged in deadlocked negotiations with the oil companies, and the price cut was interpreted by some as bringing pressure against Baghdad. Other oil-producing countries felt that their economic growth and even their survival was threatened, inasmuch as oil represented 99 percent of the revenue in Saudi Arabia, and the price cut was to hit precisely at this critical factor in their economy. Even the moderate and pro-Western shah of Iran was furious about the price cuts concerning which he had received no warning. As he told Anthony Sampson in 1975, "even if the action was basically sound . . . it could not be acceptable to us as long as it was taken without our consent." Consequently, he decided to join the conveners in the Baghdad Conference in September 1960, a conference that ended with the establishment of OPEC: "'I must admit we were just walking in the mist,' the Shah said, [continuing the story of OPEC]; 'not in the dark, but it was a little misty. There was still that complex of the big powers, and the mystical power and all the magic behind the name of all these big countries'" (Sampson, 1976: 191). And one Kuwaiti agreed: "OPEC would not have happened without the oil cartel. We just took a leaf from the oil companies' book. The victim had learned the lesson" (ibid., 193).

The aim, then, as Nadim Pachachi, OPEC's ex-secretary general, put it, was to freeze up "the managerial prerogative" of the oil companies to unilaterally fix prices. Items 1 and 2 of the first resolution of the 1960 Baghdad Conference establishing OPEC emphasize this aspect:

> 1. That Members can no longer remain indifferent to the attitude heretofore adopted by the Oil Companies in effecting price modifications;
>
> 2. That Members shall demand that Oil Companies maintain their prices steady and free from all unnecessary fluctuations; that Members shall endeavour, by all means available to them, to restore present prices to the levels prevailing before the reductions; that they shall ensure that if any new circumstances arise which in the estimation of the Oil Companies necessitate price modifications, the said Companies shall enter into consultation with the Member or Members affected in order fully to explain the circumstances (OPEC, Official Resolutions, 1983: 1).

In the 1960s, then, OPEC was just asking for "consultation" and "explanation" of oil price fixing by the companies. The 1970s saw the rise of OPEC and its success in fixing both oil prices and levels of production. The press release on the occasion of the twentieth anniversary of OPEC's establishment (September 14, 1980) noted that "to-day, 20 years later, the international oil scene presents, from *OPEC's point of view,* a totally different and healthier picture" (OPEC, Official Resolutions, 1983: 184-185, emphasis added). Thus the tables were turned: OPEC, not the Seven Sisters, could fix prices and production levels.

Yet, given its greatly increased strength in the 1970s, has OPEC's structural dependency on the outside diminished, and have its members become more immune to the vagaries of the world system? Not at all. The international oil market still remains the most crucial variable affecting OPEC rise and decline as well as the pace of its members' economies.

OPEC and the World Market

In a tight market situation (i.e., when oil demand is higher than supply) such as that of the 1979 Iranian oil crisis, increases in crude oil prices on spot markets affect OPEC's official prices. It is therefore fair to say that failure by OPEC member countries to adjust their official prices according to spot prices results in a shift of oil sale revenues from these countries to multinational oil companies and OECD Organization for Economic Cooperation and Development governments. This enables the companies, buying OPEC crude oil at official prices, to resell the same at higher spot prices.[1] OECD governments, for their part, must raise consumer taxes in order to fill the gap between OPEC official prices of crude oil and spot prices. OPEC member countries must subsequently raise their official prices in order to avoid this shift in revenues. As will be explained in the section concerning decision planning, during the Iranian oil crisis OPEC member countries raised their official prices for crude oil to avoid losses in sale revenues to international oil companies and OECD governments.

On the other hand, in a soft market situation (in which oil supply is higher than demand) such as the one experienced during the world oil glut of 1982, the residual demand model is applied to real markets. Oil supplies satisfying world demand are assumed to flow first from non-OPEC sources and then from OPEC. Therefore, a decline in world demand for oil affects only demand for OPEC supplies. OPEC member countries must therefore individually lower their respective prices and increase their respective production rates in order to compensate for the loss of their share of the world market. Again, as will be explained further, during the world oil glut of 1982 OPEC member countries lowered their official prices of crude oil and increased their oil production.

THE ORGANIZATIONAL STRUCTURE AND ITS INTERNAL POWER CHARACTERISTICS

OPEC's decision-making organizational structure is a function of the institution's objectives, especially those spelled out in items A and B of article 2 of the OPEC Statute:

> A. The principal aim of the Organization shall be the coordination and unification of the petroleum policies of Member Countries and the determination of the means for safeguarding their interests, individually and collectively.
>
> B. The Organization shall devise ways and means of ensuring the stabilization of prices in international oil markets with a view to eliminating harmful and unnecessary fluctuations.

To enable OPEC to obtain its objectives, its fourteen-article Statute was approved by the conference in Caracas in January 1961 (see Resolution 11.6, OPEC, Official Resolutions, 1983: 4-8). But given the changes in the international oil market and in the relations between OPEC members on the one hand and the oil companies and governments of developed countries on the other, the Statute has been added to and modified on at least twelve occasions between 1961 and 1980 (OPEC Statute, 1983: 26-27). However, the organizational structure remains relatively simple, as indicated in Figure 6.2. Specifically, there are three main bodies: the Conference, the Board of Governors, and the Secretariat. The Secretariat represents and carries out OPEC's common objectives, whereas the Conference represents individual national interests, with the Board of Governors falling in between but nearer in its functions to those of the Conference.

Functions

1. Article 10 of the Statute states that the *Conference* is the organization's supreme authority. The Conference consists of delegations usually headed by the ministers of oil, mines, and energy of the member countries (article 11). It meets at least twice a year, but an extraordinary meeting may be convened at the request of a member country through the secretary general (article 12). Upon convening, the Conference's first article of business is to elect its president and alternate president, both of whom hold office for the duration of the meeting of the Conference and continue to retain their titles until the next meeting (article 14). Except on procedural matters, the Conference operates on the principle of unanimity. It possesses wide-ranging and supreme authority. It decides upon any application for new membership, appoints the members of the Board of Governors, the chairman of the Board, the secretary general, and the deputy secretary general, all of whom must be nationals of the member countries. It approves any amendments to the Statute and decides upon reports and recommendations as well as the organization's budget, which is submitted by the Board of Governors. The Conference's powers are in fact wider than those explicitly stipulated; indeed, article 16 states that "all matters that are not expressly assigned to other organs of the Organization shall fall within the competence of the Conference." Thus, inasmuch as the Conference represents state-sovereignty, par excellence, against the encroachment of supranational authority, the former is considered to be at the basis of the organization and is bound to affect both the mode of deciding (i.e., bargaining among different national interests) and the decision itself (i.e., which will be much more akin to an "outcome" than to a unitary consensual choice).

150

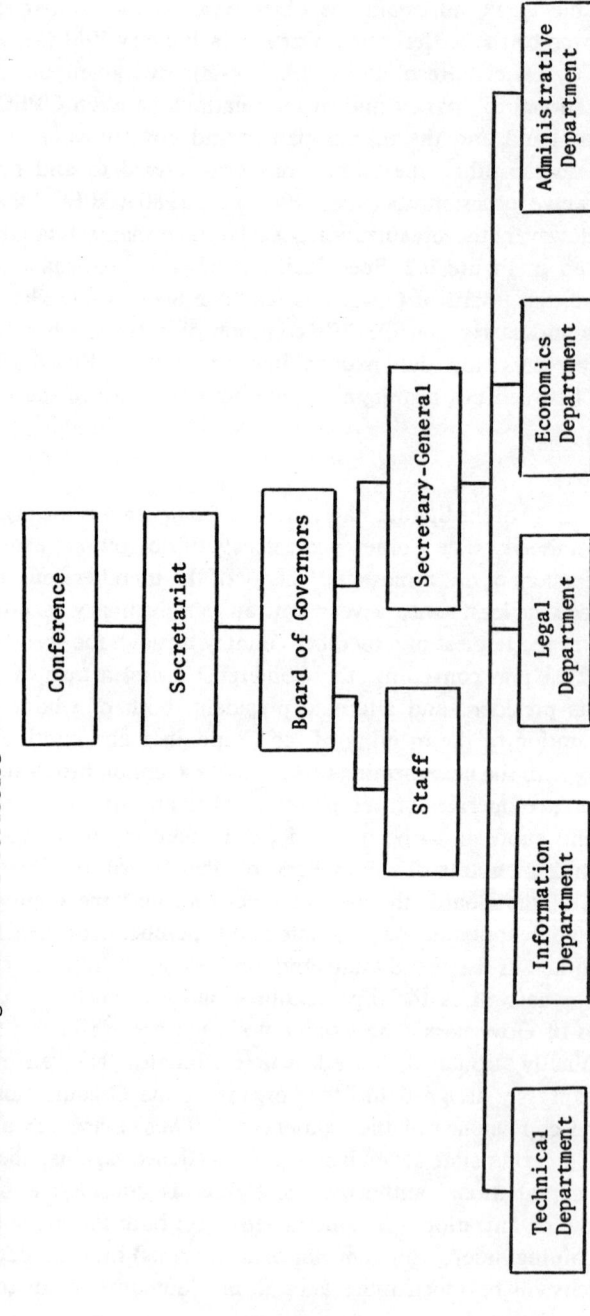

FIGURE 6.2 OPEC's Organizational Structure

Source: Al-Sowayegh, 1984:35.

2. This "state sovereignty supreme" premise is also clear with respect to the *Board of Governors,* which, according to article 17, "shall be composed of governors nominated by the Member Countries and confirmed by the Conference" for two years of service. The Board meets at least twice a year, and usually decides issues by a simple majority vote of attending governors—except when convening an extraordinary meeting, which "may be convened at the request of the Chairman of the Board, the Secretary General, or two-thirds of the Governors" (article 18b). The Board determines much of the work of the Conference, for it convenes extraordinary meetings of the Conference (article 28.8), prepares the agenda for each and every meeting, submits reports and recommendations, draws up OPEC's budget, nominates the auditor, and approves the auditor's report. In addition, the Board approves "the appointment of Directors of Divisions and Heads of Departments" (article 20.7) and directs "the management of the affairs of the Organization and the implementation of the decisions of the Conference" (article 20.1). It has thus become the necessary and influential link between the Conference and Secretariat.

3. The *Secretariat* "shall carry out the executive functions of the Organization in accordance with the provisions of this Statute under the *direction of the Board of Governors*" (article 25, emphasis added). Moreover, the secretary general, though appointed by the Conference for three years, is responsible to the Board for both his or her activities and the functions of the different departments. That is, "the Secretary General shall be assisted in the discharge of his duties by the Deputy Secretary General, a Division of Research, a Personnel and Administration Department, a Public Information Department, [and] a News Agency . . . OPECNA" (articles 33.1 and 33.2).

The organs of the Secretariat concerned with OPEC's decision-making process are (1) the Economic Commission Board, which was established in 1964 as a permanent and specialized body to assist the organization in promoting stability and equitability in international oil prices; and (2) the Division of Research, which monitors, forecasts, analyzes, and evaluates the situation of the energy and petrochemical industries. The Division of Research also analyzes economic and financial issues of significant interest and maintains and expands data services to support the research activities of the Secretariat and those of the member countries. In brief, it conducts "a continuous program of research fulfilling the needs of the Organization, placing particular emphasis on energy and related matters" (article 34). In relation to OPEC's decision-making, this division (together with any commissioned consultants or expert studies, according to article 35) represents both a brain trust and a necessary information base that could influence the decisions taken.

Thus the Secretariat seems to be the organ most identified with the role of the organization as a supranational institution and not merely as a conglomeration of individual countries, each with its own national interests. However, although nothing should "impair the efficiency of the Secretariat" (article 31), the same article requires the secretary general in his or her appointment of the officers of the Secretariat to "give due consideration, as far as possible, to an equitable nationality distribution among Members." Of course,, the secretary general (article 27b), the deputy secretary general (article 30a), and even the directors of divisions and the heads of departments (article 20.7) are selected from lists of nationals submitted by OPEC's member countries. The emphasis on the nationality of the secretary general and other top-level officers bolsters the side of state sovereignty against supranational authority, and points up the importance of the issue of membership in relation to OPEC's decision-making.

Membership

There are three categories of membership: associate, full, and founder members. (1) *Founder members* are those countries that attended the September 1960 Baghdad Conference, which established OPEC and witnessed the signing of the original document. They are Iran, Iraq, Kuwait, Saudi Arabia, and Venezuela. Not only are they similar in number to the permanent members of the UN Security Council, but on many crucial issues they also enjoy a veto power, collectively or individually. In the formative years of OPEC, these members accounted "for over 70% of all crude oil moving into the international market and well over 65% of the world's oil production" (Ajomo, 1977: 40). (2) *Full members* are those who applied later and who have been accepted by the Conference; for example, Qatar was admitted in 1961, Indonesia and Libya in 1962, Algeria in 1969, United Arab Emirates in 1970, Nigeria in 1971, and Ecuador in 1973. (3) *Associate member* is the status conferred on a country before it is accepted as a full member. Thus Gabon, for instance, was admitted as an associate member in November 1973 and became a full member only nineteen months later, on June 11, 1975. Associate members are invited to attend the Conference and to enjoy OPEC facilities (as full members do), but they do not have the right to vote. There are no associate members in OPEC at present.

Associate members, however, must satisfy the same requirements as full members. These requirements are stipulated in article 7c and are three in number. To be accepted as a member, a candidate country must

(a) be "a substantial net exporter of crude petroleum"; (b) have "similar interests to those of Member Countries"; and (c) be "accepted by a majority of three-fourths of Full Members, including the concurrent vote of all Founder Members."

These requirements have to apply conjunctively and not in isolation. For instance, if condition "a" were to be applied literally, countries such as the USSR, Canada, or the United Kingdom would qualify for OPEC membership—but this contradicts requirement "b." Indeed, the practice of OPEC shows that admission has been limited to developing countries, to those "whose financing of their development projects and the balancing of their budgets depend on revenues from oil, and who were and still are unable to exploit their oil resources without the assistance of foreigners, especially major oil companies" (Ajomo, 1977: 42). This is why article 7d comes back to this point in reiterating that "no country may be admitted to [even] Associate Membership which does not fundamentally have interests and aims similar to those of Member Countries." The primary frame of reference is that of OPEC as a group of developing countries.

This is not to say, however, that all of these countries have exactly the same power in OPEC's decision-making or see eye to eye on all issues. Indeed, the admission of a new member requires not a unanimous acceptance but only a majority of three-fourths of full members. Acceptance, however, should be unanimous among the five founding members, each of which has a veto power in this respect and some (e.g., Saudi Arabia, as we shall see later) of which have a special hegemony within the organization's informal power structure. Thus, even though there are no permanent voting blocs, *voting patterns* among OPEC members are bound to reflect variations in general political orientation (e.g., revolutionary Libya or Iran versus Saudi Arabia and other Gulf Emirates) and in the characteristics of their economies and developmental programs (e.g., Algeria or Nigeria versus Qatar or the United Arab Emirates). See Table 6.4 for a breakdown of these variations.

Yet, despite their differences, all OPEC members follow a consistent policy of raising expenditures (i.e., to meet growing development needs and pay for increasing imports) as revenues rise. Hence, in the face of a tight market, it is relatively easy for all members to adjust by raising crude oil prices as well as the quantity of crude oil output. Although squabbles among a few members might well occur as a result, there is no danger that they might undercut one another, nor is collective action at risk. On the other hand, when, in the face of a soft market, the members have to reduce both oil prices and output, there are very real difficulties

TABLE 6.4 OPEC Members and Their Characteristics

COUNTRY	AREA (sq km)	POPULATION (million)	GNP million$	GNP/ per capita$	EXPORTS/FOB (million)	IMPORTS/FOB (million)	YEAR OF ADMISSION TO OPEC
Algeria*	2,382,000	19.70	40.60	2,055.00	12,930	10,714	1969
Ecuador	281,000	8.40	11,027.60	1,319.70	2,459	2,250	1973
Gabon	268,000	0.50	3,376.00	6,171.80	2,173	674	1973 (Ass.) 1975 (Full)
Indonesia	5,193,250	147.50	60,552.96	451.21	21,908	10,834	1962
Iran	1,648,000	37.90	74,527.00	1,970.00	14,251	12,246	1960**
Iraq	438,000	13.20	39,737.00	3,010.00	26,347	13,048	1960**
Kuwait	18,000	1.37	27,247.00	19,886.00	19,762	6,548	1960**
Libya	1,760,000	2.97	3,375.60	11,335.00	22,574	4,602	1962
Nigeria	923,774	82.50	50,769.00	615.38	24,758	20,723	1971
Qatar	11,000	0.22	5,609.00	25,495.00	5,672	1,423	1961
Saudi Arabia	2,240,000	8.37	116,167.00	13,879.00	101,421	33,320	1960**
United Arab Emirates	84,000	0.90	20,773.00	23,081.00	20,747	8,746	1974 (Abu Dhabi since 1967)
Venezuela	916,000	16.50	59,923.00	3,640.00	19,976	11,130	1960**

* Algeria uses GDP (gross domestic product), not GNP (gross national product).
** All those admitted in 1960 are founder members.

Source: OPEC Member Country Profiles, OPEC Secretariat, Vienna 1983. All currency is in U.S. dollars, and data are as reported for 1980.

involved in reaching the right decision, and the organization itself is in danger. In such a situation, Saudi Arabia, which enjoys the very special status of a swing producer, increases crude oil output in a tight market to restrain price increase and, conversely, cuts output in a soft market to restrain declines in price. Saudi Arabia is the only country able, in a relatively short time and without unacceptable technical or financial consequences, to vary rates of oil production from a low of about 5 or 6 million bpd to a maximum of over 10 million bpd. Thus, instead of pursuing their professed strategy of gradual price increases, the Saudis have contributed twice to sharp price hikes (1973, 1979) and have then used their considerable production capabilities to bring about a slow decline in real prices (1974-1978, 1981-1982) (Quandt, 1982: 1). In this last instance, Saudi Arabia's production of oil fell by nearly 4 million bpd in the short period from fall 1981 to spring 1982, thereby placing Saudi Arabia at the base of OPEC's informal power structure.

Although OPEC is one of the very few supranational institutions in which the discrepancies between formal powers and real ones are not huge, an *informal power structure* has usually existed in the organization— albeit one that has undergone considerable change in the last ten years. Until the regime change occurred in Iran in 1979, Saudi Arabia and Iran held the key positions in the organization and usually managed to make other members follow their lead, however reluctantly. The degree of influence wielded by Saudi Arabia and Iran, however, depended not on the absolute share of the world oil market held by the country in question but, rather, on its flexibility as a swing producer to increase or decrease production. In this respect, Saudi Arabia was indeed the key to market control (Fesharaki and Isaak, 1983: 234-235). As the regulator of the whole system, it wielded enormous influence within the organization.

Moreover, the Saudis acted to achieve a minimum degree of stability in the world oil market, thereby maintaining a reasonable level of coherence within OPEC itself. Accordingly, during the oil glut of 1982, Saudi Arabia was ready to cut production further to maintain the $34-per-barrel price agreed upon among member countries. In addition, "when Nigeria found it difficult to sell its overpriced oil, the Saudis put some pressure on Mobil to announce its normal April level of purchases from Nigeria, then reportedly followed up by offering Nigeria a large loan to help cope with its revenue needs" (Quandt, 1982: 22). Thus the OPEC floor price was maintained—at least until the next round.

We now turn to an analysis of the decisions themselves to see how different decision factors function in reality.

THE CONTEXT OF THE DECISIONS

The Iranian Oil Crisis and the 1980 Decision

The Iranian oil crisis that erupted in 1979 can best be defined as a supply crisis. Within the country, political upheaval was the main factor leading to sharp declines in Iranian oil production. From December 1978 to March 1979, Iranian petroleum workers went on strike and oil production all but ceased. In September of 1978, Iranian oil production had reached a peak of 6 million bpd. However, it soon started to decline to 5.5 million bpd in October, to 3.5 million bpd in November, to 2.3 million bpd in December, and to its lowest level in January 1979 at 700,000 bpd. Hardly enough was left to export, although in 1979, following the success of the Islamic Revolution, the country's average oil production increased to 3 million bpd. Iranian oil production had therefore shrunk to half its peak amount within a year (Seymour, 1980: 182). To compensate for this reduction, other OPEC producers expanded production by 2 million bpd. Non-OPEC producers expanded their own production by 1 million bpd. Still, the net reduction in global oil production at that time was estimated to be 3.7 percent (El-Mallakh, 1982a: 91). Although the supply situation itself was not considered serious, panic among oil consumers (i.e., international oil companies and OECD countries) affected spot prices. Indeed, in their anticipation of oil shortages, OECD governments and international oil companies scrambled to further increase their stocks; thus created was a temporary situation of excess demand, which, in turn, resulted in skyrocketing spot prices for OPEC crude oil. For example, the price of Arabian Light marker crude[2] on the Rotterdam spot market—which had been $13.00 per barrel (pb) in October 1978—rose steadily, reached its peak in November 1979 at $40.00 pb, and stabilized at an average of $36.00 pb in spring 1980. In short, spot prices, from the beginning of the Iranian oil crisis up until the 1980 decision had been the subject of an increase of 177 percent.

The World Oil Glut and the 1982 Decision

In the spring of 1980, a soft market replaced the previous tight market and a demand crisis emerged, thereby creating excess oil supplies. World oil demand dropped to 36.8 million bpd, the equivalent of the demand that had prevailed in 1972. This decline in world oil demand was attributed to three factors: the economic recession in OECD countries, energy conservation and substitution, and oil destocking in OECD countries. As a result of the residual nature of the demand for OPEC oil, fluctuation in world demand for oil affected exclusively the same demand for OPEC oil. Therefore, OPEC output fell from 31.3 million bpd in 1979 to 16.3 million bpd in April 1982. This decline in demand led to excess supplies in OPEC oil and brought downward prices for OPEC oil. For example, in February 1982, the spot market price for Arabian Light marker crude fell to $28.50 per barrel.

DECISION PLANNING AND PARTICIPANTS

The direct participants in the decisions of 1980 and 1982 were, of course, OPEC's members, whose economic conditions and development plans were affected—to varying degrees—by the state of the international oil market. As previously noted, in a tightening oil market such as the one that prevailed during the Iranian oil crisis, the development plans of the member countries are generally revived in the light of increasing oil revenues. But as the oil market softens, the same plans are usually postponed because of the loss of forecast revenues. But some OPEC members (Algeria or Nigeria as opposed to, say, Saudi Arabia or the UAE) are more hard pressed than others—a fact that is bound to influence the collective decision-making process in its different stages.

The Iranian Oil Crisis and the 1980 Decision

In the face of market forces, OPEC members generally tend to react individually and to make uncoordinated decisions at variance with one another. For instance, in the face of increases in spot prices, both the UAE and Qatar in February 1979 imposed and implemented surcharges of up to $1.00 on their crude prices. Libya subsequently raised its own by $0.68; Kuwait, Iraq, and Oman did the same with increases ranging from $1.20 to $1.02 (Seymour, 1980: 186). Further increases by OPEC members followed in May and June of the same year.

To limit the chaos, OPEC had to intervene. OPEC oil ministers met twice in Geneva in March and June 1979 to set an OPEC price structure. During these conferences, most OPEC member countries (i.e., Iran, Iraq, the UAE, Kuwait, and Venezuela, and the producer countries in Africa) favored increases in their official crude prices and did indeed increase them. Saudi Arabia, concerned with the recessive impact the oil price increases were having on OECD economies, unsuccessfully attempted to resist these increases by imposing price ceilings. The OPEC oil ministers meeting on price policies in Caracas, Venezuela, in December 1979 broke up in disarray. During the conference, Saudi Arabia's attempts to reunify prices were counterbalanced by steady increases in crude oil prices implemented by the "maximalists/hawks"—notably, African producers and Iran—throughout the spring of 1980. In May 1980, during the Fifty-sixth

Extraordinary OPEC Conference, Saudi Arabia attempted once again to halt this upward movement of prices for crude oil. Its initiative failed badly as prices continued to rise.

The following figures illustrate the upward trend of official crude oil prices. In the spring of 1980, Iranian crude oil was selling at $35.00 pb, Libyan crude oil at $34.72 pb, and UAE crude oil at $29.00 pb. However, the official selling price of Saudi Arabia's crude oil was as low as $28.00 pb at the time it was being sold on the spot market at $35.00 pb.

Throughout the latter part of 1978 until the spring of 1980, Saudi Arabia increased its oil output to guarantee oil supplies to OECD economies and to avert price increases. By proposing price ceilings, Saudi Arabia's primary objective was to stabilize the OPEC price structure. Saudi Arabia's stance was "moderate" and "conciliatory." It had attempted to avoid a disruption of the economies of the OECD countries. The resulting pro-Western behavior of Saudi Arabia was triggered by the dependent position of Saudi Arabia's economy on OECD economies and by the political rapprochement between both parties (i.e., the government of Saudi Arabia and OECD governments). Saudi Arabia's dependent position with respect to OECD economies has many facets: commercial (pertaining to imports of industrial goods from OECD countries); technological (concerning imports of the OECD know-how for its capital-intensive petrochemical industries); military (in 1977 Saudi Arabia bought $18 billion worth of armaments from the United States); and many others (Sid-Ahmed, 1980: 255). In addition, Saudi Arabia, like other OPEC members, relies on the OECD countries to be the main customers for their crude oil. Moreover, given the geopolitics of the Middle East, Saudi Arabia has maintained a stance of political rapprochement with OECD countries as a function of its desire to bolster anti-Communist and antirevolutionary feelings within the kingdom.

The World Oil Glut and the 1982 Decision

At the OPEC Conference held in Geneva during the month of May 1981, a concerted effort was made among the member countries to reunify prices and to reduce oil surplus on the international oil market. The majority of OPEC member countries, Saudi Arabia, Iraq, and Iran excepted, agreed to cut their oil production by 10 percent. In a gesture of good will, Saudi Arabia followed suit in September 1979 and reduced its oil output from 10.3 million bpd to 9.95 million bpd. In October its production further declined to 8.5 million bpd. World demand for oil deteriorated throughout 1981 to 1982 because of the U.S. and Western European economic recession and the off-loading of excess stocks. Consequently, the demand for OPEC oil in February 1982 amounted to only 20 million bpd, contrary to a forecast of 23 million bpd. In response to this glut situation, which had brought spot prices down, Iran cut its crude oil prices by about $4 pb in order to sell at more competitive prices. But the downward pressure on prices continued as the spot market price for Arabian Light marker crude fell to $28.50 pb, whereas the official government price for the same crude was still $34.00 pb. In late February 1982, Britain greatly reduced its crude oil prices, thereby directly affecting the spot prices of similar quality oil produced by Algeria, Libya, and Nigeria.

Nigeria reacted by giving notice to other OPEC member countries that it would have to follow suit and decrease its official crude oil price. A few days before the Sixty-third Extraordinary Meeting of the OPEC Conference (March 1982), Libya accused Saudi Arabia of flooding the world oil market. Other member countries wanted Saudi Arabia to further reduce its oil production so that they could maintain or increase their share of the oil market without being forced to reduce their prices.

But Saudi Arabia championed another procedure. At the beginning of March 1982—that is, just prior to the convening of the Conference—a plan to give financial aid to Nigeria and Venezuela was agreed upon at a meeting in Qatar of OPEC's seven Arab members. The aims of this aid were to encourage the two countries not to cut their oil prices and to undermine OPEC's official pricing structure. Both countries were faced with heavy debts and a shortage of customers because of the oil glut. Under the influence of Saudi Arabia they were thus offered loans and grants to compensate for any loss of revenues that resulted from holding their prices steady.

DECISION FORMULATION

Active in the formulation of both decisions were OPEC's organs: the Conference, the Board of Governors, and the Secretariat through its various reports. The locus of decision-making was invariably the Conference itself.

The Fifty-seventh Ordinary Meeting of the OPEC Conference (Algiers, June 9-11, 1980) intended to allow for cooperation among the OPEC member countries to restore mutually and unanimously a renewed and stable OPEC price structure. It succeeded. The Sixty-third Extraordinary Meeting of the OPEC Conference held in Vienna, Austria (March 19-20, 1982), intended to allow among the OPEC member countries the cooperation required to reduce mutually and unanimously OPEC total oil output in order to alleviate the state of glut and maintain a stable OPEC price structure. It succeeded as well. Furthermore, both OPEC meetings enabled the OPEC member countries to achieve the principal objectives these countries had set for themselves as outlined in articles 1 and 2 of the Statute of OPEC.

The divergent positions held by delegates during both OPEC meetings reflected the varying politico-economic conditions of individual member countries. Moreover, Saudi Arabia's attachment to "moderation" and "stability" was evident throughout the negotiations. Indeed, Saudi Arabia managed to maintain a certain level of stability with respect to crude oil prices during the Iranian oil crisis.

The Iranian Oil Crisis and the 1980 Decision

During the Fifty-seventh Meeting of the OPEC Conference in Algiers (June 9-11 1980), delegates discussed the Report of the Economic Commission Board (from its fifty-first session) on short-term pricing policies. Notwithstanding this solid information and data base, the delegates became divided during the discussion. The "moderates/doves," who were led by Saudi Arabia, faced the "maximalists/hawks" such as Iran, Libya, and Algeria. The intermediate position was championed by Kuwait and Iraq. Production levels and price differentials of crude oil were the two key issues dividing the officials of OPEC member countries at the conference meeting. The negotiations between member countries during the debates went as follows. Tayeh Abdul-Karim, head of the delegation of Iraq, proposed a $32.00 pb benchmark price and called on OPEC's biggest producers to cut their productions in order to avoid a future oil glut. Several other producers rallied behind Iraq: Dr. Sabroto, head of the delegation of Indonesia; Abdul Aziz Bin Khalifa Al-Thani, head of the delegation of Qatar; and Ezzedin Ali Mabruk, head of the delegation of the Libyan Arab Republic.

Ali Akbar Maimfar, head of the delegation of Iran, proposed that the level of OPEC oil production be restored to the previous level of 1978 and, toward this end, demanded that Saudi Arabia and Iraq reduce their respective productions. Iran wanted to regain its share of the OPEC market in oil supply, a share it had partially lost to Saudi Arabia and Iraq during the political unrest of 1979. It agreed to cut its own production on one condition—that prices, mainly those pertaining to Arabian oil, be increased.

In response to the Iranian position, Ahmed Zaki Yamani, head of the delegation of Saudi Arabia, stated that his country was unwilling to consider any production cuts unless a unified OPEC price structure was restored. Yamani also insisted that Arabian oil prices be increased on the sole condition that the producers of higher-priced crude oil reduce their own prices. However, African producers such as Libya, Nigeria, and Algeria did not agree to a reduction of their high-quality-oil prices.

Three days of debate, negotiation, and compromise led to a unanimous decision that was effective as of July 1, 1980: (1) to set a price ceiling of $32.00 per barrel crude; (2) to require that the value differentials to be added over and above the said ceiling on the marker crude price level of $32.00 on account of quality and geographical location should not in any case exceed $5.00 per barrel; and (3) to require that this price structure would be applicable as of July 1, 1980 (OPEC Bulletin, July 1980: 2).

This new price structure aimed primarily at achieving an equilibrium between supply and demand in order to avoid further stockpiling, which would have been harmful to both producers and consumers. This decision came nearest to a compromise among the opposing views of the delegates, for it achieved an increase in the benchmark price to $32.00 pb, with Saudi Arabia keeping its crude oil price at $28.00, Nigeria and Libya lowering their crude oil prices to $37.00 pb, and Algeria and Iran setting their prices at $35.00 pb. Overall prices were thus stabilized within a flexible OPEC price structure. It is interesting to note that the benchmark price of $32.00 pb was still lower than the spot price of Arabian Light marker crude, which was traded at $36.00 pb at the time of the decision. Furthermore, an agreement was reached in regard to production levels: Each member country was to examine its respective output and determine whether cuts were necessary (*Wall Street Journal*, 11 June 1980: 2).

The World Oil Glut and the 1982 Decision

As noted earlier, the lowering of production and/or price levels is usually a painful decision for the majority of OPEC members. In the spring of 1982, as many as nine OPEC members did not produce enough oil to meet their domestic budgetary requirements, and they could not afford to cut back their production. Furthermore, Algeria and Iraq needed higher, rather than lower, oil revenues; Venezuela and Nigeria, on the other hand, had a heavy debt burden. Nigeria, with its large population, heavy commitments, and high absorption of oil revenues, was the worst affected by the glut.

The first day of the meeting (March 19, 1982) was given over to an informal consultation among oil ministers in the suite of conference chairman Mana Said Otaiba, minister of petroleum and mineral resources of the UAE. But this informal consultation soon degenerated into a heated and tense debate among the delegates over the question of allowable levels of oil production for each country. Arguments boiled down to the issue of how to distribute among the members a further reduction of 500,000 barrels per day.

In the end, however, Saudi Arabia, Kuwait, and the UAE had to bail out with financial assistance those countries worst affected by the enforced reductions in oil production. Saudi Arabia carried the heaviest burden of cuts in oil production in order to enable OPEC's members to reach agreements on allowable levels of oil production for each country. In return, Saudi Arabia's bargaining position and influence was strengthened during the Conference.

The Conference examined the current situation and decided to reconfirm the price of Arabian Light marker crude at $32.00 per barrel, as decided at the Sixty-first Extraordinary Meeting of the OPEC Conference (Geneva, October 29, 1981). Accordingly, the delegates decided to take the necessary measures for stabilizing the market. For this purpose, it was decided that, as of April 1, 1982, the total OPEC production would have a ceiling of 18 million bpd, and that this ceiling would be reviewed at the next meeting of the Conference in the light of market developments (OPEC Bulletin, May 1982).

OPEC total production at the time of the Conference was 19 million bpd. The majority of OPEC member countries blamed Saudi Arabia for the then-current oil surplus and for the related downward pressure on prices. The same majority agreed that Saudi Arabia could put an end to the glut by implementing a substantial cut in its production.

Market circumstances also pressed such member countries as Nigeria and Iran to reduce oil prices, thereby leading to a determined effort by twelve of the OPEC member countries (i.e., with the exception of Saudi Arabia) to resist the market pressure. This resistance was to be achieved through a large reduction in total OPEC oil production, the major portion of which would come from Saudi Arabia. Members, such as Nigeria, with balance-of-payments deficits and pressing financial needs were the last to compromise on this issue.

After three days of debate, negotiation, and compromise, the member countries agreed on March 20 to set a production ceiling of 18 million bpd—a reduction of 1 million bpd. The barrels-per-day quotas agreed upon were these (in millions of barrels): Iraq 1.2, Iran 1.2, Saudi Arabia 1.5, Kuwait 0.65, Neutral Zone (Kuwait) 0.3, UAE 1.2, Qatar 0.3, Nigeria 1.3, Libya 0.75, Algeria 0.65, Venezuela 1.5, Indonesia 1.3, Ecuador 0.2, and Gabon 0.15 (Field, 1982: 120).

Saudi Arabia further reduced its oil output by 500,000 bpd. The then-current price structure based on a $34.00 pb price for Arabian Light marker crude was maintained, although North African producers of high-quality crude oil were permitted to reduce their respective prices (*Newsweek*, 29 March 1982: 64).

THE IMPLEMENTATION OF THE DECISIONS

What can be said about the implementation of the 1980 and 1982 decisions? As previously noted, the Board of Governors, nominated by member countries and confirmed by the Conference for two years, implements the decisions and resolutions of the Conference and manages the affairs of the organization. However, the Board is not empowered with the legal and executory authority to impose the Conference's decisions on member countries. The implementation of OPEC's decisions rests entirely upon the member countries themselves and on the forces of the world market. We see here the manifestation of the primacy of state sovereignty and the subordination of supranational authority.

But to return to the specific decisions under study, September 1980 saw the loosening of the tight market and OPEC succeeded in achieving price unification with a single price of $30.00 per barrel for Arabian Light marker crude. But this success, due primarily to market fluctuations, was offset by the outbreak of the Iran-Iraq War. To attenuate the impact of market forces, OPEC delegates at the Vienna 1982 meeting established a committee (composed of the president of OPEC, Mana Said Otaiba, and the oil ministers of Algeria, Indonesia, and Venezuela) designed to monitor market conditions and guarantee compliance by OPEC Members with the quotas agreed upon at the Vienna meeting.

The Ministerial Committee held its first meeting in Vienna on April 21, 1982, considered a report prepared by marketing experts from the OPEC member countries on the current oil market situation, and formulated a series of recommendations that were then presented to and reviewed by OPEC's oil ministers during the Sixty-fourth Meeting of the OPEC Conference held in Pinto on May 20-21, 1982. In examining the market situation, the Conference also reviewed the report of the Fifty-sixth Meeting of the Economic Commission Board.

The OPEC quota system was effective for some time, as evidenced by Saudi Arabia's lowering of production to 6.6 million barrels a day. However, the prolonged state of glut permitted the downward pressure on prices to continue, and by September 1984 the spot price for Arabian Light marker crude was no more than $27.94 per barrel. If this trend continues, as it will likely do over the short run, OPEC member countries will have to meet again and resume their debates concerning reduction of official prices and/or output.

CONCLUSIONS

To understand OPEC's decision-making process, one must keep an eye on world market forces, OPEC's internal power structure, and especially the linkages between them. The preceding analysis of the two sets of decisions under study indicates that the OPEC decision-making process with regard to oil prices and output policies is aimed at restoring equilibrium between demand and output in the international oil market. OPEC brought about this equilibrium by counterbalancing movements in spot prices with official oil price and output policies. Accordingly, OPEC oil price and output policies sought the stabilization of a unified international oil price structure, the survival of OPEC as a credible organization, a certain predictability in the oil revenues, and the execution of the development plans of the member countries. The member countries, however, faced serious odds against attaining these objectives. Because state sovereignty—as opposed to a coordinated OPEC supranational authority—is still at the basis of OPEC's decisions and their implementation, the organization has come to be increasingly on the defensive. Faced with an oil glut, for instance, the member countries have tended to undercut each other.

Compared to the 1960s, which witnessed the birth of OPEC, and the 1970s, during which its strength was established, the 1980s have been marked by the organization's relative decline. Its share of world oil production dropped from 68 percent in 1976 to only 46 percent at the end of 1982, and its financial resources went from a peak of $109 billion in 1980 to a deficit of $18 billion in 1982 (*Time*, 7 February 1983: 34-38). It would be premature, however, to conclude that OPEC is soon to disappear. On the contrary, given the current world energy situation, OPEC is more likely here to stay.

NOTES

1. Official or posted prices are set by OPEC members while dealing with international oil companies, whereas spot prices are set on international markets such as Rotterdam according to the ratio between demand and supply.

2. OPEC's marker crude is the Arabian Light crude (from Saudi Arabia) with a 34° API (American Petroleum Institute) grading. Each crude oil is given an API degree rating in relation to its specific gravity compared to that of water.

BIBLIOGRAPHICAL NOTE

Little in the way of systematic analysis is available in English or French on the decision-making of nonstate international actors, whether they be international organizations, multinational companies, or nonstate national actors (e.g., the pre-1962 Algerian Provisional Government). Fortunately, we *can* refer to Cox and Jacobson's pioneering study (1972), with its emphasis on an explicit framework for comparative analysis and its rigorous data collection. Feld and Jordan (1983) have provided a good, straightforward introduction to the general subject of international organizations, including a chapter on decision-making. And Mansbach et al. (1976) have offered an introduction (from a behavioralist/quantitative point of view) to the whole subject of nonstate actors, but without a specific focus on decision-making itself.

Even less information exists on the subject of OPEC's decision-making processes per se. Such information is not only widely dispersed but largely unrecorded to begin with, as systematic data are hard to come by. Nevertheless, OPEC's various publications constitute an effective source of information, especially on the institutional and formal aspects of OPEC's decision-making. The works by Ajomo (1977), Al-Sowayegh (1984), Fesharaki and Isaak (1983), Mikdashi (1976), and Seymour (1980) are also very useful. The volume edited by Vernon (1976), in which Mikdashi's chapter appears, provides an excellent introduction to the global energy context and especially the crisis of the mid-1970s, whereas Peterson's book (1983) offers a multifaceted tour d'horizon with very functional appendices.

The scrutiny of the press, and of good "best-seller" journalistic accounts such as that of Sampson (1976), is essential to grasp the informal dimension of OPEC's decision-making. The reader may wish to turn first to Quandt's two studies on Saudi Arabia (1981, 1982) and Cordesman's voluminous one (1984) for an effective introduction to the important role played by Saudi Arabia in OPEC decision-making. Finally, Sid-Ahmed's work (1980) provides a good political-economy account both of OPEC as an actor in the global system and of the economic characteristics and social dynamics of its members.

7

THE FINDINGS, THE TWO ASIAN GIANTS, AND DECISION-MAKING THEORY

Bahgat Korany

INTRODUCTION

This last chapter attempts to pull the threads together and to draw some conclusions that may serve as the foundation for future research and analysis. Accordingly, the first section evaluates the findings of the different chapters in the light of the book's objectives as enumerated in the Preface, especially the attempt to balance psychological reductionism by bringing in "objective" or "real life" factors. The findings are formulated into three general propositions.

This emphasis on "objective" factors is continued in the second and third sections, in which two levels of analysis, the state-societal and the global, are illustrated by two case studies, those of China and India respectively. Data from these studies indicate that the black box of Third World society has to be opened and that national-international linkages must be emphasized. Moreover, China's case is discussed in connection with the various attempts at a definition of the Third World presented in Chapter 1 of this book.

The conclusions open avenues for future research by indicating how we may exploit and integrate the different conceptualizations available at present. Consequently, the emphasis is not only on decision-making as a group activity, but also on how group networks and patron-client relationships connect the different levels of analysis. Thus, a decision is analyzed as part, rather than instead, of the decision-making group, which in turn reflects the characteristics of "national" social processes and is also linked to the global system at large. Briefly, we need to reorient our state-centric frame of reference and instead think of state borders not as

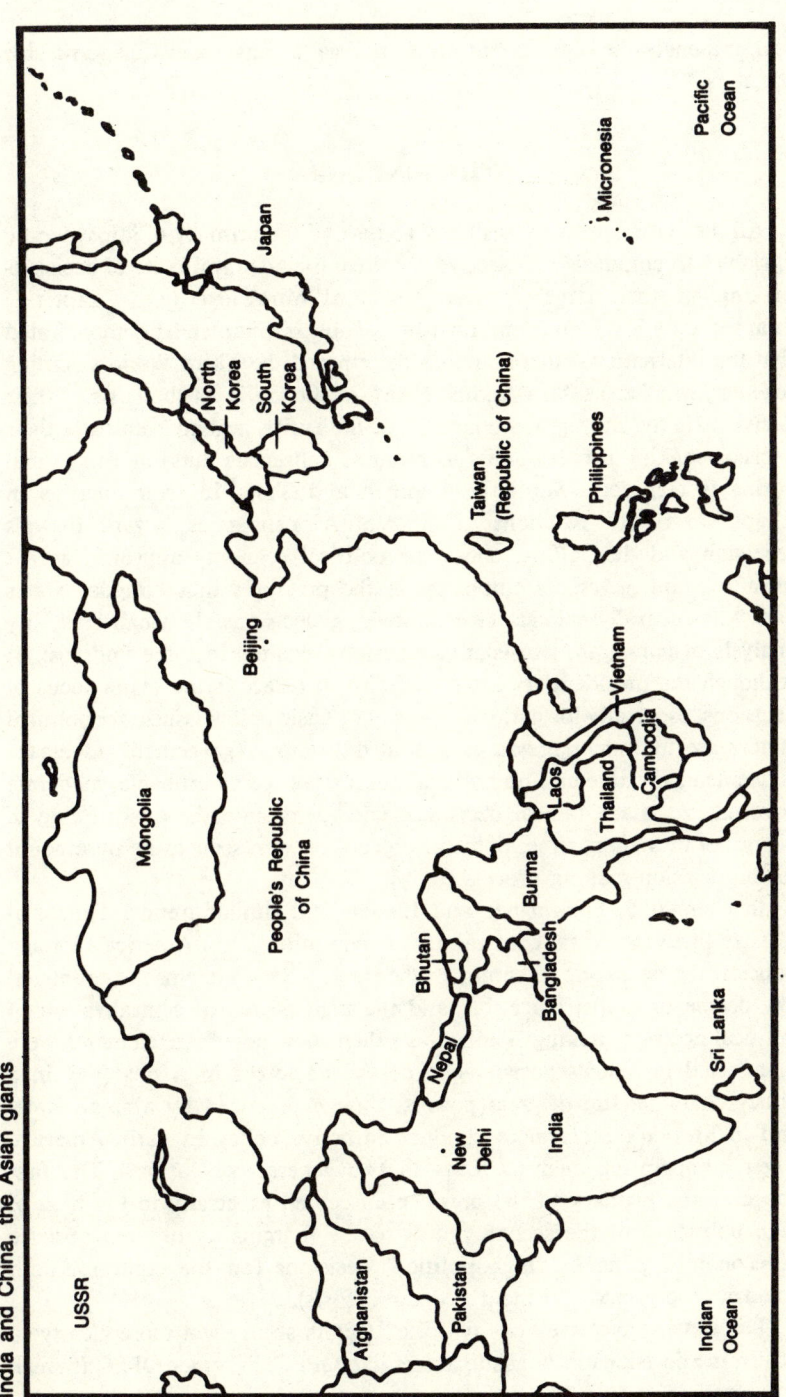

India and China, the Asian giants

real, impenetrable barriers but rather as legal arrangements for permeable societies.

THE FINDINGS

All the contributors to this book go beyond the primacy of idiosyncratic variables to emphasize "objective" or "real life" determinants of decision-making, whether at the collective all–Third World level (e.g., Chapter 1) or at the actor level (state and nonstate). Thus, in Chapter 1 I demonstrated that the international hierarchy has determined the Third World's coming together, whether as Afro-Asians, NAM, or the G-77. At the basis of their decisions is the multigroup character of the entity, and consequently their decision-making process tends to promote consensus building (no formal voting is recorded). Similarly, Daddieh and Shaw, in their analysis in Chapter 3 of the reactions of different African states toward Biafra's secession and the MPLA, chose the political economy approach as the most relevant, given its emphasis on the pressures that "fragile" states and "dependent" societies face in making decisions. In Chapter 4, my analysis of pan-Arab, pan-Islamic decisions resulted in three findings: (1) Although the presidential center or the royal palace is the major locus of decisions, especially for national security or basic policy issues, geopolitical factors are the major pressures behind decisions; (2) when the adversary is deemed inflexible and no political alternative seems probable, moderate governments make radical decisions; and (3) despite the quadrupling of oil prices in a short time, political objectives were seen to be paramount in the decision-making process.

In Chapter 5, Domínguez and Lindau find similar trends. They emphasize three structural constraints that condition Latin America's foreign policies: the persisting hierarchy of the international system, the countries' low degree of industrialization, and the high degree of centralization of political decision-making. The authors then show how these elements were manifested in Cuba's decisions to deploy its forces in Africa (i.e., in a policy characteristic of great powers, though practiced by a small state) and in Mexico's decision to conduct an active policy in Latin America. Their comparative analysis leads to two general conclusions: The first concerns the primacy of the presidential center, especially in the field of high politics, and the second points to the marginality or even absence of economic gains in "high politics" decisions (on the contrary, both countries were ready to incur economic costs).

The same "objective" or "real life" factors seem even more clearly to determine decisions in nonstate actors like OPEC. Whether OPEC is weak or strong, its decisions to determine the level of both output and prices are dominated by global system characteristics. When OPEC was weak, member countries were at the mercy of multinational oil companies. With nationalization and the increasing strength of OPEC in an energy-hungry world, OPEC's decisions are dominated by the state of the world market. This situation is even more obvious when OPEC has to make decisions to reduce oil output and/or prices during a world glut. Then OPEC member countries start to undercut each other, and OPEC's internal power structure (e.g., Saudi Arabia as a swing producer) functions smoothly but firmly. OPEC decisions are thus determined by the interaction among global factors, the characteristics of the organization's member countries, and their formal and informal power structure. The stipulation of a formal veto power in OPEC contradicts the emphasis on consensus building in all–Third World–level organizations. This might be due to the emphasis on the specific and economic character of OPEC. The decision-making process is similarly based on the presence of many groups and bargaining among them. Moreover, OPEC's formal voting procedures notwithstanding, the informal power structure seems to achieve a consensus of sorts.

The conclusions of the chapters in this book were arrived at independently, without prior consultation among the authors. This situation comes close to the reproducibility of findings so desired in the social sciences and, we hope, increases their reliability. Hence these findings can be expressed in proposition form: *Objective or "real life" factors, as distinct from the psychological traits of leaders, are primary in decision-making.*

This proposition strikes at the basis of established decision-making theory in foreign policy analysis, for one of the ongoing debates in the field is whether a country's foreign policy consists of conscious or isolatable decisions (White, 1978: 158). In other words, can one understand the whole of a country's foreign policy through the isolated analysis of one or two key decisions? The contributors to this book all independently answered this question with a resounding "No." All of them oriented the analysis of their specific decisions within the context of each country's general foreign policy. Moreover, Chapter 1 emphasizes the general context of the Third World so that the specific national or actor context of each set of decisions can be properly situated. Accordingly, as Wallace (1975) concluded after his analysis of Britain's foreign policy process, "the process of policy-making is less one of a series of discrete and identifiable decisions than a continuous flow of policy."

We should not be satisfied with a mere widening of the analysis of decisions to be integrated in the foreign policy process, the politics of policy-making à la Allison, and the bureaucratic politics model. Indeed, we must also embrace the determinants emanating from the society at large and reflecting its characteristics. In other words, foreign policy decisions (though they constitute an elitist operation that takes place behind closed doors) form only the tip of the iceberg and cannot be confined to the superstructure of state or society. The psychological school has limited itself to this aspect in its most extreme form, but the bureaucratic politics approach attempts to broaden the process while still continuing to separate bureaucratic bargaining from the wider processes of conflict and bargaining among different groups in the society at large. The critique of such perspectives leads, then, to a second proposition: *Both foreign policy decisions and the foreign policy process as a whole are part and parcel of the wider social process reflecting the characteristics of Third World permeable societies and their subordinate position in the global system.*

Chapter 1 not only focused attention on both internal characteristics of the Third World and its subordinate international position in the global hierarchy, but it also used these two dimensions to define the Third World itself. The chapter also claimed that the same two dimensions are at the basis of Third World togetherness, or Third Worldism. Even in the case of such a "powerful" actor as OPEC, these two aspects—especially the global one—have shaped its decision-making process and determined its decision. This global dimension is also the one most emphasized in this volume by Daddieh and Shaw, whereas Domínguez and Lindau focused on both the dominance of the global level and the low industrialization of Latin American societies, with all the ramifications these situations entail.

Paradoxically, an emphasis on the societal dimension of both the foreign policy process and of decision-making allows us also to reassess the impact of the leader—but in his or her proper place and keeping always in mind his or her specific (rather than all-embracing) significance. For if it is absurd to reduce the entire decision-making process to the leader's psychological traits or the individual's idiosyncrasies, it is equally absurd to exclude him or her altogether. Cybernetic approaches notwithstanding (Deutsch, 1963; Steinbruner, 1974), politics is, after all, a human activity; hence individual leaders should be assigned their proper places and their specific significance.

The question of the leader's impact on decision-making is all the more compelling, indeed, in societies such as those of the Third World, where old institutions have often been discredited or uprooted by colonial invasions and new alternatives have not yet been fully elaborated or integrated into the postcolonial state. Institutions (parliament, cabinet, constitution) do of course exist and may even proliferate; yet there is an absence of effective institutional checks on the leader. We fall into a contemporary form of the patrimonial state structure when, according to

Max Weber, "the prince organizes his political power over extra-patrimonial areas and political subjects . . . just like the exercise of his patriarchal power" (see Weber, 1978: 1007; and Callaghy, 1984, for the most recent and detailed application of patrimonialism to Zaire). In short, the exercise of patriarchal power entails the privatization of the state around the leader and his (or her) staff—*la monarchie présidentielle.*

Accordingly, the attaching of important status to the royal palace or the presidential center is thus very different from focusing on the leader as an individual atom whose "images" or "relations with his mother" are analyzed in order to reduce all the country's social complexity to this psychological level. On the contrary, the preceding analysis deals with the leader and his mode of action as part of the Third World situation, with all its socioeconomic traits of underdevelopment and its political consequences of institutional vacuum or corporatist state structures. In short, the leader is analyzed in conjunction with—rather than instead of—this Third World situation.

Other groups and individuals (national and foreign) participate formally or informally, directly or indirectly, in the decision-making process to promote specific views and shape the ultimate decision. This participation can take place by "having the king's or president's ear," by co-opting the leader, or by exercising pressure and withholding the resources necessary for carrying out a given decision. These different pressures and inducements may shape the decision's objectives, its form, and its timing—which brings us to our third proposition: *The head of state may be the sole decision-taker, but he or she is not the sole decision-maker.*

In other words, the process of decision-making is much more complicated than the literature on the Third World may lead us to believe. Therefore, we must go beyond the formal *taking* of decisions (i.e., formalizing the choices already made by others) to analyze the much more intricate process of *making* the decision. Even in the face of bureaucratic weakness and a lack of institutional checks, this latter process might still involve so much information (and misinformation), so many groups (whether internal or external, formal or informal), and so many constraints (external debts, military and/or food dependencies, and internal ethnic trouble or ethnic fractionalization) that the leader's latitude becomes extremely limited, inasmuch as many of the plausible or preferred options are practically excluded. Before the leader has the chance to decide something, a large part of the decision is already channeled in a certain way—in fact, made but not taken.

By analogy, it might be said that when one is in a Chinese restaurant, one cannot logically insist on ordering a pizza. The choices available are limited by the menu—a menu that, in our larger context, has been worked and reworked by a myriad of advisers, cronies, clique networks, social connections, and of course global constraints.

This distinction between decision-making and decision-taking in the intricate process of political outcome could protect us from going to the other extreme, away from psychological reductionism to exclude altogether the role of the individual leader. Indeed, it may even help us to integrate the existing body of theory into the analysis of Third World decision-making.

To bridge the gap between decision theory and social analysis, we will utilize two levels of analysis—the state-societal and the global-systemic. The first of these is based on groups, albeit informal ones, and the empirical example chosen to substantiate this idea is the case of China. The second level concerns the postcolonial state, a permeable one whose frontiers are legal arrangements rather than real barriers between what goes inside and outside the state. The case in point is that of India, especially its 1966 decision to devalue the rupee. Data collected by Brecher, that prolific pillar of the psychological-perceptual school, will be reanalyzed to demonstrate the primacy of global-systemic constraints.

The choice of China and India is a deliberate one. First, the Asian states have not figured prominently in this book except at the collective decision-making level (see Chapters 1 and 4). But more important, if communism has been portrayed in the literature as the most totalitarian or monolithic system of politics and then was shown here to possess a multigroup political process, this multigroup aspect would be even more characteristic of non-Communist systems. Moreover, if such a "big power" of the Third World as India is penetrated by global constraints, then what of Benin, Yemen, or Guyana? If these global constraints are demonstrated through the reanalysis of data collected within the psychological-perceptual frame of reference, the importance of systemic-global constraints will be doubly driven home.

THE COMPLEX POLITICAL PROCESS AND CHINA'S CASE

The inclusion of China's case in this book may remind some readers of the debate in the first few pages about the Third World's defining characteristics; for others, the inclusion of China as a part of the Third World might be controversial. As it falls at the intersection between "Communist Studies" and "Third World Studies," China is not fully accepted in either category.

Regarding the categorization of China as a Third World country, it has been argued that its population of 1 billion makes it a world of its own rather than a part of the Third World; that its "aligned" ideology has separated it from the (nonaligned) Third World and integrated it into one of the cold war ideological camps; and that its permanent seat in the UN Security Council has put it in the company of the great powers against which the Third World stands opposed.

But many of these aspects could be interpreted differently. Although the population issue is very real, the defining factor is quality (health standards, nutrition, literacy), not quantity. Thus, for instance, the impact of its population places tiny Switzerland in a much more advantageous position than China. Moreover, if India's 700 million people are accepted as part of the Third World, why not the Chinese? The objection against inclusion of the latter might be influenced more by China's "Communist" ideology than by any other concern, but, as we noted with respect to the Bandung Conference, even China's most vehement critics were emphasizing the differences between China's Asian communism and the Soviet/East European brand even before the Sino-Soviet conflict had developed. These differences render the conflict between Beijing and Moscow more of a structural divergence than a passing political antagonism. One might even go further to say that China is perhaps more "nonaligned" in relation to the two cold war blocs than is Cuba, and that China's emphasis on the primacy of North/South bipolarity has placed it in the company of the quasi-totality of Third World countries. Concerning its permanent seat on the Security Council, Taiwan occupied it for more than two decades without ever being suspected of resembling one of the "Great Powers." Thus a distinction should be made between historical antecedents (if not accidents) and evolving political realities. Even if it is not part of NAM (as is Vietnam, for instance), China played a major role at Bandung and in 1983 organized jointly with the Third World Foundation the South-South Conference to emphasize its integration with these countries. Last but not least, and without mentioning China's "colonial" past, we might point to the standard indicators of underdevelopment and vulnerability— that is, the level of housing and other social services, illiteracy, ratio of rural to urban population, level of technology, and terms of trade—to convince any visitor to China that it is not all that different from neighboring Third World countries.

The objections boil down to the claim that China, being "Communist," is much more "authoritarian," "totalitarian," and "monolithic" than the rest of the Third World. But, as in the study of other Third World countries, this claim is really based on the misconception that if groups are not formally present, they do not exist. Of course, social groups need not be formal; they can be quite informal. In fact—and this is precisely one characteristic of Third World societies—the presence of such informal groups is the product both of underdevelopment and of the colonial intrusion that interrupted the "normal" evolution of these societies. Formal institutions are generally imported from the outside and superficially imposed on existing indigenous structures, but without replacing them. The result is a hybrid society whose fabric and politics become mingled with ties of kinship, marriage, patronage, and clientalism (Gellner and Waterbury, 1977; Lemieux, 1977; Schmidt et al., 1977; Graziano, 1983). The politics here is in great part the one of "friends of friends," of cliques and factions, at different levels in the social hierarchy (Graham, 1968).

In the case of China, it was the arrival of the cultural revolution that liberated "China Studies" from the Mao-in-command orthodoxy. The publication of material written by the Red Guards revealed that Mao was not always the undisputed leader in command, and, in fact, that the Chinese Communist party (CCP) was dominated by factions (Nathan, 1973; Chang, 1976; Harding, 1984) and informal groups (Tsou, 1976). These groups may or may not have had a shared ideological brand, but they did share common goals and interests and were usually recruited by a leader (cf. Graham's one rallying bee in the social hierarchy characteristic of the kingdom of bees).

Indeed, an analysis even of official publications of the CCP shows that Communist leaders have assumed in their own conceptualization the "two-line" struggle ("leftists" versus "rightists," "radicals" versus "moderates"). In fact, much of the history of the CCP shows that decisions reflect the victory of one group over another (Tsou, 1976: 105-106).

Tiewes (1979) focused on the different purges of every major party leader, purges that, according to him, characterized Chinese politics. Similarly, Pye (1981) tested the different political theories against the pattern of Chinese politics in the late 1970s and found that factionalism was the most relevant. Indeed, an analysis of factions such as the Gang of Four, rural or military cadres, and economic planners provides revealing insights into Chinese political culture and modes of decision-making. In the same vein, Ra'anan (1968) and Zagoria (1968) analyzed the Chinese press during 1965 and 1966 to show how three factions (the military professionals, the civilian bureaucrats, and the Maoists) continued to exist in the face of U.S. escalation in Vietnam and how the first two coalesced against the third.

It is by examining group dynamics that the study of Third World political process can escape two extremes of underconceptualization and irrelevant conceptualization. As Tsou (1976: 113) put it in the case of China:

> On the one hand, we must try to utilize Western social science theories and concepts to help us formulate theoretical "paradigms" or "models," fully

bearing in mind that generally speaking they are culture-bound and rooted in western political values. On the other hand, we must re-examine with utmost detachment the history of political conflicts in the CCP, beginning with a careful analysis of political actors' perceptions of the nature of their opponents and their own groups, and of the processes, rules and expected outcome of political struggle.

GLOBAL CONSTRAINTS AND INDIA'S CASE

What little has been written about India's decision-making process in the 1970s and 1980s emphasizes the Great Man (or in this case Great Woman) Theory of history. During Indira Gandhi's premiership (1966–1984, with a very short absence in 1977–1978), she served well in her role as foreign minister, closely following the example of her father, Jawaharlal Nehru (1947–1964) rather than that of her predecessor, Lal Bahadur Shastri (1964–1966). As *India Today* (15 October 1983: 32) put it, "It is no great secret that like her father before her, Mrs. Gandhi is her own foreign minister. It would be logical to assume that since all political power flows from just one source, Mrs. Gandhi, it is she who decides foreign policy." From this one might conclude that the foreign policy of India or any other Third World country is a personal matter, merely a reflection of the leader's biases, prejudices, beliefs, values, and idiosyncrasies. But even if the Parliament or the Ministry of Foreign Affairs were to be side-tracked by the prime minister, how would this take place? And would the side-tracking be successful on all occasions? What of India's Foreign Affairs Committee, which, though chaired by the prime minister, comprises the ministers of finance, defense, and food and is briefed by the foreign minister? Do the information and data provided by the Policy Planning and Review Committee play any role whatsoever in "educating" the prime minister and his or her subordinates or, at least, in making them aware of certain dimensions hitherto unknown? And after excluding the influence of all these organs and affirming that the prime minister reigns supreme, does he or she do so as a person or as a power center (i.e., with his or her own bureaucracy, advisers, and networks)? We do not have answers to these questions, but not because they do not count; rather, it is because the questions were never raised before and, hence, these factors remain unanalyzed.

However, those analysts who made the effort to widen their net beyond the chief decision-maker as a *person* have had to admit to the crucial role of advisers. Tharoor (1982: 14), for instance, writes that P. N. Haksar, Indira Gandhi's principal secretary, "used his power selectively and with discretion, . . . undoubtedly functioned as *de facto* Foreign Minister during his tenure, [and] at one point even stopped foreign policy files destined for the Prime Minister from being routed via the Foreign Minister." Moreover, it was Haksar, not Indira Gandhi, who was the chief architect of the pro-Arab policy; negotiated the New Delhi conference between India and Pakistan; conducted secret talks with Mugibur Rahman during the 1971 crisis, which saw Pakistan's dismantlement and the birth of Bangladesh; and finally formulated India's general approaches to Iran (Gundevia, 1985: 70). Thus if the influence of the Foreign Ministry bureaucracy is absent in foreign policy decision-making, it is replaced not by the head of state's whims and caprices but by the latter's own power center and social bases—in short, by his or her own brand of patronage and national/international networks. Prominent among these networks and influences are the global-systemic ones.

The central case taken to demonstrate the impact of global factors revolves around the data collected by Brecher in his impressive study (1977) of India's 1966 decision to devalue the rupee. As noted in Chapter 2, Brecher, a very prominent advocate of the psychological-perceptual school, developed his conceptualization on the basis of images and attitudinal prisms. Moreover, he applied his framework in seminal empirical studies and is now testing it worldwide in his ongoing multivolume "International Crisis Behavior Project." Yet his study of India's decision can be taken to prove, through systematic reanalysis of his data, precisely the lack of impact, if not the irrelevance, of these psychological factors.

In a secret unscheduled meeting in June 1966, the fourteen-minister Indian cabinet chaired by Mrs. Gandhi decided to devalue the rupee by 57 percent. This was the second devaluation since India's independence in 1947; the first, seventeen years before, had devalued the rupee by 36.5 percent. Because of the time span involved and, even more important, because of its magnitude, this second devaluation represented a significant decision. From one day to the next, the rupee slid from 4.76 rupees per U.S. dollar to 7.5, a drop that was bound to have an immediate effect on India's trade, on Indian students abroad, and even on the daily life of the average Indian, given the potential for prices of basic imports like food grains and kerosene (if no government subsidies were offered) to rise intolerably (as, indeed, they have done). Who, then, took the decision and why?

The actual making of this decision stretched across two premierships and directly involved a number of cabinet ministers, technocrats, and even an economics professor, as well as external representatives from the United States and especially from the World Bank and the International Monetary Fund. More specifically, Indira Gandhi (who, as previously noted, chaired the cabinet meeting in which the decision was announced) succeeded Shastri, who had died suddenly on January 11, 1966, after almost two years in office. Shastri, despite his opposition to the devaluation (either for emotional reasons or because he did not like to see the rupee lose value and thus cause hardship to the public), was prevailed upon and finally became committed to the devaluation.

When Indira Gandhi succeeded Shastri, a committee intending to submit the recommendation to devalue was already at work. This committee comprised Finance Minister S. Chaudhri, Planning Minister Ashota Mehta, and Food and Agriculture Minister C. Subramanian. These ministers were in turn advised by three highly respected technocrats: the governor of the Reserve Bank of India, P. C. Bhattacharya; the secretary of the Department of Economic Affairs in the Ministry of Finance, S. Bhoothalingham; the chief economic adviser of the Ministry of Finance, I. G. Patel; and the secretary to the prime minister, L. 'Jha, who figured prominently in the decision-making group not only as a member of the committee but also because of his direct and constant contact with the prime minister. Two other persons, at a lesser level of direct influence, also participated in the decision-making process: P. Pant, secretary of India's Planning Commission, and the internationally known professor of the Delhi School of Economics, J. N. Bhagwati, who was then also serving as an economic adviser to the Finance Ministry. In addition, India's ambassador to the United States, B. K. Nehru, performed a vital intermediary function between the International Monetary Fund and the World Bank on the one hand, and the government of India on the other (Brecher, 1977: 3). Thus the influence of the outside—if only through national intermediaries—was ever present— and at the highest levels of government. To justify their pressure, "outside" sources were arguing that the deterioration of India's economic situation was a *fact*. And, indeed, both Brecher and the Reserve Bank of India have gathered data indicating the need for opponents of devaluation to come around and reconcile themselves to the situation as it stood. According to Brecher,

> Food production had declined from 89 million tons in 1964-65 to 72 million tons in 1965-66, and per capita food availability was approximately 14.02 daily, the lowest since 1952, this despite large food imports in 1965. The index of food prices in June 1966 was 167.9, the highest ever until that year and the highest until 1973. The general price level rose 13.8 per cent in 1965-66 compared with 8.8 per cent in the preceding year and 9.4 per cent two years earlier. Industrial growth had dropped from 11 per cent during the first quarter of 1965 to zero in the last quarter. The Central Government's planned budget deficit of Rs 3 crores for 1965-66 became Rs 165 crores. And the planned budget surplus for the Third Plan period (1961-66) of Rs

410 crores was transformed into a deficit of Rs 642 crores (Brecher, 1977: 9).

The Reserve Bank of India argued along the same lines:

> The twelve months, July 1965 to June 1966, were a period of very great anxiety and strain for the Indian economy, leading finally to the devaluation of the rupee. Already the economy was suffering from inflationary pressures as a result of high levels of expenditure by the Government for defence and development financed increasingly by recourse to the banking system. The strain that the Indian economy was undergoing since July 1965 was further accentuated by two unrelated developments—conflict with Pakistan which "led to the interruption in foreign aid and thereby added to the existing difficulties in the balance of payments," and the failure of the monsoon, resulting in a severe setback in agricultural production, which also resulted in "a noticeable slowing down in the rate of growth of industrial production too" (as quoted by Brecher, 1977: 9).

It is precisely the failure of partial measures and other devices to arrest the economic decline that accounts for the fact that India's economy—like that of other Third World countries—is dependent and "extraverted." As we saw, the Reserve Bank stated that India's conflict with Pakistan led to the interruption of foreign aid and thus increased the country's economic difficulties; but there are other structural problems that account for the Third World's economic dependency on the "outside": balance-of-payments deficits, international debt and its service, shortages of food, and so on. In this case, global-systemic determinants are not only present but even primary (Korany and Dessouki, 1984: 19–40).

Indeed, in tracing the decision process, Brecher finds that

> The earliest event cited by all decision-makers occurred at the annual World Bank–IMF meetings in Tokyo from 7 to 11 September 1964. The Fund's Managing Director, Schweitzer, asked India's Finance Minister very discreetly, "what do you plan to do to offset the deterioration in the value of the rupee?" According to a participant, TTK "exploded." Nevertheless, immediately upon his return to Delhi, the Government of India raised the bank rate, the first time in several years. From that time onwards the economic malaise and the possible drastic solution—devaluation—were a recurrent part of the internal debate among India's mandarins of economic policy. Then and for more than a year, however, it was a dirty word; politically it was impossible. Devaluation became a policy issue for the Government of India following the Consortium meeting in Washington on 21 April 1965: the Aid-to-India Club offered $1,007 million in aid for 1965–66, the final year of the Third Plan, if India accepted the Bell Mission recommendations (Brecher, 1977: 10).

The Bell Mission was headed by Bernard R. Bell, who had been sent by the World Bank in 1964. Its members prepared ten reports on the different sectors of the Indian economy. These reports were submitted to the president of the World Bank as late as October 1965, but its contents and the commission's advice—namely, devaluation—had already been the focus of discussions at the April 1965 Consortium meeting in Washington. Moreover, Brecher himself was acquainted with the commission's advice as early as winter 1964-1965, when he went to New Delhi for research purposes.

Another outside pressure, equal to that of the World Bank in its effect on India's decision-makers, was that exerted by the IMF. This pressure became a direct and strong influence when Pierre Paul Schweitzer (the IMF's managing director) sent a message to the Indian government informing it that the Fund would not be able to accept the withdrawal of another credit tranche in the absence of an agreement to devalue. Whether deliberate in its actions or not, the United States contributed to the external pressure on India's general economic policy, in part, as President Johnson noted in his memoirs, by putting food aid on a short-term basis in place of the long-term arrangement of earlier years (in this connection, see the detailed and eloquent quotation in Brecher, 1977: 6). Manifesting this outside influence were the visits by Indira Gandhi (March 27-29, 1966) and Ashok Mehta (April 19-May 7, 1966) to the United States. The link between such diplomatic visits and the decision to devalue was heightened by the fact that the day after Gandhi's meeting with Johnson, the president asked Congress for approval to provide India with 3.5 million tons of food. Similarly, Mehta held extensive discussions concerning aid with the World Bank as well as with members of the U.S. administration, although he insisted at the time that the question of devaluation never came up. That may indeed be the case, as the devaluation decision had already been made and had only to be announced. Because this situation was an open secret in Washington at that time, its discussion was no longer necessary. Moreover, given the cable sent by Nehru (India's ambassador in Washington) to 'Jha (Indira Gandhi's secretary) stating "that if India did not devalue the rupee she would not receive any more aid from the Bank or the Fund" (Brecher, 1977: 15), most of the decision was made but not yet taken. Hence the formal taking of the decision had to be accelerated and was made public on June 5, 1966 (although U.S. Ambassador Chester Bowles was notified a day before).

Almost all of the participants in the making of this devaluation decision concurred in their perception of the influence of external factors. By the same token, the then minister of food and agriculture maintained that the aid factor "was an important component of the decision, because devaluation envisaged substantial World Bank aid as a package. It was the necessary condition of aid" (Brecher, 1977: 4). Another prominent civil servant, while calling attention to the connection between internal and external factors in shaping the decision, also emphasized the impact of external factors: "The major stimulus to India's decision to devalue came from the fact that the rupee was so grossly over-valued that it was doing harm to our exports and was holding back the development of the country. There was, as a result of this, pressure from World Bank and the IMF which linked this with the possibilities of difficulties in aid if the rupee was not devalued" (Brecher, 1977: 5).

'Jha, who was equally emphatic about the pressures from the World Bank, the IMF, and the U.S. government, went one step further in asserting the primacy of external factors. "The devaluation," he said, "was largely a response to external pressure"—pressure, that is, exerted by the World Bank (Brecher, 1977: 4). Bhagwati concurred about the role of the World Bank: "That the measure was adopted under a heavy pressure from this source is indisputable." He even went further to describe the public resentment that had developed against the government's decision for what was deemed India's concession to world pressure: "Many people, certainly among articulate groups, felt strongly that India had capitulated to foreigners . . . and that India had been forced to adopt a measure that was almost certainly inspired by a foreign ideological position and was detrimental to her economic interests" (quoted in Brecher, 1977: 5).

Clearly, then, what might have been considered a violation of national will and sovereignty, even within the ruling Congress party, determined many of the reactions to this decision. Thus it happened that T.T.K., the ex-finance minister who was dismissed for refusing to devalue the rupee, referred during the Congress Working Committee Session to the repeated U.S. pressure exerted upon him while he was still in office to get on with the devaluation decision (Brecher, 1977: 19). Other members of the Parliamentary Party Executive characterized the decision as a "serious mistake" and as a "Himalayan blunder" (referring to China's 1962 invasion of India during which the Indian Army was overrun in the Himalayas).

The nongoverning political parties, too, were almost unanimous in their opposition to the devaluation decision. The leader of the pro-Moscow Communist party of India, S. A. Dange, described the decision as a "shameful act"—indeed, as the "blackest act of national betrayal since independence." Meanwhile, the left-of-center People's Socialist party (PSP) leader, B. B. Das, considered the decision yet another bit of evidence that the government was tying itself "to the apron-strings of foreign capital and foreign countries" (Brecher, 1977: 20). Even the Soviets interpreted the decision as a giving in to Western pressures and expressed their unhappiness to India's embassy in Moscow. When Minister Mehta went to Moscow to explain the decision, "[he] found a strong silence among them when explaining devaluation and playing down the limits to liberalization of our economy"; as he further explained, "it was a dialogue between the deaf."

In short, the decision to devalue the rupee was criticized by numerous people of varied political inclinations. Many interpreted it as a capitulation to external pressures. Psychological factors were never emphasized, however—not even by Brecher himself in his analysis of the situation. After mentioning once, and only in passing, that "objective" factors tend to coincide with perceptions, Brecher drew two major conclusions from his extensive research and data collection: "First, the devaluation crisis of 1966 is a revealing case study of the mutual interaction of domestic and external stimuli to foreign policy behaviour. Secondly, India's economic crisis spawned multiple consequences for her external relations and domestic politics and economics" (1977: 25).

CONCLUSIONS

Where to go from here? It is mandatory to go not only beyond the individual as a level of analysis but also beyond the state, however monolithic and autonomous it may appear to be. Decision-making structures and national social processes must be conceptualized as part of a more general social organization—that is, as links in the global system chain. In the early 1970s, an attempt was made to form a connection between national and international groups (see Amin, 1973, and especially Galtung, 1971). In this context, the concepts of "Center" and "Periphery" (denoting developed and developing countries, North and South, or, more generally, dominant and dominated groups) were developed at both the national and international levels. In combination, these two levels yield four categories of social groups: (1) the center of the Center (i.e., the very top elites at the global level); (2) the periphery of the Center (the underprivileged in developed countries, e.g., blacks in the United States); (3) the center of the Periphery (i.e., elites in developing countries); and (4) the periphery of the Periphery (i.e., the dominated groups in developing countries, or the "underdogs" at the global level, who lack basic needs and die from starvation, as in Ethiopia, or suffer a miserable existence, as in Haiti).

But we must also go beyond categorization and classification of social groups to specify their linkages and networks, especially those between the national and international levels. Certainly the issue of political economy has attracted attention to the role of middlemen and collaborators in the foreign policy arena. The "radical" political economy, whose original conceptualization focused on the theory of imperialism, emphasizes the importance in the Third World of *compradorization* (Hoogvelt, 1976: 100), a term derived from the Portuguese word *comprador,* meaning "interpreter" or "middleman." Historically speaking, compradors are the middlemen between foreign capitalists coming to the coast of a colony and the natives occupying the hinterland. Over time, the compradors emerged to form an externally dependent merchant class. Without conceptualizing this process of compradorization, the "liberal" school of political economy concurs with the radical school in emphasizing the phenomenon of middlemen (Robinson, 1972: 117–142). Indeed, the imperial use of local collaborating groups, whether ruling elites or landlords, "explains why Europe was able to rule large areas of the world so cheaply and with so few troops" (Robinson, 1972: 117). But the concept of middlemen and national collaborators is relevant not only to the past but also to the present: Did not Paraguay's president, Alfredo Stroessner, state publicly during a visit to Washington in March 1968 that he considered the U.S. ambassador in Ascuncion to be a member of his cabinet (Kaufman, 1977: 148)? A more formal national/international linkage at the highest level of decision-making could not be found.

Of course, national/international group linkages can be less direct than physical participation in their influence on top decision-makers, yet equally decisive. For instance, the aims associated with the political and economic intervention of external groups, whether formal or informal, may be to determine the level of resources available to the different national groups involved, to enhance the bargaining power of selected groups among them, and, consequently, to determine a certain political outcome. More specifically, a foreign power or organization (e.g., the CIA) may provide arms or any other form of "aid" to help a particular military force (or one faction within it) to direct national decision-making along a certain avenue; it might even assist the favored group in taking over the government in question, thereby permitting that group to become the legitimate authoritative decision-makers.

Such national/international group linkages may also emerge when external groups attempt to shape the frame of reference and parameters of a given decision-making process. A multinational company, for example, might co-opt a particular group of national elites and socialize its members into following certain modes of thought, standards of living, values, and exogenous patterns of behavior that serve as criteria for evaluating options and taking decisions. In short, external groups acting as unofficial but effective decision-makers can assume the role of super-patron in relation to national or local patrons.

It is undoubtedly through such emphasis on social groups and their networks at the national and international levels that decision theory can escape the psychological cul-de-sac associated with the Great Man theory of history and become linked to wider social processes, thereby profiting from advances in the various social sciences.

BIBLIOGRAPHICAL NOTE

The two basic levels of analysis utilized in this book—the global and the societal—complement the psychologistic level and are associated with two major schools in the literature: that of political economy and that of the group theory of politics. The basic works in the former category are those emphasizing concepts of dependency and imperialism and their application to the Third World. As mentioned earlier, the works of Amin (1973), Cardoso and Faletto (1979), Frank (1967, 1978), Galtung (1971), and Wallerstein (1974) are basic, whereas those of Chilcote (1984) and Gendzier (1985) provide an effective overview of this school.

The area of political economy does not, however, focus on Third World foreign policy, let alone decision-making. Inasmuch as its advocates have been concerned with the macro level (i.e., the structure and functioning of a global system of domination), they have mentioned foreign policy only in passing and in the most general way. Nevertheless, the literature of this school is important, given its emphasis on influences coming from outside the state and penetrating Third World societies—influences that seriously limit the choices available for the decision-makers in these countries.

It was necessary, then, to complement this general macro level of the global system with the societal one, which views society as a conglomeration of groups (both formal and informal) rather than as a monolithic entity. Notwithstanding Evans's (1979) effective attempt to link the two levels in the political economy school with his application to investment in Brazil, we must conclude that the analysis of groups should go far beyond one case-study application and focus primarily on foreign policy decisions.

The analysis of the role of groups in the political system goes back to the works of Bentley (1967) and Truman (1951) and a good survey is provided by Garson (1978). But this analytical approach is very much dependent on the theories of pluralism and pressure politics characteristic of developed Western political systems—hence the emphasis in this chapter on the role of informal groups and the hierarchy among them. But class analysis, which represents the major entry in this latter category, has neglected the noneconomic factors of group formation (e.g., ethnicity or kinship). It is in this context that the literature on economic anthropology, with its emphasis on patronage and clientalism, becomes useful. Lemieux (1977) and Graziano (1983) have provided very good surveys, and their empirical analyses are excellent. Graham's work (1968) and the whole collection by Schwartz (1968) are early examples that continue to be quite valid; Gellner and Waterbury (1977), whose works are much more recent, concentrate on Mediterranean cases. The huge collection of articles by Schmidt et al. (1977) is still the most complete treatment of the field, embracing the state of theory, empirical analysis, and bibliography.

The resources of both political economy and economic anthropology have not yet been exploited to complement the foreign policy conceptualization inspired mainly by political science, but a research group at the University of Montreal is now embarking on this job (Korany et al., 1984b; Gundevia, 1985; Amrani, 1985). The objective is to operationalize the advantages of building on recent advances in established foreign policy theory in order to go beyond its pitfalls and make it adaptable to the analysis of Third World conditions.

BIBLIOGRAPHY

BOOKS AND PERIODICALS

Acimovic, L., ed. (1969). *Nonalignment in the World of Today.* Beograd: Institute of International Politics and Economics.

Ajayi, A.J.F. (1982). "Expectations of Independence." *Daedalus* 3 (Spring): 1-9.

Ajomo, M. A. (1977). "An Appraisal of the Organization of the Petroleum-Exporting Countries (OPEC)." *Texas International Law Journal* 13, no. 11: 11-31.

Ake, C. (1976). "Explanatory Notes on the Political Economy of Africa." *Journal of Modern African Studies* 14 (March): 1-23.

Akindele, R. A. (1976). "Reflections on the Preoccupation and Conduct of African Diplomacy." *Journal of Modern African Studies* 14 (December): 557-576.

Akinyemi, A. B. (1982). "Africa—Challenges and Responses: A Foreign Policy Perspective." *Daedalus* 3 (Spring): 243-254.

———(1978). "Nigerian Foreign Policy in 1975: National Interest Redefined." In O. Oyedirian, ed., *Survey of Nigerian Affairs.* Ibadan, Nigeria: Oxford University Press, 1978.

Akpan, N. U. (1971). *The Struggle for Secession, 1966-1970: A Personal Account of the Nigerian Civil War.* London: Frank Cass.

Akuchu, G. E. (1977). "Peaceful Settlement of Disputes: Unresolved Problems for the OAU (A Case Study of the Nigeria-Biafra Conflict)." *Africa Today* 24 (October-December): 39-58.

Allison, G. (1971). *Essence of Decision.* Boston: Little, Brown.

———(1969). "Conceptual Models and the Cuban Missile Crisis." *American Political Science Review* 62, no. 3 (September): 689-718.

Allison, G., and M. Halperin (1972). "Bureaucratic Politics. A Paradigm and Some Policy Implications." *World Politics* (April): Supplement.

Almond, G., and J. Coleman (1960). *The Politics of Developing Areas.* Princeton, N.J.: Princeton University Press.

Al-Sowayegh, A. (1984). *Arab Petro-Politics.* London: St. Martin's Press.

Amin, S. (1973). *Le Développement Inégal.* Paris: Minuit.

———(1969). *L'Accumulation à l'Echelle Mondiale.* Paris: Anthropos.

Amrani, S. (1985). *Les Politiques Etrangères du Maroc et de l'Arabie Saoudite: Une Etude Comparative.* M.A. thesis, University of Montreal.

Amstrup, N. (1976). "The Perennial Problem of Small States." *Cooperation and Conflict* 9: 163-182.

Anderson, B., and J. Cockroft (1969). "Control and Cooptation in Mexican Politics." In Irving Louis Horowitz et al., eds., *Latin America Radicalism.* New York: Vintage Books.

Anglin, D. G. (1980). "Zambia Crisis Behavior." *International Studies Quarterly* 24 (December): 581-616.

———(1971). "Zambia and the Recognition of Biafra." *African Review* 1 (September): 102-136.

BIBLIOGRAPHY

Anglin, D. G., and T. M. Shaw (1979). *Zambia's Foreign Policy: Studies in Diplomacy and Dependence.* Boulder, Colo.: Westview Press.

Anuario Estadistico de los Estados Unidos Mexicanos (1979, 1980). Mexico D.F.: Secretariz de Programacion y Presupuesto.

Aron, R. (1962). *Paix et Guerre entre les Nations.* Paris: C. Levy.

Art, R. (1973). "Bureaucratic Politics and American Foreign Policy: A Critique." *Policy Sciences* 4: 467–490.

Asso, B. (1976). *Le Chef d'Etat Africain.* Paris: Albatros.

Auma-Osolo, A. (1977). "Rationality and Foreign Policy Process." *Yearbook of World Affairs:* 257–288.

Azar, E., and T. Sloan (1975). *Dimensions of Interaction.* Pittsburgh: International Studies Association.

Azevedo, M. J. (1977). "Zambia, Zaire and the Angolan Crisis Reconsidered: From Alvor to Shaba." *Journal of Southern African Affairs* 2 (July): 275–293.

Bach, D. (1980). "Le Général de Gaulle et la Guerre Civile au Nigéria." *Canadian Journal of African Studies* 14, no. 2: 259–272.

Baker, R. K. (1970). "The Role of the Ivory Coast in the Nigeria Biafra War." *African Scholar* 1, no. 4: 5–80.

Ball, D. (1974). "The Blind Men and the Elephant: A Critique of Bureaucratic Politics Theory." *Australian Outlook* 28 (April): 71–93.

Barraclough, G., and R. Wall, eds. (1960). *Survey of International Affairs 1955–1956.* London: Oxford University Press, Royal Institute of International Affairs.

Bentley, A. (1967). *The Process of Government.* Cambridge, Mass.: Belknap Press. (Originally published in 1908.)

Bill, J., and R. Hardgrave (1973). *Comparative Politics: The Quest for Theory.* Columbus, Ohio: Merrill.

Bon, D., and K. Mingst (1980). "French Intervention in Africa: Dependency or Decolonization?" *Africa Today* 27: 5–20.

Bond, R., ed. (1977). *Contemporary Venezuela and Its Role in International Affairs.* New York: New York University Press.

Boulding, K. (1959). "National Images and International Systems." *Journal of Conflict Resolution* 3 (June): 120–131.

Bozeman, A. (1960). *Politics and Culture in International History.* Princeton, N.J.: Princeton University Press.

Bozeman, A. B. (1976). *Conflict in Africa: Concepts and Realities.* Princeton, N.J.: Princeton University Press.

Braibanti, R., and F. Al-Farsy (1977). "Saudi Arabia: A Developmental Perspective." *Journal of South Asian and Middle Eastern Studies* 1 (September): 3–43.

Brecher, M. (1980). *Crisis Decision-Making: Israel 1967 and 1973.* Berkeley: University of California Press.

———(1979). "State Behavior in International Crisis: A Model." *Journal of Conflict Resolution* 23: 446–480.

———(1978). "A Theoretical Approach to International Crisis Behavior." *Jerusalem Journal of International Affairs* 3: 5–24.

———(1977). "India's Devaluation of 1966: Linkage Politics and Crisis Decision-Making." *British Journal of International Studies* 3 (April): 1–25.

———(1974). *Decisions in Israel's Foreign Policy.* London: Oxford University Press.

———(1972). *The Foreign Policy System of Israel.* London: Oxford University Press.

Brecher, M., B. Steinberg, and J. Stein (1969). "A Framework for Research on Foreign Policy Behavior." *Journal of Conflict Resolution* 13 (March): 75–102.

Bukarambe, B. (1983). "Conflict and Conflict Management in Africa: The Role and Impact of the OAU in Management of African Conflict." *Survival* 25 (March-April): 50–58.

Burgess, P., and R. Lawton (1972). *Indicators of International Behavior.* Beverly Hills, Calif.: Sage.

Burton, J. (1965). *International Relations: A General Theory.* London: Cambridge University Press.

Callaghy, T. (1984). *The State-Society Struggle: Zaire in Comparative Perspective.* New York: Columbia University Press.

Cardoso, F., and E. Faletto (1979). *Dependency and Development.* Berkeley: University of California Press.

Castaneda, J. (1981). *Comércio exterior de Mexico* (English edition) 27, no. 10 (October): 427–431.

Castro Ruz, F. (1979). "Discurso Pronunciado por el Comandate en Jefe Fidel Castro Ruz, Primer Secretario del CC del Partido Comunista de Cuba y Presidente de los Consejos de Estado y de Ministros, en la clausura del II periodo de sessiones de 1979 de la Asamblea Nacional del Poder Popular. Palacio de la Convenciones, 27 de diciembre de 1979."

———(1977). *Verde Olivo* 18, no. 3 (March): 3.

Chang, P. (1976). "The Passing of the Maoist Era." *Asian Survey* 16 (November): 997–1011.

Chazan, N. (1983). *An Anatomy of Ghanaian Politics:Managing Political Recession, 1969–1982.* Boulder, Colo.: Westview Press.

Chazan, N., and T. M. Shaw (1982). "Limits of Leadership: Africa in Contemporary World Politics." *International Journal* 37 (Autumn): 543–554.

Chilcote, R. (1984). *Theories of Development and Underdevelopment.* Boulder, Colo.: Westview Press.

Chilcote, R., and J. Edelstein, eds. (1974). *Latin America: The Struggle with Dependency and Beyond.* Cambridge, Mass.: Schenkman Publishing Co.

Choucri, N. (1969). "The Perceptual Base of Nonalignment." *Journal of Conflict Resolution* 13 (March): 37–57.

Clapham, C., ed. (1977). *Foreign Policy-Making in Developing States: A Comparative Approach.* London: Saxon House.

Cohen, B., and S. Harris (1975). "Foreign Policy." In F. Greenstein and N. Polsby, eds., *Handbook of Political Science,* Vol. VI. Reading, Mass.: Wesley.

Collier, D., ed. (1979). *The New Authoritarianism in Latin America.* Princeton, N.J.: Princeton University Press.

Colombo Nonaligned Summit (1976). "Documents of the Fifth Conference of Heads of State or Government of Non-Aligned Countries," United Nations Document A/31/110.

Comité Estatal de Estadisticas (1980). *Anuario estadistico de Cuba.* Havana.

Conference of Nonaligned Countries (Second Summit) (1964). *Review of International Affairs* (Beograd) 15, no. 350 (November 5, 1964).

Conference of Nonaligned Countries (Third Summit) (1970). *Review of International Affairs* (Beograd) 24, nos. 563–564 (September 20 and October 5, 1973).

Cordesman, A. (1984). *The Gulf and the Search for Strategic Stability.* Boulder, Colo.: Westview Press.

Cox, R., and H. Jacobson (1972). *The Anatomy of Influence.* New Haven, Conn.: Yale University Press.

Cronje, S. (1972). *The World and Nigeria: The Diplomatic History of the Biafran War, 1967–1970.* London: Sidgwick & Jackson.

Cutler, R. (1982). "The Formation of Soviet Foreign Policy: Organizational and Cognitive Perspectives." *World Politics* 34 (April): 418–437.

BIBLIOGRAPHY

Daddieh, C. K. (1985). "Foreign Policy and Political Economy of the Ivory Coast." In O. Aluko and T. M. Shaw, eds., *The Political Economy of African Foreign Policy: A Comparative Analysis*. Aldershot, England: Gower.

———(1983a). "Review Article—Mark W. Delancey, African International Relations: An Annotated Bibliography." *International Journal of African Historical Studies* 16.

———(1983b). "Crisis Management in an African State: The Case of Houphouet Boigny Versus Ivorian Students." Paper presented at the Center for African Studies, Dalhousie University (February).

Dahl, R. (1961). "The Behavioral Approach in Political Science: Epitaph for a Movement to a Successful Protest." *American Political Science Review* 55 (December): 763–772.

Davis, H., and L. Wilson (1975). *Latin America Foreign Policies: An Analysis*. Baltimore: Johns Hopkins University Press.

Dawisha, A. (1980). *Syria and the Lebanese Crisis*. New York: St. Martin's Press.

———(1977). "The Middle East." In C. Clapham, ed., *Foreign Policy-Making in Developing States: A Comparative Approach*. London: Saxon House.

———(1976). *Egypt in the Arab World: Elements of Foreign Policy*. London: Macmillan Publishers.

Dawisha, K. (1984). *The Kremlin and the Prague Spring*. Berkeley: University of California Press.

———(1979). *Soviet Foreign Policy Toward Egypt*. London: Macmillan Publishers.

Dayan, M. (1977). *Story of My Life*. New York: Warner Books.

DeLancey, N. W. (1981). *African International Relations: An Annotated Bibliography*. Boulder, Colo.: Westview Press.

De St. Jorre, J. (1982). "Africa: Crisis of Confidence." *Foreign Affairs* 61, no. 3: 675–691.

———(1972). *The Nigeria Civil War*. London: Hodder & Stoughton.

Destler, I. (1974). *Presidents, Bureaucrats, and Foreign Policy*. Princeton, N.J.: Princeton University Press.

Deutsch, K. (1963). *The Nerves of Government*. New York: Free Press.

Dibaco, T., ed. (1977). *Presidential Power in Latin American Politics*. New York: Praeger Publishers.

Domínguez, J. (1982a). "Political and Military Limitations and Consequences of Cuban Policy in Africa." In Carmelo Mesa-Lago and June Belkin, eds., *Cuba in Africa*, Latin American Monograph and Document Series, no 3. Pittsburg: University of Pittsburgh, Center for Latin American Studies.

———(1982b). "Revolutionary Politics: The New Demands for Orderliness." In J. I. Domínguez, ed., *Cuba: Internal and International Affairs*. Beverly Hills, Calif.: Sage.

———(1978a). "Cuban Foreign Policy." *Foreign Affairs* 57, no. 1: 83–108.

———(1978b). *Cuba: Order and Revolution*. Cambridge, Mass.: Harvard University Press.

———(1978c). "Consensus and Divergence: The State of the Literature on Inter-American Relations in the 1970s." *Latin American Research Review* 13, no. 1: 87–126.

———(1971). "Mice that Do Not Roar: Some Aspects of International Politics in the World's Peripheries." *International Organization* 25, no. 2: 175–208.

Duguid, S. (1970). "A Bibliographical Approach to the Study of Social Change in the Middle East: Abdallah Tariki as a New Man." *International Journal of Middle East Studies* 1: 195–220.

East, M. (1973). "Size and Foreign Policy Behavior: A Test of Two Models." *World Politics* 25 (July): 556–576.

Ebinger, C. K. (1976). "External Intervention in Internal War: The Politics and Diplomacy of the Angolan Civil War." *Crisis* 20 (Fall): 669–699.

Eicher, C. K. (1982). "Facing up to Africa's Food Crisis." *Foreign Affairs* (Fall): 151–174.

Elaigwu, J. I. (1977a). "The Nigerian Civil War and the Angolan Civil War: Linkages Between Domestic Tensions and International Alignments." *Journal of Asian and African Studies* 12 (January and October): 215–235.

———(1977b). "South Africa and the Angolan Conflict." *Africa Today* 24 (April–June): 35–46.

El-Khawas, M. A. (1976). "Power Struggle in Angola: Whose Struggle? Whose Power?" *Journal of Southern African Affairs* 1 (October): 53–67.

El-Mallakh, R., ed. (1982a). *OPEC: Twenty Years and Beyond*. Boulder, Colo.: Westview Press.

———(1982b). *Saudi Arabia: Rush to Development*. London: Croom Helm.

Emmanuel, A. (1972). *Unequal Exchange: A Study of the Imperialism of Trade*. New York: Monthly Review Press.

Evans, P. (1979). *Dependent Development*. Princeton, N.J.: Princeton University Press.

Feld, W., and R. Jordan, with L. Hurwitz (1983). *International Organizations: A Comparative Approach*. New York: Praeger Publishers.

Ferris, E., and J. Lincoln (1981). *Latin American Foreign Policies: Global and Regional Dimensions*. Boulder, Colo.: Westview Press.

Fesharaki, F., and D. Isaak (1983). *OPEC, the Gulf, and the World Petroleum Market*. Boulder, Colo.: Westview Press.

Field, M. (1982). "Oil in the Middle East and North Africa." In *The Middle East and North Africa*. London: Europa Publications.

Fox, A. B. (1968–1969). "The Small States in the International System: 1919–1969." *International Journal* 24: 751–764.

Frank, A. (1978). *Dependent Accumulation and Underdevelopment*. London: Macmillan Publishers, and New York: Monthly Review Press.

———(1967). *Capitalism and Underdevelopment in Latin America*. New York: Monthly Review Press.

———(1966). "The Development of Underdevelopment." *Monthly Review* 18 (September): 17–31.

Freedman, L. (1976). "Logic, Politics and Foreign Policy Processes: A Critique of the Bureaucratic Politics Model." *International Affairs* 52 (July): 434–449.

Galtung, J. (1971). "A Structural Theory of Imperialism." *Journal of Peace Research* 2: 81–117.

Garcia Marquez, G. (1977a). "Castro in the War Room: Tactical Advice to Angola." *Washington Post* (January 11).

———(1977b). "Colombian Author Writes on Cuba's Angola Intervention." *Washington Post* (January 20): A14.

———(1977c). "Operation Carlota." *Tricontinental Bimonthly* 53: 4–25.

Garson, G. D. (1978). *Group Theories of Politics*. Beverly Hills, Calif., and London: Sage.

Gellner, E., and J. Waterbury, eds. (1977). *Patrons and Clients*. London: Duckworth.

Gendzier, I. (1985). *Managing Political Change: Social Scientists and the Third World*. Boulder, Colo.: Westview Press.

George, A. (1980). *Presidential Decisionmaking in Foreign Policy*. Boulder, Colo.: Westview Press.

Ghali, B. (Egypt's Minister of State for Foreign Affairs) (1985). Personal communication, January.

Graham, B. (1968). "The Succession of Factional Systems in the Utter Pradesh Congress Party, 1937–66." In M. Schwartz, ed., *Local-Level Politics*. Chicago: Aldine Publishing Co.

Graziano, L., ed. (1983). *Political Clientalism and Comparative Perspectives*. Beverly Hills, Calif.: Sage. (A special issue of *International Political Science Review* 4 [October]).

Grimaud, N. (1984). *La Politique Extérieure de l'Algérie*. Paris: Karthala.

Gundevia, M. (1985). "La Politique Etrangère de l'Inde." M.A. thesis, University of Montreal.

Hagen, E. (1962). *On the Theory of Social Change*. Homewood, Ill.: Dorsey Press.

Halperin, M. (1974). *Bureaucratic Politics and Foreign Policy*. Washington, D.C.: Brookings Institution.
Hansen, R. (1971). *The Politics of Mexican Development*. Baltimore, Md.: Johns Hopkins University Press.
Harding, H. (1984). "The Study of Chinese Politics." *World Politics* 36 (January): 284–307.
Heikal, M. (1978a). "Egypt's Foreign Policy." *Foreign Affairs* 56 (July): 714–727.
———(1978b). *The Sphinx and the Commissar*. New York: Harper & Row.
———(1975). *The Road to Ramadan*. New York: Ballantine.
Helmes, C. M. (1981). *The Cohesion of Saudi Arabia*. Baltimore, Md.: Johns Hopkins University Press.
Hermassi, E. (1980). *The Third World Reassessed*. Berkeley: University of California Press.
Herrera, R. (forthcoming). *Mexico, La Politica Exterior en Transicion*. Mexico: El Colegio de Mexico.
Herzog, G. (1975). *The War of Atonement*. Boston: Little, Brown.
Hill, C. (1977). "Theories of Foreign Policy-Making for the Developing Countries." In C. Clapham, ed., *Foreign Policy-Making in Developing States*. London: Saxon House.
Hilsman, R. (1971). *The Politics of Policy-Making in Defense and Foreign Affairs*. New York: Praeger Publishers.
———(1958). "Congressional-Executive Relations and the Foreign Policy Consensus." *American Political Science Review* 52: 725–744.
Hoffman, S. (1978). *Primacy or World Order: American Foreign Policy Since the Cold War*. New York: McGraw-Hill.
Holsti, K., et al. (1982). *Why Nations Realign*. London: Allen & Unwin.
———(1967). *International Politics: A Framework for Analysis*. Englewood Cliffs, N.J.: Prentice-Hall.
Holsti, O. (1962). "The Belief System and National Images: A Case Study." *Journal of Conflict Resolution* 6 (September): 244–252.
Hoogvelt, A. (1976). *The Sociology of Developing Societies*. London: Macmillan Publishers.
Houphouet-Boigny, F. (1968). "Biafra: A Human Problem, A Human Tragedy." *African Scholar* 1 (August–November): 10–13.
Hunter, S. (1984). *OPEC and the Third World*. Bloomington: Indiana University Press.
Hutchful, E. (1979). "A Tale of Two Regimes: Imperialism, the Military and Class in Ghana." *Review of African Political Economy* 14 (January–April): 36–55.
Ibrahim, S. (1982). *The New Arab Social Order*. Boulder, Colo.: Westview Press.
Inter-American Development Bank (1982). *Economic and Social Progress in Latin America, 1980–1981*. Washington, D.C.
Jabber, P. (1982). "Oil, Arms, and Regional Diplomacy: Strategic Dimensions of the Saudi-Egyptian Relationship." In M. Kerr and S. Yassin, eds., *Rich and Poor States in the Middle East*. Boulder, Colo.: Westview Press.
Jackson, R. (1983). *The Nonaligned, the U.N. and the Superpowers*. New York: Praeger Publishers.
Jalee, P. (1968). *The Pillage of the Third World*. New York: Monthly Review Press.
Jankowitsch, O., and K. Sauvant, eds. (1978). *The Third World Without Superpowers*. Dobbs Ferry, N.Y.: Oceana Publications.
Jansen, J. (1966). *Afro-Asia and Nonalignment*. London: Faber & Faber.
Jones, R. (1967). *The Functional Analysis of Politics*. London: Routledge & Kegan Paul.
Kalb, M., and B. Kalb (1974). *Kissinger*. New York: Dell.
Kanovsky, E. (1981). "The Diminishing Importance of Middle East Oil: A Harbinger of the Future?" In C. Legum, H. Shaked, and D. Dishon, eds., *Middle East Contemporary Survey*, Vol. V. London and New York: Holmes & Meier.

Kaufman, E. (1977). "Latin America." In C. Clapham, ed., *Foreign Policy-Making in Developing States: A Comparative Approach*. London: Saxon House.

Kegley, C., and R. Skinner (1976). "The Case for Analysis Problem." In J. Rosenau, ed., *In Search of Global Patterns*. New York: Free Press.

Khalaf, N. (1971). *Economic Implications of the Size of Nations*. Leiden, Holland: Brill.

Kissinger, H. (1982). *Years of Upheaval*. Boston: Little, Brown.

———(1957). *Nuclear Weapons and Foreign Policy*. New York: Harper.

Koehane, R., and J. Nye (1977). *Power and Interdependence*. Boston: Little, Brown.

Korany, B. (1986). "Stratification Among the Underdogs," *Third World Affairs Yearbook* 2.

———(1984a). "Foreign Policy in the Third World: An Introduction." In B. Korany, ed., Foreign Policy Decisions in the Third World (a special issue of *International Political Science Review* 5 [January]: 7–21).

———(1984b). "Une, Deux, ou Quatre . . . Les Ecoles de Relations Internationales." In B. Korany, ed., La Crise de Relations Internationales: Vers un Bilan (a special issue of Etudes Internationales). Quebec: University of Laval Press.

———(1983a). "Structure et Processes dans le Système International Arabe 1961–1983." In *Le Moyen-Orient: Evolution et Enjeux*. Quebec City: Presses de l'Université Laval (Collection Choix).

———(1983b). "Retribalization of Politics and the Crisis of the Arab System." *International Journal of Middle East Studies* 15 (November): 571–577.

———(1983c). "The Take-Off of Third World Studies: The Case of Foreign Policy." *World Politics* 35 (April): 465–487.

———(1983d). "Allah's Wish? Premises and Promises of Contemporary Arab Political Economy." Paper presented at the South-South Conference on Strategies of Cooperation, Development and Negotiations, Beijing (April).

———(1982a). "Arabia Saudita: da Culla dell'Islam a Petrolpotenza." *Politica Internazionale* 1: 79–91.

———(1982b). "The Difficult Equation in the Foreign Policy of Developing Countries: The Case of Egypt." *International Studies Quarterly* (Cairo) 18 (July): 133–148.

———(1978a). "Dépendence Financière et Comportement International." *Revue Française de Science Politique* 23 (December): 1067–1093.

———(1978b). "Societal Variables and Foreign Policy in the Third World: Hypothesis and Data." *Journal of the Social Sciences* 6 (October): 273–294.

———(1976). *Social Change, Charisma and International Behavior: Toward A Theory of Foreign Policy-Making in the Third World*. Leiden, Holland: Sijthoff.

———(1974). "Foreign Policy Models and Their Relevance to Third World Countries." *International Social Science Journal* 26 (March): 70–94.

Korany, B., and A. Dessouki et al. (1984). *The Foreign Policies of Arab States*. Boulder, Colo.: Westview Press.

Korany, B., J. Balladier, and J. B. Gauthier (1984). "Dépendance et Politique Etrangère au Monde Arabe: Le Cas de la Tunisie," *Etudes Arabes* (Montréal) 4.

Kraus, J. (1983). "Revolutions and the Military in Ghana." *Current History* 82 (March): 115–132.

———(1980). "The Political Economy of Conflict in Ghana." *Africa Report* 25 (March-April): 9–16.

Lackner, H. (1978). *A House Built on Sand: The Political Economy of Saudi Arabia*. London: Ithaca Press.

Larrabee, S. (1976). "Moscow, Angola and the Dialectics of Detente." *World Today* 32 (May): 173–182.

Leifer, M. (1977). "Southeast Asia." In C. Clapham, ed., *Foreign Policy-Making in Developing States: A Comparative Approach*. London: Saxon House.

Lemieux, V. (1977). *Le Patronage Politique: Une Etude Comparative*. Quebec: University of Laval Press.

Leogrande, W. (1982a). "Cuban-Soviet Relations and Cuban Policy Africa." In Carmelo Mesa-Lago and June Belkin, eds., *Cuba in Africa*, Latin American Monograph and Document Series, no 3. Pittsburgh, Pa.: University of Pittsburgh, Center for Latin American Studies.

———(1982b). "Foreign Policy: The Time of Success." In J. I. Domínguez, ed., *Cuba: Internal and International Affairs*. Beverly Hills, Calif.: Sage.

Leys, C. (1982). "African Economic Development in Theory and Practice." *Daedalus* 3 (Spring): 99–124.

Libby, R. T. (1976). "External Cooptation of a Less Developed Country's Policy-Making: The Case of Ghana, 1969-1972." *World Politics* 29 (October): 67–89.

Lister, F. (1984). *Decision-Making Strategies for International Organizations: The IMF Model*. Denver: University of Denver, Monograph Series in World Affairs.

Lloyd, P. (1968). *International Trade Problems of Small Nations*. Durham, N.C.: Duke University Press.

Lopez Portillo, J. (1980). "Cuarto Informe Presidencial." *Comercio Exterior* 30, 9 (September): 1006–1026.

Lowenthal, A. (1983). "Research in Latin America and the Caribbean on International Relations and Foreign Policy: Some Impressions." *Latin American Research Review* 18: 143–155.

Lyon, P. (1963). *Neutralism*. London: Leicester University Press.

Malloy, J. (1977). *Authoritarianism and Corporatism in Latin America*. Pittsburgh, Pa.: University of Pittsburgh Press.

Mansbach, R., Y. Ferguson, and D. Lampert (1976). *The Web of World Politics*. Englewood Cliffs, N.J.: Prentice-Hall.

Marcum, J. (1978). *The Angolan Revolution: Exile Politics and Guerrilla Warfare (1962-1976)*. Cambridge, Mass.: MIT Press.

Marei, S. (1979). *Political Papers*, Vol. III. Cairo: El-Maktab El-Misri El-Hadith. (In Arabic.)

Mathews, K., and S. S. Mushi, eds. (1981). *Foreign Policy of Tanzania, 1961-1981: A Reader*. Dar es Salaam: Tanzania Publishing House.

Matter, G., and A.E. Hillal Dessouki (1979). *The Arab Regional System*. Beirut: Center for Arab Unity Studies. (In Arabic.)

Mazrui, A. (1967). *Towards a Pax Africana: A Study in Ideology and Ambition*. London: Weidenfeld.

McClelland, D. (1961). *The Achieving Society*. Princeton, N.J.: Van Nostrand Reinhold Co.

McClosky, H. (1956). "Concerning Strategies for a Science of International Politics." *World Politics* 7 (January): 281–295.

Mesa-Lago, C. (1981). *The Economy of Socialist Cuba: A Two-Decade Appraisal*. Albuquerque: University of New Mexico Press.

Mikdashi, Z. (1976). "The OPEC Process." In R. Vernon, ed., *The Oil Crisis*. New York: Norton.

Miller, J. (1966). *The Politics of the Third World*. London: Royal Institute of International Affairs (Chathom House Essays).

Modelski, G. (1964). "Kautilya: Foreign Policy and International Systems in the Ancient Hindu World." *American Political Science Review* 58 (September): 549–560.

Morgenthau, H. (1961). "A Critical Look at the New Neutralism." *New York Times Magazine* (August 27): 25, 76–77.

Mortimer, R. I. (1983). "Succession and Recession." *Africa Report* (January-February): 4–7.

———(1980). *The Third World Coalition in International Politics*. New York: Praeger Publishers.

Moulin, R. (1978). *Le Présidentialisme et la Classification des Régimes Politiques.* Paris: Librarie Générale de Droit et Jurisprudence.

Moyano-Martin, D. (1979). *Handbook of Latin American Studies: Social Sciences,* no. 41. Austin: University of Texas Press.

Munton, D., ed. (1978). *Measuring International Behavior: Public Sources, Events and Validity.* Halifax, Canada: Center for Foreign Policy Studies.

Myrdal, G. (1968). *Asian Drama.* London: Penguin.

Nasser, G. (1970). *Speeches: 1967-1970.* Cairo: Al-Ahram.

Nasser, G. (n.d.). *Speeches, Declarations and Press Interviews 1952-1970.* Cairo: Information Department.

Nathan, A. (1973). "A Factionalism Model for CCP Politics." *China Quarterly* 53 (January-March): 34-66.

Nehru's Speeches, Delhi (n.d.). Ministry of Information and Broadcasting.

Neustadt, R. (1970). *Alliance Politics.* New York: Columbia University Press.

Ninsin, K. (1983). "Ghana: The Failure of a Petty-Bourgeois Experiment." *Africa Development* 7 (July-September): 37-67.

Noble, P. (1984). "The Arab System: Opportunities, Constraints and Pressures." In B. Korany and A. Dessouki et al., *The Foreign Policies of Arab States.* Boulder, Colo.: Westview Press.

Nwanko, A. A., and S. U. Ifejika (1969). *The Making of a Nation: Biafra.* London: C. Hurst.

Nweke, G. A. (1980). *Harmonization of African Foreign Policies, 1955-1975: The Political Economy of African Diplomacy.* Boston: African Studies Center.

Ogunbadejo, O. (1980). "Nigeria's Foreign Policy Under Military Rule, 1966-1979." *International Journal* 35 (Autumn): 748-765.

Ogunsanwo, A. (1980). *Nigerian Military and Foreign Policy 1975-1979: Processes, Principles, Performance, and Contradictions.* Princeton, N.J.: Center of International Studies.

Ojeda, M. (1976). *Alcanes y limites de la politica exterior de Mexico.* Mexico: El Colegio de Mexico.

OPEC (1983a). *OPEC Official Resolutions and Press Releases 1960-1983.* Vienna.

OPEC (1983b). *Member Country Profiles.* Vienna.

OPEC (1983c). *The OPEC File, 1982.* Vienna.

OPEC (1982). *Energy and Development: Options for Global Strategies,* OPEC Seminar, 1981. Vienna.

Organization of American States (1975-1982). Departamento de Asuntos Culturales, secretaria General (1982) Bibliografia de articulos sobre las relaciones internacionales de America Latina y el Caribe, SG/Ser. L/1.3. Washington, D.C.

Oxaal, I., et al. (1975). *Beyond the Sociology of Development.* London: Routledge & Kegan Paul.

Paige, G. (1968). *The Korean Decision, June 24-30, 1950.* New York: Free Press.

Panter-Brick, S. K. (1968). "The Right to Self-Determination: Its Application to Nigeria." *International Affairs* 44 (April): 254-266.

Pellicer, O. (1981). "Mexico's Position." *Foreign Policy* 43 (Summer): 88-92.

Peterson, J., ed. (1983). *The Politics of Middle Eastern Oil.* Washington, D.C.: Middle East Institute.

Polhemus, J. H. (1977). "Nigeria and Southern Africa: Interest, Policy and Means." *Canadian Journal of African Studies* 11: 42-66.

Post, K.W.J. (1968). "Is There a Case for Biafra?" *International Affairs* 44 (January): 26-39.

Purcell, S. K. (1975). *The Mexican Profit-Sharing Decision: Politics in an Authoritarian Regime.* Berkeley: University of California Press.

Pye, L. (1981). *The Dynamics of Chinese Politics.* Cambridge, Mass.: Oelgeschlager, Gunn & Hain.
Quandt, W. (1982). *Saudi Arabia's Oil Policy.* Washington, D.C.: Brookings Institution.
―――(1981). *Saudi Arabia in the 1980s.* Washington, D.C.: Brookings Institution.
―――(1976). *A Decade of Decisions: American Policy in the Middle East 1967–1976.* Berkeley: University of California Press.
Queille, P. (1965). *Histoire de l'Afro-Asiatisme jusqu'à Bandoung.* Paris: Payot.
Ra'anan, U. (1968). "Peking's Foreign Policy Debate 1965–1966." In T. Tsou, ed., *China in Crisis.* Chicago: University of Chicago Press: 23–72.
Raghavan, C. (1985). "UNCTAD and the Group of 77 at Twenty-One: Hope or Uncertainty." *Third World Affairs* 1: 54–65.
Rentz, G. (1980). "The Saudi Monarchy." In W. Beling, ed., *King Faisal and the Modernization of Saudi Arabia.* Boulder, Colo.: Westview Press.
Reubens, E., ed. (1981). *The Challenge of the New International Economic Order.* Boulder, Colo.: Westview Press.
Robinson, E., ed. (1960). *Economic Consequences of the Size of Nations.* New York. St. Martin's Press.
Robinson, J. (1972). "Non-European Foundations of European Imperialism: Sketch for a Theory of Collaboration." In E. Owen and B. Sutcliffe, eds., *Studies in the Theory of Imperialism.* London: Longman.
Roca, S. (1982). "Economic Aspects of Cuban Involvement in Africa." In Carmelo Mesa-Lago and June Belkin, eds., *Cuba in Africa,* Latin American Monograph and Document Series, no. 3. Pittsburgh, Pa.: University of Pittsburgh, Center for Latin American Studies.
Rodney, W. (1974). *How Europe Underdeveloped Africa.* Washington, D.C.: Howard University Press.
Rosenau, J. (1984). "A Pre-Theory Revisited: World Politics in an Era of Cascading Interdependence." In *International Studies Quarterly,* 28/3 (Sept.): 245–305.
―――(1980). *The Scientific Study of Foreign Policy.* London: Francis Pinter.
―――(1976). "Restlessness, Change, and Foreign Policy Analysis." In J. Rosenau, ed., *In Search of Global Patterns.* New York: Free Press.
―――(1975). "Comparative Foreign Policy: One-Time Fad, Realized Fantasy, and Normal Field." In C. Kegley and R. Skinner, eds., *International Events and the Comparative Analysis of Foreign Policy.* Columbia, S.C.: University of South Carolina Press.
―――(1967). "The Premises and Promises of Decision-Making Analysis." In J. Charlesworth, ed., *Contemporary Political Analysis.* New York: Free Press.
―――(1966). "Pre-Theories and Theories of Foreign Policy." In B. Farrell, ed., *Approaches to Comparative and International Politics.* Evanston, Ill.: Northwestern University Press.
Rosenau, J., T. Burgess, and C. Herman (1973). "The Adaptation of Foreign Policy Research: A Case Study of an Anti-Case Study Project." *International Studies Quarterly* 17 (March): 119–144.
Rostow, W. (1960). *The Stages of Economic Growth: A Non-Communist Manifesto.* Cambridge, England: Cambridge University Press.
Rothstein, R. (1977). *The Weak in the World of the Strong.* New York: Columbia University Press.
―――(1968). *Alliances and Small Powers.* New York: Columbia University Press.
Roxborough, I. (1979). *Theories of Underdevelopment.* Atlantic Highlands, N.J.: Humanities Press.
Rubinstein, A. (1970). *Yugoslavia and the Nonaligned World.* Princeton, N.J.: Princeton University Press.
Sabri, M. (1974). *Documents of the October War.* Cairo: El-Maktab El-Misri. (In Arabic.)

Sadat, A. (1978). *In Search of Identity.* London: Collins.
———(1977). *Speeches 1970–1975.* Cairo: State Department of Information. (In Arabic.)
Sampson, A. (1976). *The Seven Sisters.* New York: Bantam.
Sauvant, K. (1982). "Organizational Infrastructure for Self-Reliance." Paper presented to the Twelfth World Congress of the International Political Science Association, Rio de Janeiro, August.
———(1981). *The Group of 77.* New York, London, and Rome: Oceana.
Sayegh, F., ed. (1964). *The Dynamics of Neutralism in the Arab World.* San Francisco: Chandler Publishing Co.
Schelling, T. (1962). *The Strategy of Conflict.* New York: Oxford University Press.
Schmidt, S., et al., eds. (1977). *Friends, Followers and Factions.* Berkeley: University of California Press.
Schneider, R. (1976). *Brazil: Foreign Policy of a Future World Power.* Boulder, Colo.: Westview Press.
Schwartz, M., ed. (1968). *Local-Level Politics.* Chicago: Aldine Publishing Company.
Servan-Schreiber, J. (1980). *Le Défi Mondial.* Paris: Fayard.
Seymour, J. (1980). *OPEC: Instrument of Change.* London: Macmillan Publishers.
Shaw, T. M. (1983). *Africa's International Affairs: An Analysis and Bibliography.* Halifax, Canada: Centre for Foreign Policy Studies.
———(1982). "Zambia after Twenty Years: Recession and Repression Without Revolution." *Issue* 12 (Spring-Summer): 53–58.
———(1980). "Foreign Policy, Political Economy and the Future: Reflections on Africa in the World System" (review). *African Affairs* 79 (April): 260–268.
Shaw, T. M., and O. Aluko, eds. (1983). *Nigerian Foreign Policy: Alternative Perceptions and Projections.* London: Macmillan Publishers.
Shaw, T. M., and O. Fasehun (1980). "Nigeria in the World System: Alternative Approaches, Explanations and Projections." *Journal of Modern African Studies* 18 (December): 551–573.
Shazli, S. (1980). *The Crossing.* San Francisco, Calif.: American Mideast Research.
Sid-Ahmed, A. (1980). *L'OPEP: Passé, Présent et Perspectives.* Paris: Economica, and Alger: Office des Publications Universitaires.
Singer, J. D., ed. (1968). *Quantitative International Politics.* New York: Free Press.
———(1961). "The Level of Analysis Problem in International Relations." *World Politics* 14: 77–92.
Singer, M. (1977). *The Weak in the World of the Strong.* New York: Free Press.
Smith, A. (1973). *The Concept of Social Change.* London: Routledge & Kegan Paul.
Snyder, G., and P. Diesing (1977). *Conflict Among Nations.* Princeton, N.J.: Princeton University Press.
Snyder, R., H. Bruck, and B. Sapin (1962). *Foreign Policy Decision-Making.* New York: Free Press.
Snyder, R., and G. Paige (1958). "The United States Decision to Resist Aggression in Korea." *Administrative Science Quarterly* 3 (December): 342–378.
Sotumbi, A. O. (1981). "Nigeria's Recognition of the MPLA Government of Angola: A Case Study in Decision-Making and Implementation," Monograph Series no. 9. Nigerian Institute for International Affairs.
Sprout, H., and M. Sprout (1965). *The Ecological Perspective on Human Affairs.* Princeton, N.J.: Princeton University Press.
———(1957). "Environmental Factors in the Study of International Politics." *Journal of Conflict Resolution* 1 (March): 309–328.
Stein, J. (1978). "Can Decision-Makers Be Rational and Should They Be?" *Jerusalem Journal of International Affairs* 3 (Winter-Spring): 316–339.

BIBLIOGRAPHY

Steinbruner, J. (1974). *The Cybernetic Theory of Decision*. Princeton, N.J.: Princeton University Press.
Stephens, R. (1971). *Nasser*. London: Allen Lane.
Stremlau, J. (1977). *The International Politics of the Nigerian Civil War*. Princeton, N.J.: Princeton University Press.
Tanzania Government (1968). *Statement on the Recognition of Biafra* (April 13). State House.
Teiwes, F. (1979). *Politics and Purges in China*. White Plains, N.Y.: Sharpe.
Tharoor, S. (1982). *Reasons of State: Political Development and India's Foreign Policy Under Indira Ghandi 1966–1977*. New Delhi: Viking Publishing House.
Thompson, S. (1967). *Ghana's Foreign Policy 1957–1966*. Princeton, N.J.: Princeton University Press.
Truman, D. (1951). *The Governmental Process*. New York: Alfred A. Knopf.
Tsou, T. (1976). "Prolegomenon to the Study of Informal Groups in CCP Politics." *China Quarterly* (January): 98–114.
Uwechue, R. (1977). *Reflections on the Nigerian Civil War: Facing the Future*. New York: Africana.
Valdes, N. (1982). "Cuba's Involvement in the Horn of Africa." In Carmelo Mesa-Lago and June Belkin, eds., *Cuba in Africa*, Latin American Monograph and Document Series, no. 3. Pittsburgh, Pa.: University of Pittsburgh, Center for Latin American Studies.
Valenzuela, J. S., and A. Valenzuela (1978). "Modernization and Dependency: Alternative Perspectives in the Study of Latin American Underdevelopment." *Comparative Politics* 10 (July): 535–558.
Vatikiotis, J. (1962). "Foreign Policy of Egypt." In R. Macridis, ed., *Foreign Policy in World Politics*. Englewood Cliffs, N.J.: Prentice-Hall.
Vayrynen, R. (1971). "On the Definition and Measurement of Small Power Status." *Cooperation and Conflict* 6: 91–102.
Verba, S. (1961). "Assumptions of Rationality and Non-Rationality in Models of the International System." In K. Knorr and S. Verba, eds., *The International System*. Princeton, N.J.: Princeton University Press.
Vernon, R., ed. (1976). *The Oil Crisis*. New York: W. W. Norton and Company.
———(1963). *The Dilemma of Mexico's Development*. Cambridge, Mass.: Harvard University Press.
Vital, D. (1967). *The Inequality of States*. Oxford: Clarendon Press.
Wallace, W. (1975). *The Foreign Policy Process in Britain*. London: Royal Institute of International Affairs.
Wallerstein, I. (1974). *The Modern World-System: Capitalist Agriculture and the Origins of the European World-Economy in the Sixteenth Century*. New York: Academic Press.
Waugh, A., and S. Cronje (1969). *Biafra: Britain's Shame*. London: Michael Joseph.
Weber, M. (1978). *Economy and Society*, 2 vols. Edited by Guenthor Roth and Claus Wittich. Berkeley: University of California Press.
Weinstein, F. (1976). *Indonesian Foreign Policy and the Dilemma of Dependence*. Ithaca, N.Y.: Cornell University Press.
———(1972). "The Uses of Foreign Policy in Indonesia." *World Politics* 24 (April): 356–381.
White, B. P. (1978). "Decision-Making Analysis." In T. Taylor, ed., *Approaches and Theory in International Relations*. New York: Longman.
Whiteman, K. (1968). "The OAU and the Nigerian Issue." *World Today* 24 (November): 449–453.
Willetts, P., ed. (1981). *The Nonaligned in Havana*. London: F. Pinter.
———(1978). *The Nonaligned Movement*. London: F. Pinter, and New York: Nichols Publishing Co.

Williams, E. (1981). "Mexico's Central American Policy: Revolutionary and Prudential Dimensions." Paper presented at the Annual Meeting of the Caribbean Studies Association, St. Thomas, Virgin Islands, May.

———(1969). "Comparative Political Development: Latin America and Afro-Asia." *Comparative Studies in Society and History* 2 (March): 342–353.

Wolf-Phillips, L. (1979). "Why the Third World?" *Third World Quarterly* (January): 105–117.

Worsley, P. (1964). *The Third World.* London: Weidenfeld & Nicholson.

Zagoria, D. (1968). "The Strategic Debate in Peking." In T. Tsou, ed., *China in Crisis.* Chicago: Chicago University Press.

Zartman, W. (1966). *International Relations in the New Africa.* Englewood Cliffs, N.J.: Prentice-Hall.

Zinnes, D., R. North, and H. Koch (1961). "Capability, Threat and the Outbreak of War." In J. Rosenau, ed., *International Politics and Foreign Policy.* New York: Free Press.

NEWSPAPERS, MAGAZINES, YEARBOOKS, AND OTHER DATA SOURCES

Al-Ahram (Cairo)
Annuaire du Tiers Monde (Paris)
Christian Science Monitor
Documents of the Group of 77
Documents of the Nonaligned Conferences
Economist
El-Hawades (Beirut)
Facts on File
Granma (Havana)
Granma Weekly Review (Havana)
Keesing's Archives
Latin America Political Report
Latin America Weekly Review
Le Monde
Middle East and North Africa Yearbook
Middle East Economic Digest
Newsweek
New York Herald Tribune
New York Times
Nouvel Observateur
OAPEC Monthly Bulletin (Kuwait)
OPEC Bulletin (Vienna)
OPEC Statute (Vienna)
Survey of International Affairs
Time
Wall Street Journal

ABOUT THE CONTRIBUTORS

Bahgat Korany is director of the University Arab Studies Program and professor in the Department of Political Science at the University of Montreal. He has also been visiting professor at the universities of Carleton, Dakar, Harvard, and McGill, and is a founding member of the Organization South-South Cooperation (Beijing, April 1983). Some of his writings have been translated into and published in Chinese, Italian, and Spanish.

Selma Akbik is a doctoral candidate at the University of Montreal, with a specialization in political economy. She has been accorded a number of grants to finish her studies in the Middle East, Europe, and North America.

Cyril Kofie Daddieh is currently involved in the Program for National Development at the University of Iowa. He has been a contributor to both *The Political Economy of African Foreign Policy* (1984) and *Africa Projected: From Dependence to Self-Reliance by the Year 2000* (1984).

Jorge I. Domínguez is a professor in the Department of Government, a member of the Executive Committee, Center for International Affairs, and chairman of the Committee on Latin American and Iberian Studies—all at Harvard University. He is a former president of the Latin American Studies Association and has authored (or edited) seven books, three booklets, and more than forty articles on international relations and Latin American politics.

Juan Lindau is currently preparing his doctoral dissertation on Mexican-Cuban relations at Harvard University. He obtained an M.A. in Latin American Studies from Stanford University and another in Political Science from Harvard. In 1982–1983, he was the executive secretary of the Harvard-MIT Joint Seminar on Political Development.

Timothy M. Shaw is professor of Political Science and director of the Centre for African Studies at Dalhousie University. He has taught at Makerere University (Uganda), the University of Zambia, and the University of Ife (Nigeria), and is coauthor (or co-editor) of a series of books on African international relations, including *Alternative Futures for Africa* (1982), *Africa and the International Political System* (1982), *Nigerian Foreign Policy* (1983), *Southern Africa in the 1980s* (1984), and *The Political Economy of African Foreign Policy* (1984). He is also vice-president of the Canadian Association of African Studies and editor of Macmillan's *International Political Economy* series.

INDEX

Aba (Nigeria), 74
Abdel-Wahab, Sheikh, family, 94
Abdul-Karim, Tayeh, 160
Aburi, 69
Action Program for Economic Cooperation (1979) (NAM), 19, 20, 23
Afghanistan. *See under* Soviet Union
Africa, 138
  conservative, 70
  economies, 72, 83, 84
  foreign policy, 41, 64–65, 69, 71–72, 77–78, 81–82, 83, 84–85
  Islamic, 71
  isolationist impulse, 83
  leadership, 64, 75, 79, 82, 83, 84–85
  maps, 61–63
  radical, 70, 82
  religious bias, 71, 72, 78
  See also Biafra; *individual countries*
Afro-Asian countries, 1, 3, 5, 6, 34
  Bandung summit (1955), 6, 8–11, 12, 15, 18, 35
  Bandung II (1965), 11
  and communist countries, 8, 12
  and nonalignment, 8–9, 12, 15
  and the West, 8, 12
Agriculture, 19, 178
Ahram, al- (Egyptian publisher), 97, 104
Aid-to-India Club, 178

Air India airline explosion (1955), 10
Akinyemi, A. B., 81
Alfonso, Perez, 146
Algeria, 84, 111, 154(table)
  and Bandung II (1965), 11
  and G-77, 21, 28
  and NAM, 28–29
  and nationalization of oil, 110
  and Nigeria, 71
  oil prices, 159, 161
  oil production, 162
  oil reserves, 144(fig.)
  oil revenues, 141(table), 161
  and OPEC, 152, 153, 154(table), 157, 160
  and UN, 29
Alliances and Small Powers (Rothstein), 5
Allison, Graham, 52, 53, 54, 55, 56, 169
Almond, G., 17
American Political Science Review, 53
Amin, Idi, 78
Andean Pact, 116(table)
Anglin, D. G., 77
Anglo-Iraqi treaty (1932), 13
Angola
  civil war, 65, 66, 67, 68, 70
  government, 78, 79, 80, 83, 84
  maps, 62–63
  natural resources, 66–67, 79, 81
  See also under Cuba; Nigeria
Ankra, Joseph, 69
Anticolonialism, 12

199

Arab countries, 87(fig.). *See also individual countries*
Arab-Israeli conflict
  1967, 86, 89, 90
  See also October War
Arab League (1945), 13, 111, 138, 146
  Collective Security Pact (1950), 14
  headquarters transfer (1979), 111
  Oil Experts Committee (1951), 146
  Petroleum Department (1954), 146
Arab nationalism, 14. *See also* Arab League; Pan-Arabism
Arab oil embargo (1973), 88, 89, 99–101, 110, 116(table)
  lifted (1974), 111
  planning, 103–109
Arab Petroleum Congress (1959), 146
Arab summit (1967), 93, 99
Aramco (oil company), 96, 107, 108(fig.)
Argentina, 116(table). *See also under* Great Britain
Aron, Raymond, 138
Arusha Conference (1979), 32
Asia, 40, 138, 167(fig.). *See also* Afro-Asian countries; *individual countries*
Asian Drama (Myrdal), 2
Asian Joint Communiqué (1954), 9
Assad, Hafez, 102
Attrition War (1969–1970), 86
Authoritarian political systems, 115
Awolowo, Chief, 76

Badr (final offensive plan), 98
Baghdad Conference (1960), 147, 152
Baghdad Pact (1955), 13, 15
Bandaranaike, S. W. R. D., 25, 27, 28

Bandung. *See* Afro-Asian countries, Bandung summit
Bangladesh, 176
Bank of England, 140
Barlev Line, 86, 106
Bashir, Tahseen, 57
Basic human needs, 18
Bay of Pigs invasion (1961), 29
Behavioral revolution, 48
Belgian Congo. *See* Zaire
Belize, 133
Bell, Bernard R., 179
Bell Mission, 178–179
Ben Bella, Ahmed, 11, 16
Benguela railroad, 67, 79, 82
Bhagwati, J. N., 177, 180
Bhattacharya, P. C., 177
Bhoothalingham, S., 177
Biafra, 61(fig.), 64, 65, 66, 67, 68–69, 70, 71, 73–74, 75, 76, 81, 82, 83, 168
  oil, 76–77
  support for, 70, 71, 74–75, 76–77, 78
  telecommunications blockade of, 72
Bolivia, 116(table)
Borchgrave, A. de, 91, 92
Botswana, 70, 75
Boulding, Kenneth, 51
Boumedienne, Houari, 7, 11, 21, 28, 34, 71
Bourguiba, Habib, 23, 71
Bowles, Chester, 179
Bozeman, Adda, 69
Brazil, 115, 116(table)
Brecher, Michael, 42, 44–45, 46–47(fig.), 51, 57, 172, 176, 177, 178, 179, 181
Brezhnev, Leonid, 98
Brezhnev Doctrine, 30
Brioni. *See* Nonaligned Group, Brioni Tripartite Summit
British Petroleum (oil company), 142, 144, 145(table)
Bureaucratic-organizational school, 48, 52–56, 170

INDEX   201

Bureaucratic Politics and Foreign Policy (Halperin), 53
Bureaucratic politics model, 54, 55
Burma, 6, 9

Cairo Radio, 13
Cameroon, 72
Camp David Accords (1978), 31, 110, 111. *See also* Peace treaty
Canada, 144(fig.)
Caracas Program of Action (CPA) (G-77), 32
Carazo Odio, Rodrigo, 126
Castañeda, Jorge, 127, 130, 131
Castro, Fidel, 7, 25, 30, 115, 119, 120, 123, 126
CCP. *See* China, People's Republic of, Communist party
Center concept, 181
Central America, 114(fig.). *See also* individual countries; *under* Mexico
Central American Common Market, 129
Central Intelligence Agency (CIA), 79, 182
Ceylon. *See* Sri Lanka
Chad, 64, 71, 72, 83, 84. *See also under* Libya
Chaudhri, S., 177
Chile, 116(table)
China, People's Republic of, 8, 166, 172
  and Bandung Conference, 9–10, 11, 173
  Communist party (CCP), 174, 175
  cultural revolution, 174
  factionalism, 174
  ideology, 172–173
  map, 167
  oil reserves, 144(fig.)
  population, 172, 173
  purges, 174
  Red Guards, 174
  and Soviet Union, 173
  and UN, 173
  underdevelopment, 173
  See also India, and China war
Chou En-lai, 8, 10
Christian Democratic-military regime (El Salvador), 130
CIA. *See* Central Intelligence Agency
Cohen, Bernard, 40
Cold war. *See* East-West conflict
Coleman, J., 17
Colonialism, 173–174
Commonwealth Prime Ministers' Conference, 35
Communism, 77, 88
  differences, 8, 173
Compradorization, 182
Consensus, 34–36, 37, 168, 169
Copper, 82
Costa Rica. *See under* Mexico
CPA. *See* Caracas Program of Action
Cronje, S., 71, 74
Cuba
  and Angola, 29, 83, 115, 116(table), 117, 118, 119, 120, 122–124
  armed forces, 119, 120
  canned fish, 124
  centralized political system, 119, 121, 134
  Communist party, 30, 119–120
  economy, 119, 124, 125, 135, 136
  and Ethiopia, 30, 116(table), 117, 118, 119–120, 121, 122, 123, 124, 135
  exports, 123–124
  foreign policy, 119–125, 134, 135
  as global power, 136, 168
  gross social product (GSP), 122
  map, 114
  military capabilities, 117
  and NAM, 25, 28, 29–30, 116(table), 119
  National Assembly, 119, 120

petroleum imports, 122
and revolutionary movements, 121, 134
and Soviet Union, 29, 30, 121–122, 123, 135
sugar, 122, 123, 124
and United States, 29, 117, 119, 125, 134, 135
See also under Mexico
Cuban missile crisis (1962), 16, 53, 54, 55
Cutler, R., 48
Cyprus, 31

Daddieh, Cyril Kofie, 168, 170
Dahomey, 70, 75
Dange, S. A., 180
Das, B. B., 180
Dawisha, Adeed, 40
Dayan, M., 93
Decision-making, 168, 171
 crisis, 66
 defined, 49
 economic, 115, 116(table), 178
 and geopolitical factors, 110, 168
 interventionist, 66, 67, 68, 78, 84, 133, 182
 military, 110, 111, 115, 116(table), 117, 121
 models, 44–45, 46–47(fig.), 49–56, 138
 noninterventionist, 66, 68, 69, 133
 objective, 168, 169
 political, 110, 115, 116(table), 117, 121, 168
 and pragmatism, 69
 and social analysis, 172, 181, 182–183
 See also Arab oil embargo; October War, planning; Third World, collective decision-making; Third World, foreign policy; *under* Foreign policy
Decision-taking, 171–172
Decolonialization, 17, 22, 69, 84

Deen and donia (religious and political authority), 94
de Gaulle, Charles, 75, 76
Delhi School of Economics, 177
Democratic Revolutionary Front (FDR) (El Salvador), 131
Dependency, 17
Destler, I. M., 53
Development. *See* Third World, development process; Underdevelopment
Díaz Arguelles, Raúl, 120
Diori, Humani, 69, 72
do Mascimento, Lopo, 80
Domínguez, Jorge I., 168, 170
Domino effect, 67
 reverse, 81
Duarte, José Napoleón, 130, 132
Dulles, John Foster, 9

East-West conflict, 4, 13, 67, 70
ECDC. *See* Economic Cooperation Among Developing Countries
Echeverría, Luis, 128
Economic Conference (1962) (NAM), 34
Economic Cooperation Among Developing Countries (ECDC) (G-77), 32, 34
Economic growth, 18
Economist, The (journal), 94, 95
Ecuador, 116(table), 154(table)
 oil, 141(table), 162
 and OPEC, 152, 154(table)
 See also Peru-Ecuador war
Egypt, 64
 army, 97
 and Baghdad Pact, 15
 Center for Political and Strategic Studies, 97, 103
 and colonialism, 88
 economy, 91, 94
 and Iraq, 13, 14
 and Israel, 15, 88, 91, 92, 110, 111. *See also* Arab-Israeli conflict; October War
 leadership, 89, 94
 and Libya, 100

INDEX 203

and NAM, 15, 31, 91
and Nigeria, 71
oil reserves, 144(fig.)
and oil weapon, 103–109
social structure, 88
and Soviet Union, 88, 90–91, 98, 110
and Suez, 15, 90
and United States, 88, 91–92, 93, 98, 104, 110
See also under Saudi Arabia
Elaigwu, Isawa, 66, 68
ELF. *See* Eritrean Liberation Front
El Salvador, 116(table), *See also under* Mexico
Eritrea, 72, 123
Eritrean Liberation Front (ELF), 72–73
Essence of Decision (Allison), 53
Esso. *See* Exxon
Ethiopia, 69, 73
and Angola, 78
and NAM, 29
and Nigeria, 72, 73, 74
See also under Cuba
Ewe, 69
Experts on Private Foreign Investment (NAM), 19
Export earnings, 6, 154(table)
Exxon (oil company), 142, 145(table)

Facts on File, 41
Fahd (king of Saudi Arabia), 99
Faisal (king of Saudi Arabia), 41, 95, 96, 99, 100, 106–109
Farabundo Martí National Liberation Front (FMLN) (El Salvador), 131
Fawzi, Mohmoud, 104
FDR. *See* Democratic Revolutionary Front
Finance and development aid (G-77), 21
Fisheries, 19
FLEC. *See* Front for the Liberation of Cabinda Enclave

FLS. *See* Front Line States
FMLN. *See* Farabundo Martí National Liberation Front
FNLA. *See* Front for the National Liberation of Angola
Foreign capital flows, 6
Foreign policy
constraints (Latin America), 115
decision-making, 45, 48–56, 59, 169–170, 175
independent variables, 44, 45
theory, 42–45, 46–47(fig.), 65, 182
See also Mexico, and Central America; *under* Cuba; India; Third World
Fox, Annette Baker, 4
France
and Biafra, 70
and Egypt, 88
and El Salvador, 131
and FLEC, 79
and Nigeria, 72, 76
Front for the Liberation of Cabinda Enclave (FLEC) (Angola), 79, 84
Front for the National Liberation of Angola (FNLA), 66, 78, 79, 80, 81, 82, 83, 84
Front Line States (FLS), 76, 82, 83

Gabon, 70, 76, 154(table)
oil, 141(table), 162
and OPEC, 152, 154(table)
Gamassy military document, 93, 96
Gambia, 74
Gandhi, Indira, 25, 27, 28, 175–177, 179
Gang of Four, 174
Garba, Joseph, 80
GATT. *See* General Agreement on Tariffs and Trade
Gaza, 15

General Agreement on Tariffs and Trade (GATT), 116(table)
Genocide, 71, 75, 131
Ghana, 64, 74
 National Liberation Council (NLC), 69
Ghorbal, Ashraf, 57
Golan Heights, 86
Government of National Unity (Angola), 78, 79, 80
Gowon, Yakubu, 66, 76, 81
Granite Two, 98
Great Britain, 53, 169
 and Argentina, 115, 116(table)
 and Baghdad Pact, 13–14
 Hong Kong colonial authorities, 10
 and Nigeria, 70
 oil, 144(fig.), 159
Great Man Theory of history, 175, 183. *See also* Individual-psychological variable
Grenada, 115
Group networks, 166, 172, 174–175, 182
Group of Experts on the Establishment of the Solidarity Fund for Economic and Social Development in Nonaligned Countries
 Legal Committee, 2–3
 See also Solidarity Fund for Economic and Social Development of Nonaligned Countries
Group of 77 (G-77) (1967), 1, 6, 7, 11, 16, 139
 Caracas meeting (1981), 32
 charter (1967), 7, 21
 and developed countries, 36
 and economic issues, 20, 21, 34
 institutionalization, 32
 membership, 7, 21, 34
 ministers of foreign affairs meetings, 22
 and NAM, 22, 32
 and national leaders, 7
 1967 meeting, 7, 21
 regional groups, 36
 structure, 33(fig.), 36
 and UNCTAD, 20, 21, 34
 See also Consensus
G-77. *See* Group of 77
GSP. *See* Cuba, gross social product
Guatemala. *See under* Mexico
Guinea, 71, 81
Gulf (oil company), 142, 145(table)

Haifa (Israel) oil pipeline, 146
Haile Selassie (emperor of Ethiopia), 69
Haksar, P. N., 175, 176
Halperin, Morton A., 53, 55, 56
Harris, Scott, 40
Hausa, 72
Hawadess, Al- (Beirut weekly), 100
Heikal, Mohamed H., 92, 97, 104, 105
Hierarchy of international system, 115, 136, 168, 170
High Minarets plan, 98
Hill, C., 2
Hilsman, Roger, 53
Holsti, Ole, 51
Honduras, 116(table)
Hong Kong, 9–10
Houphouet-Boigny, Felix, 70, 76, 77, 82
Human rights, 116(table), 130
Hussein (king of Jordan), 100

Ibn Abdel-Aziz, Nawaf, 106
Ibo, 72, 74
IGOs. *See* Intergovernmental organizations
Ikhwan, Al-, 94
IMF. *See* International Monetary Fund
Imperialism, 13, 15, 21, 29, 79, 182
Income, 6

INDEX

India, 9, 34, 166, 172
  budget, 177–178
  and China war (1962), 16, 180
  Communist party of, 180
  Congress party, 180
  economy, 177, 178, 179, 180
  food, 177, 178, 179
  foreign policy, 176–181
  industry, 177
  and Iran, 176
  leadership, 175–177
  map, 167
  and NAM, 25, 28
  oil reserves, 144(fig.)
  and Pakistan, 92, 176, 178
  Parliamentary party, 180
  People's Socialist party (PSP), 180
  population, 173
  pro-Arab policy, 176
  rupee devaluation, 176–177, 178, 179–181
  technocrats, 176, 177
  and United States, 179, 180
  See also under Soviet Union
India-Pakistan War, 92
India Today, 175
Individual-psychological variable, 44, 45, 56–58, 65, 169, 170–172. *See also* Africa, leadership
Indonesia, 6, 9, 154(table)
  oil, 141(table), 144(fig.), 162
  and OPEC, 152, 154(table)
Industrialization, 115, 168, 170
Industrial sector, 6
Information and Press Group (NAM), 19
Institutionalization. *See under* Group of 77; Nonaligned Movement
Interest groups, 3, 126
Intergovernmental Follow-up and Coordination Committee (G-77), 32
Intergovernmental Group on Raw Materials (NAM), 19
Intergovernmental organizations (IGOs), 138–139

"International Crisis Behavior Project" (Brecher), 176
International Herald Tribune, 41
International Monetary Fund (IMF), 142, 176, 177, 178, 179, 180
Iran, 154(table)
  and Baghdad Pact, 13
  and Bandung Conference, 8, 12
  defense expenditures, 140
  and G-77, 32
  and NAM, 8
  oil, 142, 146–147
  oil crisis (1979), 148, 156, 160
  oil prices, 158, 159, 161, 162
  oil production, 151, 162
  oil reserves, 144(fig.)
  oil revenues, 141(table)
  and OPEC, 152, 153, 154(table), 155, 160
  and U.S. hostage crisis, 111
  See also Iran-Iraq war; *under* India
Iranian Consortium, 146
Iran-Iraq war, 89, 111, 163
Iraq, 154(table)
  and Baghdad Pact, 13–14
  and Bandung Conference, 8, 12
  and NAM, 8, 28, 31
  oil prices, 157
  oil production, 162
  oil reserves, 144(fig.)
  oil revenues, 141(table), 161
  and OPEC, 152, 154(table), 160
  See also Iran-Iraq war
Iraq Petroleum Company, 146
Islamic Law and Contemporary Issues (Yamani), 96
Ismaïl, A., 98
Ismail, Hafez, 91–92, 93
Israel, 13
  foreign policy, 44–45
  Gaza attack (1955), 15
  and Ivory Coast, 84
  and Lebanon, 110, 111
  and Liberia, 84

military, 86, 97
   and Nigeria, 74
   and oil, 146
   and Zaire, 84
   See also Arab-Israeli conflict;
      October War; *under* Egypt;
      Syria; United States
Ivory Coast, 64, 70, 76–77, 82.
   See also under Israel

Japan, 122
Jayewardene, J. R., 27
Jerusalem, 93, 95
'Jha, L., 177, 179, 180
Johnson, Lyndon B., 179
Joint Declaration of the Seventy-
   seven (1964), 21, 22
Jordan, 100. *See also under*
   Saudi Arabia; Syria

Kadhafi, Muammar, 94, 100
Kampuchea, 31
Kaufman, Edy, 3, 40
Kaunda, Kenneth, 22, 27, 28,
   70, 77, 82
Keesing's Archives, 41
Kegley, Charles, 42
Kennedy, John F., 19
Kenya, 20
Khalil, Mustafa, 103, 104, 106
Khawas, El-, M. A., 81, 82
Khrushchev, Nikita, 19
Kissinger, Henry, 53, 92, 98
Korany, Bahgat, 65
Korea, 31
Kuomintang agent, 10
Kuwait, 154(table)
   oil prices, 157
   oil production, 162
   oil reserves, 144(table)
   oil revenues, 141(table)
   and OPEC, 152, 154(table),
      160, 161

Latin America, 3, 7, 32
   centralization, 115, 119
   economies, 115, 170

foreign policy, 40, 113,
   115–118
See also individual countries
LDCs. *See* Less Developed
   Countries
League of Nations, 138
Lebanon. *See under* Israel; Syria;
   United States
Leifer, Michael, 40
Less Developed Countries
   (LDCs), 2
Liberia. *See under* Israel
Libya, 94, 97, 154(table)
   and Chad, 111
   and NAM, 31
   and Nigeria, 71
   oil prices, 157, 158, 159, 161
   oil production, 162
   oil reserves, 144(fig.)
   oil revenues, 141(table)
   and OPEC, 152, 153,
      154(table), 160
   See also under Egypt
Lindau, Juan, 168, 170
Liquidity surplus effects, 140,
   142
López Mateos, Adolfo, 128
López Portillo, José, 117, 126
Lumumba, Patrice, 22
Lyon, P., 2

Mabruk, Ezzedin Ali, 160
Machel, Samora, 82
Maimfar, Ali Akbar, 160
Malaysia, 6, 144(fig.)
Mali, 71, 72
Mali Federation, 75
Manufactured goods, 21
Mao-in-command orthodoxy, 174
Mao Zedong, 174
Mareï, Sayed, 104, 105, 107, 109
Market system, 6. *See also* Oil,
   international market
"Measures for Economic
   Development of
   Underdeveloped Countries"
   (1951) (UN), 2
Mecca (Saudi Arabia), 93
Medina (Saudi Arabia), 93

INDEX

Mehta, Ashok, 179, 181
Mehta, Ashota, 177
Meir, Golda, 92
Mengistu Haile Mariam, 73
Menon, Krishna, 2
Mexico
  Armed Forces, 127
  and Central America, 116(table), 117, 118, 125-134, 135, 168
  and Central American Common Market, 129
  centralized power, 126-127, 134
  Congress, 127
  and Costa Rica, 126
  and Cuba, 126
  domestic policy, 128
  economic capabilities, 117
  economy, 126, 129, 133-134, 135, 136
  and El Salvador, 128, 130-131, 132, 133
  and G-77, 32
  and Guatemala, 125, 128, 130, 131-132
  left-leaning diplomacy, 127-128
  map, 114
  and Nicaragua, 126, 128, 129-130, 133
  oil, 126, 128-129, 131-133, 135. *See also* PEMEX
  oil reserves, 144(fig.)
  political party. *See* Party of the Institutionalized Revolution
  as regional power, 132, 136
  and social change, 128
  and United States, 117, 126, 129, 130, 132, 134, 135
  and Venezuela, 128, 132-133
Middle East
  and communism, 14
  decisions, sample of, 110-111
  foreign policy, 40
  map, 87
  and nonalignment, 15
  and the West, 13-14, 15

  See also individual countries
Miller, J. B., D., 2
Mobil (oil company), 142, 145(table), 155
Mobutu Sese Seko, 82
Modernization, 17, 18
Monetary-financial cooperation, 19
Montgomery, Bernard, 88
Morgenthau, Hans, 4, 138
Morocco, 71, 84
  Green March (1975), 111
Moslem brotherhood, 71
Mossadeq, Mohammed, 142
Mozambique, 81
MPLA. *See* Popular Movement for the Liberation of Angola
Multinational companies, 7, 115, 139, 140, 148, 182. *See also* Organization of Petroleum Exporting Countries, and multinational oil companies
Myrdal, Gunnar, 2

NAM. *See* Nonaligned Movement
Namibia, 83
Napoleon (emperor of the French), 88
Nasser, Gamal Abdal, 7, 12, 13, 14, 15, 25, 27, 64, 71, 90, 91, 93-94, 97
  daughter, 98
Nasserism, 17
National interest, 75, 134
National/international group linkages, 181-183
National Union for the Total Independence of Angola (UNITA), 66, 78, 79, 80, 81, 82, 83, 84
Nation-state, 49, 51, 138
Nehru, B. K., 177, 179
Nehru, Jawaharlal, 2, 7, 10, 11, 12, 22, 25, 27, 35, 175
  death (1964), 16
  and nonalignment, 15
Neto, Agostinho, 29, 61, 82
Neustadt, Richard, 52-53

Neutral Zone, 162
New International Economic
    Order (NIEO), 19, 34
    Declaration (1974), 29
Newsweek, 91
New York Herald Tribune, 9
New York Times, 53
New Zealand, 7, 20
Nicaragua, 115, 126. *See also
    under* Mexico
NIEO. *See* New International
    Economic Order
Niger, 69, 72
Nigeria, 61(fig.), 64, 66, 67, 70,
    81, 83, 84, 154(table)
    Air Force, 71
    and Angola, 66, 69, 79-81
    civil war. *See* Biafra
    Moslem North, 71
    natural resources, 66
    oil prices, 159, 161, 162
    oil production, 162
    oil reserves, 144(fig.)
    oil revenues, 141(table), 161
    and OPEC, 152, 154(table),
        155, 157, 159
    petro-naira, 80
    and regional trade, 72
    support for, 71, 72, 73, 75
    See also under Soviet Union
Nixon, Richard M., 88, 92, 93,
    98, 107, 108
Nkrumah, Kwame, 2, 7, 16, 64,
    77
NLC. *See* Ghana, National
    Liberation Council
Nonaligned Group, 1, 2, 3, 6,
    11, 12-15
    Brioni Tripartite Summit
        (1956), 15, 22, 25, 27
    Cairo Tripartite Summit
        (1961), 27
    New Delhi Tripartite Summit
        (1966), 27
    and the West, 13-14
    See also Nonaligned
        Movement
Nonaligned Movement (NAM)
    (1961), 15, 37, 139, 173

Conference of Foreign
    Ministers (1972), 23, 28
Coordination Bureau (1973), 8,
    23, 29, 30-32
crisis of leadership, 16-17
crisis of orientation, 16
and development, 18
economization of, 15, 18-19,
    34
First Summit (Belgrade 1961),
    6, 15, 16, 19
Second Summit (Cairo 1964),
    16, 23
Third Summit (Lusaka 1970),
    16(table), 22, 23, 25, 28
Fourth Summit (Algiers 1973),
    16(table), 25, 26(fig.), 28, 30,
    31, 41
Fifth Summit (Colombo 1976),
    16(table), 18-19, 26(fig.), 30,
    31, 35
Sixth Summit (Havana 1979),
    16(table), 19, 29, 31, 32, 35
Seventh Summit (Delhi 1983),
    6-7, 16(table), 31, 35, 36
institutionalization of, 15, 16,
    22-32
membership, 6, 15, 16, 31, 34
ministerial meetings, 25,
    26(fig.), 27, 30, 31
moderates, 16, 29
organization structure, 24(fig.)
and political issues, 34
radicals, 16, 28, 29, 30
revitalization (1970s), 20
sophistication, 19-20
technical groups, 19-20
and UN, 30, 34
and the West, 29
See also Consensus; *under*
    Group of 77
Non-OPEC oil producers, 156
North Korea, 29
North-South relations, 7, 21, 28,
    29, 116(table), 173
Norway, 144(fig.)
Nu, U, 12
Nuclear testing, 72

INDEX

Nweke, G. Aforka, 70, 71, 72, 75
Nwokedi, Francis, 76, 82
Nyerere, Julius, 6, 32, 70, 82

OAPEC. *See* Organization of Arab Petroleum Exporting Countries
OAS. *See* Organization of American States
OAU. *See* Organization of African Unity
October War (1973), 57, 58, 86, 88, 89, 92, 104, 106, 110, 112(n1)
   planning, 96–99, 101–103, 109, 110
OECD. *See* Organization for Economic Cooperation and Development
Oil
   companies, 108(fig.)
   glut, 99, 144, 148, 155, 156–157, 159, 161, 163, 164, 169
   international market, 147–148, 155, 157, 162, 163, 164, 169
   pipeline, 146
   production, 105(table)
   reserves, 144(fig.)
   spot prices, 148, 156, 157, 158, 159, 163, 164(n1)
   See also Arab oil embargo; Organization of Petroleum Exporting Countries; *individual OPEC countries*
Ojukwu, Chukwuemeka, 73, 74, 75, 82
Oman, 144(fig.), 157
OPEC. *See* Organization of Petroleum Exporting Countries
Operation 41, 98
Organizational process model, 54, 55
Organization for Economic Cooperation and Development (OECD), 20, 148, 157, 158
Organization of African Unity (OAU) (1963), 61, 64, 65, 138
   Addis summit (1969), 76
   Algiers summit (1968), 71, 73, 74, 75
   and Angola, 78, 80, 83
   Charter, 68
   Consultative Committee (1967), 70, 73, 74, 75
   Foreign Ministers' conference, 74
   Kinshasa summit (1967), 70
   and Nigeria, 68, 69, 71
Organization of American States (OAS), 126
Organization of Arab Petroleum Exporting Countries (OAPEC), 88, 108, 109, 139(fig.)
Organization of Petroleum Exporting Countries (OPEC) (1960), 105(table), 111, 139, 144, 147, 154(table)
   aid contributions, 142, 143(table), 159, 161, 164
   Board of Governors, 149, 150(fig.), 151, 159, 162–163
   capital transfers, 142
   Conference, 149, 150(fig.), 152, 159, 163
   Division of Research, 151
   Economic Commission Board, 151, 160, 163
   economies, 158
   Fifty-seventh Ordinary Meeting (1980), 139, 159, 160
   Fifty-sixth Extraordinary Conference (1980), 157–158
   gross national product (GNP), 154(table)
   as international actor, 139, 140, 142, 164, 168–169, 170
   labor imports, 140
   marker crude, 164(n2)
   members, 139, 154(table)
   membership categories, 152–153

and multinational oil companies, 142, 144–147, 169
oil exports, 140
oil price ceiling (1980), 139, 157, 158, 161, 163
oil prices, 140, 144, 146, 148, 153, 157, 158, 159, 160, 162, 163, 164
oil production, 142, 144, 145(table), 148, 153, 155, 156, 157, 158, 160, 161–162, 164
oil production ceiling (1982), 139, 159, 162
oil reserves, 144(fig.)
oil resources, 140
oil revenues, 141(table), 164
power structure, 139, 148–155, 163, 169
Secretariat, 149, 150(fig.), 151–152, 159
Sixty-first Extraordinary Meeting (1981), 162
Sixty-third Extraordinary Meeting (1982), 139, 159
Sixty-fourth Meeting (1982), 163
voting patterns, 153, 157, 160
See also Oil, international market
Otaiba, Mana Said, 161, 163
Owerri (Nigeria), 74

Pachachi, Nadim, 147
Page, Howard, 146
Paige, G., 52, 57
Pakistan, 8, 9, 13, 32, 176. *See also* India-Pakistan War; Turko-Pakistani Treaty
Palestine, 31
Palestine Liberation Organization (PLO), 111
Pan-American Common Market, 116(table)
Pan-Arabism, 13, 88, 89, 90, 94, 168
Pan-Islamism, 88, 89, 168
Pant, P., 177

Paraguay, 116(table)
Party of the Institutionalized Revolution (PRI) (Mexico), 127
Patel, I. G., 177
Patrimonial state structure, 170–171
Patron-client relationships, 166, 174, 182
Pax Americana, 88, 110
Peace treaty (1979), 88
Pellicer, Olga, 127
PEMEX (Mexican state oil monopoly), 127
Perez Guerero, Manuel, 32
Periphery concept, 41, 181
Peru, 116(table)
Peru-Ecuador war (1981), 115
Petrodollars, 140
Pharaon, Rashad, 106, 108
Philippines, 8, 12, 32
PLO. *See* Palestine Liberation Organization
Podgorny, Nikolai, 90
Poland, 30
Polhemus, J. H., 81
Political development indicators, 3
Political economy, 18, 34, 64, 168, 181–182
Political science, 48, 49, 51
Politics of Policy-Making in Defense and Foreign Affairs (Hilsman), 53
Popular Movement for the Liberation of Angola (MPLA), 66, 67, 74, 78, 79, 80, 81, 82, 83, 84, 118, 120, 122, 168
Port Harcourt (Nigeria), 74
Portugal, 66, 76, 81
Power assumption, 4
Pragmatism. *See under* Decision-making
Prebisch, Raoul, 21
PRI. *See* Party of the Institutionalized Revolution
Productivity, 6

INDEX

PSP. *See* India, People's Socialist party
Psychological-perceptual school, 48–52, 56, 65, 172, 176, 183. *See also* Individual-psychological variable
Psychologism, 39, 56
Public enterprises, 19
Public Enterprises and Multinational Companies (NAM), 19
Public sector, 6
Puerto Rico, 30
Pye, L., 6, 174

Qadi, El-, Saad, 106
Qatar, 154(table)
  oil prices, 157
  oil production, 162
  oil reserves, 144(fig.)
  oil revenues, 141(table)
  and OPEC, 152, 153, 154(table)
Quaddafi, Muammar. *See* Kadhafi, Muammar

Ra'anan, U., 174
Radio Biafra, 74
Rahman, Mugibur, 176
Rational actor model, 53, 54, 134
Raw materials, 21
Red Sea, 72
Reserve Bank of India, 177, 178
Richardson, E., 91
Rio Treaty, 116(table)
Roberto, Holden, 82
Roel, Santiago, 127
Rogers, William, 91
Rommel, Erwin, 88
Rosenau, James, 42–44, 45
Rostow, W., 17
Rothstein, R., 3, 4, 5–6
Rotterdam spot market, 156, 164(n1)
Rwanda, 70, 75

Sabroto, 160

Sadat, Anwar, 57, 58, 88, 91, 92–93, 94, 96, 99, 100, 104, 105, 106, 110, 111
Sadek, Hatem, 97, 98
Sadiq, Mohamed, 91
Sahara, 72
Salem, Salah, 14
Sampson, Anthony, 147
Sandinistas, 128, 129–130, 133
San José oil facility agreement (1980, 1983), 128, 133
Saqqaff, El-, Omar, 107
Saud (king of Saudi Arabia), 95, 99
Saud (prince of Saudi Arabia), 100
Saud, Al-, family, 94
Saudi Arabia, 154(table)
  and communism, 88, 158
  Council of Ministers, 95
  defense expenditures, 140
  and Egypt, 93, 94, 99, 100, 106–109
  and IMF, 142
  and Islam, 93, 94–95
  and Jordan, 99
  leadership, 89, 93, 94, 99
  and NAM, 41
  and OECD, 157, 158
  oil prices, 158, 161
  oil production, 88, 93, 95, 99, 100, 101, 105(table), 107, 109, 155, 158, 159, 162, 163. *See also* Arab oil embargo
  oil reserves, 144(fig.)
  oil revenues, 93, 106(table), 141(table), 146
  and OPEC, 139–140, 152, 153, 154(table), 155, 157, 158, 159, 160, 161, 162, 169
  per capita income, 89
  population, 88–89, 154(table)
  social structure, 88
  technocrats, 95, 96
  and United States, 88, 95–96, 99, 100, 101, 107–108, 109, 110, 158
Sauvy, A., 2
Savimbi, Jonas, 82

Schelling, T., 53
Schweitzer, Pierre Paul, 179
Science, Technology, and
    Research (NAM), 19
Scientific and technological
    cooperation, 19
Scott, J., 6
Secession, 70, 71, 72, 73, 75, 84
Security, 5
Self-determination, 77, 133
Self-employment, 6
Senegal, 64, 69, 70, 71, 75, 76
Senghor, Leopold Sedar, 11, 64,
    71, 75
Sepulveda, Bernardo, 127
Seven Sisters (oil companies),
    142, 144, 147
Shaba I and II, 84
Shah of Iran, 146–147
Shastri, Lal Bahadur, 175, 177
Shaw, Timothy M., 41, 168, 170
Sheikh, Al-, family, 95
Shell (oil company), 142,
    145(table)
Shukeiry, El-, A., 11
Sid-Ahmed, A., 140
Sierra Leone, 70, 75, 76, 82
Sinai, 98
Singer, M., 5
Sistemo Economico Latino-
    Americano, 116(table)
Size concept, 4–5
Skinner, Richard, 42
Snyder, Richard, 48, 49, 51, 52,
    57
Socal (oil company), 142,
    145(table)
Social Science Research
    Committee, 17
Solidarity Fund for Economic
    and Social Development of
    Nonaligned Countries
    (NAM), 19
Somalia, 118. *See also* Cuba,
    and Ethiopia
Sotumbi, A. O., 80
South Africa, 66, 67, 76
    and Angola, 78, 79, 80, 81,
    83, 84, 118–119, 120

South East Asia, 40
South Korea, 21
South-South Conference (1983),
    173
South-South Cooperation
    principle (G-77), 32
South Vietnam, 21
Soviet Union, 8, 13, 41
    and Afghanistan, 30
    and Angola, 83, 123
    and India, 180–181
    and Latin America, 115
    and Middle East, 110
    and Nigeria, 70, 77
    oil reserves, 144(fig.)
    See also under China; Cuba;
    Egypt; United States
Sparkle (code name), 102
Sprout, Harold, and Margaret,
    44, 51
Sri Lanka, 9, 25, 27–28
*Stages of Economic Growth,
    The: A Non-Communist
    Manifesto* (Rostow), 17
Stevens, Siaka Probyn, 76
Stremlau, John, 74
Stroessner, Alfredo, 182
Subramanian, C., 177
Subsistence production, 6
Sudan, 71
Suez aggression (1956), 15, 90
Suez Canal, 86, 91, 101–102
Sugar. *See under* Cuba
Sukarno, Ahmed, 7, 9, 12, 16
Switzerland, 173
Syria
    and Israel, 111
    and Jordan, 110
    and Lebanon, 111
    See also October War

Taiwan, 10, 173
Tanks, 86, 88, 112(n1)
Tanzania, 31, 32, 64, 70, 76, 77
Tariki, Abdullah, 96, 146
Technocrats. *See under* India;
    Saudi Arabia
Telli, Diallo, 69, 71

INDEX

Texaco (oil company), 142, 145(table)
Thani, Al-, Abdul Aziz Bin Khalifa, 160
Tharoor, S., 175
Third World
  characteristics of, 6, 170, 172, 173
  collective decision-making, 1, 34–36, 37, 168
  collective identity, 1, 2, 3–4, 7, 36, 37
  concerns, 7
  development process, 17–18, 20
  foreign policy, 39–41, 52, 56–59, 65, 89
  global-systemic context, 6–7, 11, 12, 13, 14, 17, 36–37, 116(table), 138–139, 169, 170, 172, 182
  groups, 1, 2–3, 6. *See also specific names*
  leadership, 7, 168, 171–172
  non-nuclear, 2
  radicalized, 7
  UN membership, 138
  See also individual countries
Third Worldism. *See* Third World, collective identity
Tiers Etat, 2
Tiers Monde, 2
Tiewes, F., 174
Tito, Josip Broz, 7, 15, 25, 27, 28
Togo, 74
Traditional sector, 17, 18
Tripartite aggression (1956), 15
Tsou, T., 174
T. T. K. (Indian finance minister), 180
Tunisia, 23, 70, 71, 75, 76
Turkey, 8, 12, 13
Turko-Pakistani Treaty (1953), 13, 14

Uganda, 70, 75, 78
Ulama and umara (religious scholars and princes), 94

Umuahia (Nigeria), 74
UNCTAD. *See* United Nations Conference on Trade and Development
Underdeveloped countries, 2, 3, 5–6, 115
Underdevelopment, 17, 173
UNITA. *See* National Union for the Total Independence of Angola
United Arab Emirates, 154(table)
  oil prices, 157, 158
  oil production, 162
  oil reserves, 144(fig.)
  oil revenues, 141(table)
  and OPEC, 152, 153, 154(table), 157, 161
United Nations, 2, 7, 12, 20, 22, 29, 30, 34, 138, 173
  Resolution 242 (1967), 101
United Nations Conference on Trade and Development (UNCTAD), 20, 22, 32
  I (1964), 7, 20, 21
  II (1968), 7, 21
  III-VI (1972, 1976, 1979, 1983), 21
United States, 53
  and Angola, 67, 81, 118, 123
  and Bandung Conference, 9
  and Israel, 88, 92, 99, 107
  and Latin America, 113, 117, 125
  and Lebanon, 110
  and Nigeria, 74
  oil reserves, 144(fig.)
  and Soviet Union, 98
  See also Arab oil embargo; Central Intelligence Agency; *under* Cuba; Egypt; India; Mexico; Saudi Arabia
Upper Volta, 72
Uruguay, 116(table)

Vayrynen, R., 4
Venezuela, 116(table), 154(table)
  oil prices, 157
  oil production, 162
  oil reserves, 144(fig.)

oil revenues, 141(table), 161
and OPEC, 152, 154(table), 159
Vietnam, 29, 134
Vital, David, 4, 5,

Wallace, W., 169
Waugh, A., 71, 74
Weak in the World of the Strong, The (Singer), 5
Weber, Max, 171
Weinstein, F., 6
Western Sahara, 64, 83, 84
Whiteman, Kaye, 70, 73
Willetts, Peter, 41
Williams, E., 3
Women, 19
World Bank, 140, 142, 176, 177, 178, 179, 180

World War II, 88
Worsley, Peter, 2
Wushishi, 79

Yamani, Ahmed Zaki, 96, 99, 160
Yemen, 89, 93
Yom Kippur, 101
Yugoslavia, 13, 15

Zagoria, D., 174
Zaire, 22, 67, 70, 81, 82, 84. *See also under* Israel
Zambia, 57, 64, 67, 70, 76, 77
and Angola, 79, 81, 82
economy, 82
and NAM, 27, 30
Zinsou, Emile-Derlin, 70, 75
Zionism, 13, 15, 95, 100